NO ONE
TELLS YOU
THIS

A Memoir

GLYNNIS MACNICOL

Simon & Schuster

New York   London   Toronto   Sydney   New Delhi

Simon & Schuster
1230 Avenue of the Americas
New York, NY 10020

First Simon & Schuster hardcover edition July 2018

SIMON & SCHUSTER and colophon are registered trademarks of
Simon & Schuster, Inc.

For information about special discounts for bulk purchases, please
contact Simon & Schuster Special Sales at 1-866-506-1949 or
business@simonandschuster.com.

The Simon & Schuster Speakers Bureau can bring authors to your
live event. For more information or to book an event, contact the
Simon & Schuster Speakers Bureau at 1-866-248-3049 or visit our
website at www.simonspeakers.com.

Interior design by Carly Loman

Manufactured in the United States of America

10 9 8 7 6 5 4 3 2 1

Library of Congress Cataloging-in-Publication Data
Names: MacNicol, Glynnis, 1974– author.
Title: No one tells you this : a memoir / Glynnis MacNicol.
Description: New York : Simon & Schuster [2018]
Identifiers: LCCN 2018000331| ISBN 9781501163135 (hardcover :
  alk. paper) | ISBN 9781501163142 (trade paper : alk. paper) | ISBN
  9781501163159 (e-book)
Subjects: LCSH: MacNicol, Glynnis, 1974– | Single women—New York
  (State)—New York—Biography. | Canadian Americans—New York
  (State)—New York—Biography. | Man-woman relationships—New York
  (State)—New York. | Caregivers—Family relationships—Canada—
  Toronto. | Middle-aged women—Family relationships. | Mother and child. |
  Self-realization in women. | Women authors, American—21st century—
  Biography. | Women authors, American—21st century—Family relationships.
Classification: LCC HQ800.4.U6 M33 2018 | DDC 306.7—dc23
LC record available at https://lccn.loc.gov/2018000331

ISBN 978-1-5011-6313-5
ISBN 978-1-5011-6315-9 (ebook)

For my mother and my sister

CONTENTS

There are years that ask questions and years that answer.

Zora Neale Hurston

You're lonely? Get a cat. They live thirteen years. Then you get another one, and another one after that. Then you're done.

Katherine Olson to her daughter Peggy, *Mad Men*

Numerology

For someone who has always been bad at math, I have a weird fixation on numbers.

Take my mother's death. Officially my mother died on March 20. A Monday. This is the date on her death certificate, and the date on her gravestone. This is also what the staff at the nursing home north of Toronto, where my mother had lived for the past twenty-six months, told my father when they called him at seven that morning. My mother, they said, had died overnight.

I wanted more details, though. "Overnight" felt too nebulous. When my sister, Alexis, and I arrived the next day to retrieve the last of my mother's possessions, it was the first thing I inquired about. Who *exactly* had found her? I asked the nursing attendant manning the staff desk that oversaw my mother's wing, hoping this would lead to the specifics I was searching for.

The nurse was an older blond woman and she seemed puzzled by my question. "When a person is that ill," she said, "we send someone in to see them every hour." Behind her on the wall, in the frame reserved for pictures of recently deceased residents, was a picture of my mother. IN LOVING MEMORY read the gold-plated plaque nailed to the bottom of the frame. It was a terrible picture, taken recently. My mother's face was thin and frail, the confusion that had eaten up her mind apparent in the angry, taut expression. It made her look like a stranger. My mother, always so careful with her appearance, would have been horrified by the photo. She wasn't even wearing lipstick.

I turned back to the nurse. I understood her confusion; there was exactly nothing mysterious about my mother's death. She had been sick for a long time; the previous Wednesday a specialist had told us she probably had six months, "give or take."

Still, I tried again. I concentrated on sounding calm—I'd long ago learned this was the best way to deal with medical staff—as if I was just making casual conversation. But the truth was that since the previous morning, when my father and then, minutes later, my sister had called to tell me the news, I'd been preoccupied with this small bit of information: I wanted to know the exact minute my mother had died. And barring that, I wanted a time stamp on the last instance they'd seen her alive. I had obsessively time-stamped my journals as a child, carefully watching the second hand on my Mickey Mouse alarm clock, and then furiously scribbling down the numbers before it ticked on, as if this detail would give more authenticity to my record. I wanted to be able to do the same for my accounting of the end of my mother's life. It felt like a loose thread in an otherwise perfectly woven tapestry I was trying to reattach correctly.

I hadn't yet shed a single tear. I had a vague sense they were on the horizon, but the tsunami of emotions brought on by her loss wouldn't reach me for a while yet. In the meantime, I set about constructing a narrative around my mother's death that made sense, a path I could funnel everything down when grief arrived and tried to wreak havoc on me. So many of the decisions I'd made in my life had been the result of stories I'd read, or heard, or was trying to emulate—there was a safety there, I knew. I also knew there was an irrefutability to numbers that I could rely on to nail everything else down.

The number I was looking for that day was nineteen. The 19th was Maddy's birthday. Maddy, my oldest friend in New York, the person who had for nearly two decades stood in so many times as my unconditional support system, my emergency contact. That my mother would depart the world on the same date Maddy had entered it seemed to me a perfect conclusion to the story I was creating for myself about her death. It made sense. I deeply wanted proof from the nursing home staff that it was possible "overnight" meant my mother *could* have died before midnight and simply hadn't been found until the 20th. This was my first foray into the house of mirrors that I later came to recognize as the early days of grief, and I was confident I was being entirely rational.

But no one knew. As far as the world was concerned, my mother had died, alone in her room. Peacefully in her sleep, as they say. After a lengthy battle with Parkinson's and forty-nine years of marriage to my father.

My sister and I wrote those lines, in fact, composing her obituary in the car on the way to the funeral home the next afternoon. I dictated sentences from the driver's seat and Alexis typed them into her phone and then read them back to me, making corrections and suggestions as she went. It all *sounded* so normal. Practically comforting. The sort of benign obituary one passes over and thinks: *long life, well-lived, no tragedy here.*

In the four months since the 2016 election, I'd greeted nearly every reported death of a person over seventy with a sort of mental hat doffing, as if to say *good for you, this definitely feels like an excellent time to make an exit.* But now that the person exiting belonged to me, it didn't feel that way at all. As it turned out, standing by death's door, no matter how long you may spend there with a person, no matter how comfortable you think you are with its presence, is a great deal different than having that person walk through it.

Everything felt like a set of nearly-but-not-quite symmetrical numbers to me that week. At forty-three I was one year younger than my mother had been when her own mother died. I'd done the math as I was driving up to Alexis's house after landing at the airport in Toronto. Even the roads that morning seemed slightly off, which was especially odd since I'd been born here. I had grown up traveling these highways to swim meets, to visit relatives, to sneak out to downtown dance clubs. In the last few years, as my mother's health had failed and my visits home increased, I'd done this drive an average of every six weeks, and yet on this trip I dimly stared ahead wondering why it all seemed so strange. It wasn't until I was halfway home that I realized I was on the wrong highway. I'd taken the wrong exit out of the airport but had no recollection of doing so. This would be the first of many wrong exits I would take off familiar routes over the next few days.

More numbers: My mother had been married to my father for eighteen years by the time she'd attended her own mother's funeral. She'd had two children, Alexis and me, nine and eleven, respectively. She'd blazed through university, the first in her family to do so. It was my father who insisted we include in my mother's obituary the fact she'd completed two master's degrees on full academic scholarship and received straight As throughout her education. He'd always been just as enamored with her brain as the rest of us.

Not long after they'd married, however, she'd opted to become a stay-at-home mother. In pictures snapped on our front lawn from the year my grandmother died, my mother *looks* forty-three: thoroughly middle-aged, from her overlarge eyeglasses to her taupe wraparound skirt and orthotic shoes. It's almost as though she'd walked out of a museum exhibit about mid-eighties motherhood in the suburbs. She appeared sensible and respectable, someone you would expect to be carting her children around to various activities (in the hulking brown Oldsmobile, visible behind us in many snapshots), rising early to make our breakfast before swim practice and to carefully pack lunches, complete with sliced carrots wedged into Tupperware containers holding just enough water to keep them fresh. Which is what she did. She never traveled. She never went anywhere on her own. I can't remember a single day when she wasn't waiting for us when we arrived home from school. Always modestly dressed, she never left the house without lipstick on.

I appeared to be none of these things. I lived in New York by myself. I had no children. My main mode of transportation was a bicycle, which I wielded through the streets of the city like a weapon. I traveled as much as I could. I enjoyed being alone. I often walked to the corner store in my pajamas (though rarely without lipstick, it's true).

In short, I had not become my mother. Which was not an accident. I loved my mother very much, but the truth—a truth I couldn't escape even after her death, when the world called on me to create pleasing truths—was that she had never been an example for me. Never been a source of wisdom or guidance. I hadn't come to her with problems I needed solving. I hadn't sought her approval. Once, when I was small, four or five at most, a therapist she'd been seeing to deal with her then near-paralyzing agoraphobia—or perhaps it was her claustrophobia; she battled many anxiety-related phobias for most of her life—had told her, "You have a very powerful child there, Mrs. MacNicol." I'd loved this anecdote growing up. Even at a young age I was already marking the gap between my mother and the heroines I liked to read about in books. I was powerful like them! And now I had proof! Only years later did it occur to me that I had been, in part at least, the subject of that visit. That my relentlessness had always been a challenge for her.

I had known early on that I did not want my mother's life. If anything, I actively *unwanted* it. She must have known this, too, but if it hurt her, she never let on. I was certainly never made to feel bad about it. Instead of filling this gap between us with guilt or anger or fear, she gave me stories. Nearly every night of my childhood we sat in the living room, where the dog was not allowed to enter, on the white couch my parents had purchased as newlyweds, in a room now reserved for holidays and company (even though we rarely had any of the latter), while she read to me. *The Chronicles of Narnia, Little House on the Prairie, The Hobbit, The Lord of the Rings, The Black Stallion, Anne of Green Gables* (I was always tasked with reading aloud the chapter where Matthew dies, my mother too choked up to get out the words). Like the blue atlas I continually pulled out of the bookcase to mark Laura Ingalls's trek across the American Midwest—eventually rubbing off small towns completely with my repeated attention—my mother spent my childhood supplying me with these literary maps of the world. What she had been unable to provide for me as a lived example—fearlessness, adventure, ambition—she made sure I had in abundance in tales. An ever-expanding blueprint for life, doled out to me chapter by chapter, night after night, while she scratched my back with her long, elegant fingers and well-filed nails and read on in her calm, articulate voice.

As much as anything my mother did, or didn't do, the lessons learned from those books made me the person I became, often in ways that I'm sure made my mother wish she'd handed me something more practical instead, like a guide to economics, or even a cookbook. These stories directed my entire life. Until they didn't.

Which returns us again to the question of numbers. Or one number. Forty.

Are you aware that you are, perhaps, the most discussed animal in the universe?

Virginia Woolf

1. The Forecast

Eight hours before my fortieth birthday, I sat alone at my desk on the seventeenth floor of an office building in downtown Manhattan, unable to shake the conviction that midnight was hanging over me like a guillotine. I was certain that come the stroke of twelve my life would be cleaved in two, a before and an after: all that was good and interesting about me, that made me a person worthy of attention, considered by the world to be full of potential, would be stripped away, and whatever remained would be thrust, unrecognizable, into the void that awaited.

It was ridiculous. Deep down, I *knew* it was ridiculous. However, knowing this did not keep me from anxiously glancing at the clock out in the hallway as if the hands on it were actual blades.

I thought of my mother, of course. Whether or not we actually resemble the image we see, our mothers are our first, and most lasting, reflection of ourselves: a mirror we gaze into from birth until death.

I was eight when my mother turned forty, and while I could

no longer recall the exact details of that day, I did have a vague memory of it being surrounded by the sort of manic hysteria I associated with the *Cathy* cartoons that were sometimes clipped and taped to our fridge. My mother loved the comics; she found joy in their simple, two-dimensional humor. For most of her life she would try to hand the comic strip section of the newspaper to me over the breakfast table or read them aloud, so I could enjoy them too. I never did. I was baffled that anyone found them interesting; they were so bloodless. At age eight, the appeal of the *Cathy* cartoon, about a single woman with heavy thighs, who dimly battled with her weight, her dating life, and her job, all with pathetic aplomb, was especially confusing. My interest in those days was almost exclusively directed at Princess Leia and Laura Ingalls. This sad Cathy creature, so often pictured feverishly trying to shove herself into bathing suits in department store changing rooms, struck me as the exact version of life I would happily expend all my future energy avoiding. Which is largely what I did.

My strongest impression of my mother's birthday, however, was that it was an ending. I sensed an *abandon all hope, ye who enter here* message woven into the colorful birthday cards that arrived in the mail for her. As if simply by turning forty, my mother had somehow failed at something. And now here I was so many years later, about to turn forty myself, gripped by those identical fears despite all my determination to be otherwise. Eight-year-old me would have been revolted.

My desk faced north. Through the wall of windows that made up half of the corner office I was in, I had a panoramic view of the island. Below me Manhattan stretched out like a toy city, all sharp angles, silver rectangles, and the unbroken lines of the avenues running north. Even from this height the city exuded purpose, like an engine exhaust. Right then it was shimmering in the late afternoon, early September sun. The light cast a golden hue on everything. It was the sort of light that caused even the most hell-bent New Yorker to look up with renewed awe. I pulled out my phone, automatically angled my head in a well-practiced tilt, and took a selfie. I contemplated the result with some satisfaction, but I didn't need the picture evidence. I was aware that to the outside world I could not have appeared less like a woman who should be worried about her age, less like someone who was now spending the last hours before her birthday seized by the belief she was being marched to her demise. In all likelihood, even my friends would have been surprised to hear it. I was not known as a person who tended to cower; I was a person who kept going, who took care of things, who always had the answer, who rarely asked for help. I had been on my own since I was eighteen years old. I had taken myself from waitress to well-paid writer to business owner and now back to writer without stopping to consider whether any of these things were plausible to anyone but me. I knew what I wanted, and what I liked, which was probably why most of my friends had taken me at my word when I said I didn't want a birthday party; they were accustomed to me knowing my own mind. I wasn't so sure anymore, however.

Currently my mind felt split, as though there were two voices in my head debating the importance of my birthday, and like the pendulum on a grandfather clock I was swinging from one to the other. The rational voice kept pointing out that it was not only shameful, but also a waste of time, to cower before age. Wouldn't my energies be better spent contemplating how lucky I was? *Lucky* was too weak a word. Did I really need reminding that by nearly every metric available, there had never been a better time in history to be a woman? (Sometimes this voice merely noted how universally horrific it had been to be a woman up until *very* recently.) After all, I hadn't been raised by a mother who responded to fifth grade homework questions, like "How many wives did Henry VIII have?" with a detailed explanation of the War of the Roses, only to arrive at this point in my life without a deeply ingrained sense of the larger picture.

Who cares, said the other voice. Sure, fine, technically it might be true I was lucky. But this so-called luck was no more interesting to me than the meals I'd been commanded to finish as a child because "there are starving children in the world": knowing I was fortunate did not make the plate before me any more palatable. The only truth this increasingly feverish voice recognized was the sort that had been gleaned from stacks of literature, countless movies, and decades of magazine purchases I'd made: it was a truth universally acknowledged that by age forty I was supposed to have a certain kind of life, one that, whatever else it might involve, included a partner and babies. Having acquired neither of these, it was nearly impossible, no matter how smart, educated, or lucky I was, not to conclude that I had officially become the wrong answer to the question of what made a woman's life worth living. If this story wasn't going to end with a marriage or a child, what then? Could it even be called a story?

I very much wanted to muster a good *fuck you* to these voices. I reminded myself what the manager of the Greenwich Village tavern where I worked in my twenties as a waitress had once said to me (after listening to me lament my upcoming twenty-fifth birthday, no less): "You'll never be younger than you are today." But instead I laid my head on my desk and closed my eyes. *Bring on the blade*, I thought. I was so tired of my own mind it would be a relief.

My phone vibrated beside me and my heart leapt from long habit, like a dog that believes every noise of a package being opened holds the promise of food. But it was just my friend and now business partner, Rachel. Since leaving the office for a meeting a few hours ago, she had texted me some variation of *PARTY?* every fifteen minutes or so.

There's still time! Party Party Party???? YES PARTY

Rachel had been offering to throw me a party all week. Her fortieth birthday party, two years prior, had taken place in a vast loft with a liquor sponsor. I had no doubt that if I'd wanted the same she would have managed to provide it, probably in the next two hours if I really made a fuss. She'd already put together a gift bag for me from twenty friends.

No Party, I wrote back.

She wasn't the only one. People had asked and offered. There were a half dozen friends I could text right now, who would meet me at any place I chose. Whatever else it was, my birthday was not the story of a lonely woman. But I did not want a party. I couldn't shake the feeling that the years ahead, if they were to be lived in a way that didn't leave me feeling like I was standing in a corner watching the action but never living it, would require me to transform into a person I could not yet recognize and was not totally convinced even existed. A party felt like a delay tactic. A distraction. A weakness. If it was true that I was likely going to be alone for the rest of my life, *let's see how alone I could be.*

This little spark of defiance had brought me comfort in recent days, but now I could barely strike it before it faded away. Not even the view could save me this time, it seemed. Right now, all it revealed was who I had been. I needed only to glance out the window to see my own history laid out before me. Live in the same place long enough and it eventually becomes a map to all your past lives: a different you waiting around every corner. And there had been plenty of versions of New York City me. From this vantage, I could practically trace my path beginning with my first heady year here, when I'd stumble out of after-hours clubs at 9:00 a.m. and be forced to walk home in the too-bright sun, having spent all the money I'd made the night before. The diner, somehow still in business, where Maddy and I would scrounge together our change and split $1.50 egg sandwiches. The shadowy ridge of midtown buildings, where I'd had my first office job in publishing, at age thirty-one, after deciding it was time to get my professional act together. The subway stop that I had walked through every day for six months, hoping to "accidentally" bump into the man who'd told me the "timing just wasn't right." And down there, too, was the office in SoHo where, after leaving publishing, I'd begun my mad charge up the media career ladder until it all came crashing down a few years later, shortly before I turned thirty-seven. Sitting here now thinking of those years, it occurred to me this birthday panic might not actually be such a recent development. If I was honest with myself it was probably truer to say I'd been turning forty for the past three years.

•

If someone had drawn a cartoon of me at age thirty-seven there would have been two equally sized thought bubbles over my head. Instead of words the first bubble would have contained an equation representing the sad reality that nearly everything in my life had become a shifting math problem with an immutable result: a baby. The calculation went something like this: I had x amount of activities in a week. If I met someone at one of them, how long would we have to get to know each other—a year seemed reasonable—before we'd need to be married so that it would leave enough time—six months perhaps?—to get pregnant before the cutoff (the cutoff being forty, the year in which a baby ceases to be a mathematical certainty and becomes a lucky roll of the dice). (Babies are never mathematical certainties, obviously, but that is one of those truths that is never true for you until it is true for you.) As thirty-seven became thirty-eight became thirty-nine the calculations became even more pressing and less feasible. Married next week, and pregnant the next morning? Time ticked on. Eventually there was no way to make the numbers add up. I couldn't outrun my own clock.

The second bubble would simply have been a picture of me getting on a plane on short notice and leaving. By the time I turned thirty-seven, I was almost as consumed with the idea of getting away as I was with the conviction I was running out of time. Not traveling per se, just leaving. I was a media reporter in New York then, and I started my long work days from home. To the outside observer my job was glamorous: television appearances and glitzy parties. The reality was that it required me to chase website traffic like a shady lawyer going after an ambulance—clicks, no matter how ill-gotten, were the coin of the realm. Increasingly, early mornings had found me sitting at my desk in my tiny, sun-filled studio apartment ("It's exactly the sort of apartment you dream of living in when you dream of living in New York," my friend John said when he first saw it) where I paid twice as much rent as I'd ever paid in my life, listening to the garbage truck heave its way down the leafy streets of Brooklyn Heights, and wishing with every molecule of my being that I was the trash collector hanging off the back of it. All I could think as I gazed at it was: *There is no internet on that garbage truck.* Hunched over my desk, my BlackBerry buzzing like a trapped fly against a window, chat windows exploding on my screen with the urgency of dispatches being sent from a war zone, I spent months nearly paralyzed by my desire to be anywhere else.

That these two visions of my life were in direct contradiction with each other never once occurred to me. Not even a little bit. Neither did the fact that I wasn't actually doing anything to make either outcome a reality. If anything, I was doing the opposite. When I wasn't dating wildly inappropriate men, with whom there was little to no chance of building anything resembling a stable long-term relationship, I was working eighteen-hour days, nearly every day. Had I ever stopped long enough to consider things, I might have recognized the truth, which was that I'd never bothered to seriously question whether I actually wanted to be married with kids, or even just with kids (I'd at least Googled airplane ticket prices). I had simply taken it as a given, like financial security and regular exercise, obvious outcomes sane people generally aimed their lives toward. This lack of self-awareness was especially galling considering the singular focus with which I'd pursued other goals in my life. On paper at least, I was, by the time I turned thirty-seven, precisely where I had always wanted to be. I was a New Yorker; I was a full-time writer. Not just that. I was a full-time writer making a six-figure salary, plus excellent benefits, regularly appearing on TV to talk about subjects I'd written on. It was a position I had achieved less than five years after waiting my last table.

It hadn't come easily. I had worked for it, relentlessly. For most of my thirties, I'd been on fire with determination. I'd been a pyre of ambition, fueled by what I considered all the lost time of my twenties. Which worked out admirably well, until I also went up in smoke. Or so it felt like to me. Life on the internet, the very thing that had allowed me to skip over the years of drudgery I knew had been required of nearly every established writer I'd admired, eventually caught up to me. There are no speed bumps in the digital world. No clocking out. No off switch. It was as though my career was a car racing across an endless plain, on a road with no speed limits, pedal to the floor: the only thing that was going to stop me was me. And that was exactly what happened. Five years into my career, at the top of my game, I didn't so much stop as buckle under my own momentum. The fiery ambition that had once driven me to work eighteen hours a day, seven days a week, for years, consumed me until I burned up. Burned out.

Burned out. Another weak phrase—as if borrowed from a subway advertisement for bubble bath or resort vacations—to describe something that felt so shattering. It had started slowly and the early warning signs were easy to ignore. When I started thinking of writing as punishment instead of fortune, for instance, people said it was just the subject matter, I should switch beats. When I started approaching my workday with dread instead of eagerness, people told me I just needed a vacation. But it turned out this was like telling someone whose house has been destroyed in a natural disaster that they simply needed a fresh coat of paint. The hours I'd been clocking for years on end had pushed me past the point of quick fixes—past the point of caring about finding a fix, it turned out. I simply went through my day on autopilot, resentful but too worn out to make any changes. Then, three months after my thirty-seventh birthday, I was called into a meeting with the company's manager, where it was gently but firmly suggested I figure out how to get a better attitude, *or else* (the *or else* was not said out loud, but the implication was impossible to miss). Without thinking, I opened my mouth to promise I would try harder (in this instance, rational me was thinking about salary and health benefits and the fact I'd just been quoted in a full page ad in the *New York Times*), but instead what came out was "I'm done." I was given the weekend to think it over, but I didn't need to; some fundamental part of me had taken the wheel and was pulling me off the road. Instead, I cleared my desk out and walked home over the Brooklyn Bridge feeling giddy with my new freedom. This sensation lasted for a few weeks, buoyed along by plenty of *good for yous!* and *I wish I could do that.* I've noticed it's almost always people who are living the exact opposite lives than you, and facing none of the risks, who are most encouraging. Eventually the rush wore off and reality began to set in, and yet I found myself unable to stop doing nothing. Panic, my reliable companion, the thing that had kicked me into gear at other times in my life when I'd veered too close to the cliff's edge, was nowhere to be found. I knew I *should* be panicked, but try as I might I couldn't muster it. I felt like I'd had a lobotomy. (Later a therapist would tell me this was not my imagination, that true burnout left one "numb," operating in "survival mode," though the latter phrase again struck me as absurd, considering actual *survival* had seemingly ceased to be a concern to me during this time.)

During those months of doing nothing, I watched the numbers in my savings account disappear, as though observing a weather report from a far-off land. When I thought about it at all, I sometimes considered how differently I'd be behaving if, for instance, I had a child to support. Presumably the necessity of a paycheck to keep someone else alive might have eclipsed the manner in which I earned it. Other days I wondered what it would be like not to be in this alone, to know there was someone else to pick up the financial slack. (I sometimes regarded my married friends who had health benefits thanks to their husbands' jobs with the same envious and irrational gaze I'd formerly laid on the garbage truck drivers.) Perhaps this imagined partner might say something like: "You've worked hard enough, honey, I'll cover the rent this month," or "Take the time you need, your happiness is important, I've got this." But I was alone—my parents had never been a source of financial support, and thirty-seven-year-old employable women did not go to friends, who themselves now had families to think about, and ask for loans. Instead I did nothing. In fact, my only source of enjoyment during those bleak months was telling people I did nothing. (Nothing stops New York cocktail party conversation quite as abruptly as the phrase *I do nothing*.) I felt like I was playing chicken with myself. I could see the cliff's edge—would I drive myself off? How close could I get? Did it matter? I was the only person relying on me, and I did not seem to care what happened.

It took a gutted bank account (something I'd never allowed to happen before) and, until my cable and internet were cut off for nonpayment, many afternoons of watching *Golden Girls* reruns (the envy I felt toward fictional retired women living in Florida *before the internet* was unlike any I'd experienced—I wanted to crawl into my TV screen *Poltergeist*-style) before I really hit rock bottom and began piecing my professional life back together. It had taken two years, but I was now approaching solid ground.

•

I returned my gaze to the city skyline. It was precisely the sort of view that belonged to a "master of the universe" character in a Tom Wolfe novel. Which was fitting, I supposed—I was now, if nothing else, master of my own universe, *self-made*, my own boss. From this office, Rachel and I ran our small, newly sustainable networking business—the old boys' club for women, we called it. Our partnership had been conceived of in the black center of my burnout; it was a pinpoint of light I could walk toward, and more practically speaking, something to do that might keep me from looming eviction. After much trial and error, we'd made it work. In addition to this, I was slowly but surely reassembling my freelance writing career in a way that made me want to come to the computer instead of flee from it. I could once again pay my rent. And yet, despite all this, here I was still feeling unsteady.

The city gazed back at me in all its triumphant, unapologetic power. The city did not care that I was determined to ignore my birthday. It would quite happily ignore my birthday right along with me if I so chose. It was my job to convince the city I was worth paying attention to at all. It was now five o'clock. Was I really going to go home? Sad, sad Glynnis retreating to her studio apartment, defeated by her age. This could not be the story of my birthday. More than anything, it was just too boring. In an effort to avoid appearing pathetic, it was starting to occur to me that I was being very pathetic. At the very least I'd take myself out for a drink at the Bemelmans Bar, the Upper East Side institution on the ground floor of the Carlyle Hotel. The walls of Bemelmans were illustrated by its namesake, Ludwig Bemelmans, author of the *Madeline* children's books, who had stayed as a guest there for many months. It was as old-school as it was possible to get in New York, and if the city was my sanctuary, Bemelmans was my sanctuary within it in my lowest moments.

Newly fired up by my plan, I opened my computer and looked up hotel room rates at the Carlyle. I could pack a pair of silk pajamas, have a martini at Bemelmans, and wake up to a stroll in Central Park.

Good Lord.

I closed the tab almost as quickly as I'd opened it. Not even the most acrobatic, panicked, you-only-turn-forty-once rationalizations could justify half a month's (already obscenely high) rent on one night in a hotel. I might not know what sort of life awaited me, but I was certain whatever shape it took I would still have to pay my bills. Even so, I'd hit on the missing piece. I was desperate to be in motion. To have a destination on a day that was leaving me feeling paralyzed and without purpose. It was too late for a road trip now, though I suddenly understood clearly that's what I should have done. I thought of all the motels I'd stayed in over the years on various cross-country road trips. The promise of their glowing neon signs, the rooms' brief answers to the quintessential question of the road: where to next? That's what I needed.

I turned over the city in my head. Most of the hotels were in Times Square and full of tourists. I had never been a tourist, and I wasn't about to start now. Suddenly I recalled the newly opened motel out in the Rockaways I'd heard people talking about over the summer. The Rockaways were technically a part of Queens, a little peninsula that jutted out into the water southeast of Coney Island and lined on all sides with beaches. The area had been a summer destination for city dwellers looking to escape the heat since the mid-nineteenth century, and had come in and out of fashion ever since. The neighborhood had the feel of a beach town even though it was possible to see the city's skyline in the distance. Another world inside the same city, only a subway ride away. It was one of New York's better magic tricks. I Googled the hotel. It was open! A few more clicks and I had booked a seventy-five-dollar room. Just like that, I'd managed to tilt the world just enough to let it refill with some possibility. I packed my things and took one last look out the window. The sinking sun had tinged the silver buildings gold, giving me the sensation of being granted a glowing send-off.

anywhere new after dark. Except I was literally just taking a subway ride. I was going to Queens. I'd been there a hundred times, *hundreds* of times. Still, this felt different.

Down on the subway platform a man in shapeless, filthy clothes was weaving along dipping his hand into the garbage bins, fishing out empty fast-food packages, and then tossing them back in a rage before lurching onward to the next bin. I could hear him angrily muttering to himself. Instinctively I took a step back from the edge and leaned against one of the thick vertical beams that lined the platform, making it impossible for someone to push me into an oncoming train. I'd been doing this pillar shuffle for as long as I could remember. It was one of a handful of little rituals that promised to forever separate me from the poor folk who ended up on the front pages of the tabloids, victims of the city's randomness. I also didn't step on manhole covers in the summer for fear of being electrocuted, and I avoided walking over the groaning sidewalk cellar doors for fear they would collapse (of all my city-induced neuroses, this was by far the most realistic). I had a healthy respect for New York's heartless peculiarities.

When I'd first arrived in New York in the late nineties, just as Giuliani was campaigning for a second term as mayor, the front pages of the city tabloids were the equivalent of a great Greek chorus, weighing in with operatic judgment on the activities of its citizens. Often they told the sensational tale of a girl (pretty, young, white) who'd had one too many shots, or done one too many lines, and then: stumbled into the wrong cab, gone home with the wrong bartender, said yes to drinks with the wrong man, and was now dead. Or DEAD! MURDERED! MANGLED! Depending on her appearance, and how much drink or drugs or sex had been involved, she was either asking for it, or an innocent victim of the evil metropolis. Either way, a tragedy of lost potential. At twenty-three, largely on my own in New York, or at least bereft

2. Husband Material

Nothing about the Jay Street–MetroTech subway station
downtown Brooklyn suggested it was, to paraphrase Tennyson
Ulysses (a man also trying to escape his age . . . not to men
tion his "aged wife"), an arch through which anything gleamed
Some subway stations in New York bustled and snapped with
energy (even if it was just the energy of anxious, irritated com
muters), or even managed to feel airy despite being under
ground. Not here. The Jay Street station was dark, dingy, and
depressing. A place to get through, often with head down and
shoulders hunched. It felt slightly ominous.

Which perhaps at least partially explained the strange case
of nerves I'd suddenly come down with as I descended the final
set of stairs into the sauna below. It was the same feeling I
sometimes got when I was about to embark on a long trip, unsure of what I would find at the other end. It was true I was dis-
obeying one of my cardinal rules for travel, one I'd established
long ago as a teenager backpacking across Europe: never arrive

of any oversight, those headlines filled a space normally taken up by concerned parents or partners. Before long, my cautionary inner voice began resorting to tabloid speak. I'd gauge just how stupidly I was behaving by anticipating what sort of cover story it might make. If my night went badly, would I be regarded as the good girl for taking the subway at 4:00 a.m. after a long shift in order to save money, or the reckless girl for doing lines in the VIP bathroom at a club with two men I didn't know, or the stupid girl for walking everywhere, alone, at every hour? Even though it had never gone badly, or badly enough to warrant front-page treatment, the habit had stuck with me. Now as I stood there, braced behind the pole against the uncertain movements of the man digging through the trash and anyone else who might come along, I couldn't help but imagine the worst-case headline:

FOREVER YOUNG: On the eve of her 40th birthday, woman pushed into oncoming train by madman.

I envisioned packed cars of people folding back the paper, shaking their heads, horrified and grateful in equal measure to read of every New York City subway rider's worst nightmare. Afterward they'd look up and say to themselves, or their neighbor, or later their coworker: *At least she didn't have any children.* It was clear to me, even in the imaginary stories I was telling to myself, that after today I would be a person who would forever be measured by what I didn't have.

A long rumbling from the dark tunnel and the A train pulled in. I boarded, squeezing into a corner seat by the door, as the rush-hour crowds behind me made their well-practiced move farther into the train car. I leaned back as we pulled out of the station and looked around at all the faces, something I rarely did anymore—people on subway cars were something to be navigated around, not contemplated—and thought about all the lives and complications that must lie behind them. All the fears and insecurities. I was just another face here. I thought about how I had been so many faces already in my life. So many different women. How I'd hurled myself into different versions of life to try them on, sometimes keeping them, sometimes leaving them behind like apartment addresses in neighborhoods I rarely returned to. Up until now the transformation had always thrilled me.

Before coming down to the subway platform I'd texted both Rachel and Maddy, and also my friend Mauri, to tell them what I was doing. Then I'd taken my phone and shoved it as far down into my backpack as I could, below the silk pajamas I'd rushed home to grab, and the lumpy freezer Ziploc I used as a vanity bag. It had largely been a gesture—there was no Wi-Fi on the train and it would be an hour before we'd come aboveground and I'd be able to get a signal—but I wanted my phone as far away from me as possible. I'd considered leaving it behind entirely; the idea of being unreachable had felt like the most luxurious present I could give myself. But then what if there was an emergency?

Based on the last few months, this was a not unlikely possibility. One of the reasons it felt like my birthday panic had arrived in such late fashion, rushing, it seemed, to catch me like a commuter making the last train, was that my life had recently been overrun with actual emergencies that had left little time for concern about much else. Before I'd done my weird, frustrating morph into a woman, a *single, childless woman* (the words continued to pound in my head like a sentencing gavel), on the eve of her fortieth birthday, I'd been spending much of the year being the good daughter, the good sister, the good friend.

At some point in the last few years my mother had been diagnosed with Parkinson's. *At some point.* That I, with my head for dates, couldn't remember when this diagnosis had happened was a measure of how nonchalantly I'd greeted the news. It barely made a dent. My mother was a constant, gentle white noise in our lives. It had been my father's health that had been the bell that tolled in our family since childhood. For as long as I could remember, he'd been plagued by back problems that laid him out on the living room floor for hours at a time. "Your father's back is bothering him" was practically a slogan in our house, and my mother relied on it to explain all his last-minute absences. When I was a teenager, my father had been diagnosed with bipolar disorder. This was long before the term had entered the public consciousness, or carried with it any understanding or empathy. It's possible his condition contributed to his losing his job as an executive at a large bank when I was fourteen; I had no idea. I was a teenager and my awareness didn't reach far beyond my immediate sphere. I did know that he never found his footing again, and when I was in eleventh grade, not long before my parents filed for bankruptcy, he went to work behind the counter at the local pizza joint, alongside my best friend who lived next door. A year later I was out of the house for good, but returned home for a stretch sometime after my thirtieth birthday to help my mother after he'd had a heart attack while driving home and required multiple bypass surgery and weeks of care.

So, when my mother floated into the kitchen one afternoon while I was home for a visit and gently announced, as though remarking on casual news she'd picked up during a trip to the mall, that the doctor had determined she had Parkinson's, I don't recall that I even stopped eating. I don't remember why I was home, or what season it was. Or even if my sister, Alexis, had children yet. The news made no impression; it was so outside the narrative of our family, it refused to plant itself in a timeline. I do recall a brief sense of confusion. Wasn't Parkinson's the disease that made you shake? My mother had no discernible tremble—she had no discernible anything—how could they know? Apparently, they knew.

Years passed, or maybe just a year, and then quite suddenly, we also knew. Since Christmas—nine months by the calendar, but an eternity in my head—the disease had whipped through her like a match on dry tinder, at times leaving only shadowy hints of her former self. The violent tremors never appeared as forecast. Instead the thing that was consuming her had arrived like an alien invasion, skipping over her body and going straight for her mind. I remembered every detail of that holiday, right down to the classical music that was playing on the stereo, and the exact shade of blue afternoon light that the snow outside was reflecting into the living room when this new version of my mother appeared. I had been sitting on the couch reading when she suddenly came dancing through, waving her arms and pirouetting like a small child performing a made-up dance routine.

"I feel wonderful!" she said, clapping her hands together. "Let's go on a trip!"

I frowned. My parents didn't travel. "We can go for a walk," I said absentmindedly, assuming this would likely put an end to things, and we'd shortly end up in the downstairs family room watching a movie and ordering pizza, which is how she and I had spent most of our evenings together. My mother also didn't exercise. My sister and I had been athletic our whole lives. Before having kids, Alexis had run marathons. My mother drove two blocks to the corner store.

"Yes! You are brilliant, my sweet, let's do that." She did another pirouette.

Maybe this was a New Year's resolution I didn't know about; every year she talked about making them, but they rarely lasted a full twenty-four hours. I loved walking; if she wanted to go, I was game. I got up to retrieve our coats, but when I returned to the living room a few moments later it was as though the air had gone wavy with an electric charge. I looked around before I realized it was coming from my mother. It was like she'd been plugged into a socket and currents were shooting through her body. Later I would learn to recognize those afternoon dances for what they were: evidence of dangerous storm clouds forming on the horizon of her mind, but at that moment I was aware only that she had slipped from strangely happy to something else.

She sat down, then she stood up, she walked in a circle around the room, and sat down again. Our black Labrador, Medley, the first family dog my mother could claim as hers, followed her movements with perked ears. The rest of the house was silent. Even though it was only late afternoon, my father was already in his bedroom and down for the night.

"Do you want to go outside?" I held up her coat encouragingly, not knowing what else to do.

"I'd like to go home," she said, staring at me accusingly, standing up again and peering around as if looking for something. "I want to make sure I'm ready."

"Ready for what, Mom?" I thought she might be looking for her purse; she had spent much of my childhood looking for her purse. I wondered whether she meant my sister's home (Alexis and her husband and two children lived twenty minutes away).

"For when we leave," she said. Then she gazed at me in alarm. "Is everyone else dressing up?"

"Dressing up for what?" I asked.

"For the event. I think I've decided after all, I don't want to stay."

I put her coat down and swallowed, making an effort to keep the growing alarm out of my voice. "What event?"

She turned and looked directly at me, her pupils swallowing up her eyes.

"Do you work here?" A metallic twang I'd never heard before had slipped into her voice. "I'm ready to go home," she said, as though someone had locked her in.

I've always been told I was good in emergencies. In that

moment, some instinct to remain absolutely calm rose up and gripped me. "You *are* home, Mom."

I watched a wave of horrific amazement sweep over her, and for a minute I was reminded of the exaggerated acting in the old *Twilight Zone* episodes we used to watch on Saturday afternoons when I was a kid. Suddenly her face contorted with unmistakable rage.

I had no understanding of how to deal with rage from my mother. To my knowledge, she had never been rageful at anything in her life, let alone me. On the rare occasions she got angry it was a toothless anger that left me feeling guilty rather than fearful. Only once, when the girls on my swim team had singled me out to be bullied, the way preteen girls do sometimes, turning on me inexplicably like a flock of birds shifting flight, had I seen anything resembling this. On that occasion, my mother, having glimpsed the scratches they'd left on my legs during the previous practice, stood on deck and glared fiercely at them for an hour straight. Even underwater I could feel the fury radiating off her. I remember being overwhelmed with gratitude by this gesture—so out of character for her—and so comforted. After that night, the girls left me alone, and things soon returned to normal. Now that fierce gaze was being directed at me, and I was so shocked by it I couldn't even be upset, let alone speak. All those years I'd complained she was too nice, too content to let things be, that she'd never just say what she was feeling. Here finally was the creature I had thought I wanted her to be—as though summoned by my teenage self, two decades too late—and I had no idea what to do.

She looked wild. Her eyes darted back and forth. The Parkinson's tremors, normally so subtle as to be invisible, jerked her body this way and that. It was as if my mother had disappeared and been replaced with . . . I had no idea. I fought back the sensation that I'd also been dropped into another world. Maybe if

I stayed calm I could help her return to safer ground. I squared my shoulders and lowered my voice as if I were talking to a small child, the way I talked to my niece or nephew.

"You *are* home," I said. "This is your house. You live here with Dad. I'm your daughter." There was a pause.

"I don't have a daughter."

She laughed cynically, another emotion that was wildly out of character, as if catching me in a lie. And then she looked around the room as though she had never seen it before. "I do *not* live here."

The rage disappeared like a wave retreating out of her face as quickly as it had washed in, and was immediately replaced by terror. The blue of her iris had disappeared completely, and her eyes were completely black now.

"Why won't you let me go home?" She spat the words at me. "Who *are* you?"

It took me an hour to get her to bed that night, and many more to calm her down. I'd spent the remainder of that holiday furiously Googling her symptoms, which was how I learned there was something called Parkinson's disease dementia, except every piece of information I read assured me it was nearly unheard of in a patient who'd so recently been diagnosed. I sent long, descriptive emails to the wife of my close friend Kimberly, who was an expert in the Parkinson's field. She sent equally long, incredibly kind replies back, concluding that what I was describing was "unusual" and "troubling." The doctor's offices had been closed for the holiday, and I wasn't able to get my mother in to see someone till after the new year, at which point things had calmed down. Temporarily it turned out. In the months that followed, my frequent trips home had largely revolved around getting both my father and the doctors to recognize the severity of her condition.

•

That so much of the responsibility for my mother's well-being had fallen on me was as much the result of circumstance as anything. My sister was eighteen months younger than me. When we were in our early twenties I'd once overheard her remark hotly to a friend that she'd be the one tasked with caring for our parents in their old age. The remark had stuck with me, lodging itself in my mind like a disturbing crystal ball reading. I'd been out of the house on my own for nearly five years at that point. I'd never considered what would happen to my parents when they aged. Never considered my role in it, or hers for that matter. But others likely would have agreed with my sister. By any of the usual metrics, Alexis was the responsible one. I'd joked during my speech at her wedding that it had often felt as if she were the older sister. She'd let me crawl into bed with her when I had nightmares. She had the nine-to-five job in the marketing department of a large company. She married at thirty-two a man she'd been with for a number of years, and a year later gave birth to my nephew. My niece arrived a year and a half after that. Except for two years at university, Alexis had never lived more than a forty-minute drive from my parents. But the certainty those sorts of descriptors provide on paper is so rarely mirrored by the experience of real life. Not long after my mother's catastrophic Christmas, Alexis and her husband separated; shortly after that she discovered she was carrying their third child, due in late October. My trips home had increasingly been split between racing against my mother's illness and helping my sister manage two small children and prepare for the arrival of the new baby.

And then everything got worse.

Since July, I'd been in three different emergency rooms. Once to bring my sister the clothes she needed to stay overnight with my niece who was there for observation after banging her head in a swing-set mishap. Once to retrieve my mother who'd woken up alone and confused in the house and called 911. Since there had been no one else home, the fire department was required by law to take her to the hospital. And then, finally, gut-wrenchingly, for a friend who'd had a stillbirth.

At thirty-nine, I'd been through more than a few of my friends' pregnancies, and nearly as many miscarriages. In my twenties, it had been about getting people through their abortions: lending money, being the drop-off or pick-up person. In my thirties I held hands through miscarriages, gave condolences and then gentle, encouraging talks about how common miscarriage was and that there was no doubt a healthy pregnancy was on the way. But there was no way for anyone to prepare for this. My friend had arrived at her doctor's the morning after her due date only to discover there was no heartbeat. That's what the text had said: *Glyn, my baby has no heartbeat.* I still had it on my phone. The text before it said *thanks for the baby gifts!* In between there was an extra wide white space to mark the passage of time, twenty-four hours, a small gap that held in it the upending of one person's entire life. *I'm on my way,* I'd written back, and biked the hundred blocks up Third Ave., through the thick summer heat and empty August New York streets, and held her hand while she delivered, the loud cries of live babies echoing in the hallways around our terribly silent room.

Two days later I was back in another hospital in Canada, except this time in a specialist's office for my mother. Two weeks after that, just days before my birthday, I had watched as my best friend, Mauri, was dreamily married at City Hall in New York. Somewhere in there Rachel, age forty-one and single, discovered she was pregnant, which meant our newly stable business now needed to start thinking about how to support a single mother and baby.

Far from spending the summer panicking about my age, I had instead occasionally wondered whether the world was conspiring to do me a very cruel favor. It sometimes felt as though all the things a single, childless woman on the eve of her forties is supposed to be most fearful of never having attained—the right guy, the happy marriage, the babies, the not-dying-alone— had been lined up for my inspection and then, one by one, unveiled to reveal the worst-case scenario. It wasn't that I was missing out on happy endings; there were no happy endings! It was much harder to be devastated over not being the dreamy bride, the new mother, the settled wife, when so much of my life was currently requiring me to be the fill-in for husbands missing in action. But it was also too easy to be cynical, to slip into the belief that nothing ever worked out. I knew, too, that to let myself do so would be worse for me in the long run. Still, maybe it wasn't so shocking I wanted to be alone, or that I'd been thrown for a loop by this late-stage panic: I hadn't been a going concern in my own life for a while now.

I came back to myself as orange light flooded into the car. The train finally pulled aboveground and rolled out across the marshy waters that surrounded JFK. We were deep in Queens now. In the distance, I could make out the city skyline glowing gold against a red sky. Deep down in my bag I could feel my phone vibrating through the leather of my backpack.

3. Messages from Invisible Sources

I waited until I got off the train at Broad Channel before I retrieved my phone from the depths of my bag. It was cooler out here, away from the city and closer to the ocean. The breeze was stronger and had a hint of fall to it. Unlike on the weekends, when the platform was packed with beachgoers and surfers, there was only a handful of people now waiting for the S shuttle to bring us the rest of the way out. My phone vibrated again, but still I refused to look at it.

If there had been a soundtrack to my life in recent years it was the buzz of my phone. If there was one thing I wanted to leave behind in my thirties, it was my phone. It felt like a narcotic. I'd lived with enough smokers, and seen the wrong end of the sunrise after nights fueled by lines of white powder, to recognize my own twitchy symptoms. The device itself was not entirely the problem, so much as the fact that it held incontrovertible evidence of the series of bad relationship decisions I'd made over the past few years. It was like carrying around a court transcript of my personal crimes and misdemeanors, proof of a person I didn't want to be but had been . . . repeatedly.

She was always waiting for me. If I scrolled up (and up and up) I'd eventually reach that first innocuous *hey* that had unleashed her. Men and their *heys.* I'd come to see them as a "dead end" road sign: nowhere to go past this point. This particular *hey* was from a married man, and it had been sent a year and a half ago at 1:48 a.m. and received the following morning when I woke in the hotel room where I was staying at the conference I was attending. I was, at that point, twelve months out from my career-halting burnout and still in the early stages of putting my life back together. This married man had laid eyes on me the evening before, across a large, packed hotel lobby that was doubling as an event space. I could feel the gaze; it was as if we were in one of those comics where lasers shoot out of an alien's eyes. Out of the corner of my eye I'd watched as he raced around the perimeter of the room to put himself directly in my path. It worked. We spent the next two hours on a couch talking. We'd parted at midnight. He'd *hey*'d me not long after.

It's not as if I didn't know not to get involved with a married man. I, like nearly every woman I knew who worked in New York media, had been dodging the advances of married men for so long it sometimes felt similar to walking down a crowded New York City sidewalk, one more annoying thing to maneuver around as I went through life. Not this time. This time, it was a direct collision, and I was laid flat. A weekend at a convention away from home turned into a series of clandestine rendezvous back in New York. In the aftermath, I'd often asked myself *why.* Why this time? When I mentioned to friends that I was involved with a married man, trying to figure out how to extricate myself, nobody seemed terribly shocked. But I knew it was a bad decision nonetheless. Not that it stopped me. He was successful and determined and sure of himself: three things I definitely was not in that moment. All the usual clichés had been uttered: he was unhappy, his marriage was basically over, it was just a matter of him figuring out how to leave and when. I'd heard it all before to varying degrees from men I'd walked away from, or at least kept at arm's length while they cried on my shoulder over drinks. But I hadn't kept this person at arm's length; I wanted him as close as possible, and so I accepted these assertions as truths. I believed him. Instead of turning my back I responded with patience and understanding. Later it occurred to me that, more than anything else, these were the two things he likely wanted most. Even afterward, when it all spectacularly imploded and I could only shake my head at my own stupidity, I still remembered how alive it had made me feel. How exciting it had been to be excited about someone, to have him excited about me. In the numb aftermath of quitting my job, that excitement felt like a lifeline. Proof I wasn't wasting the time I had left. Proof there was still hope for me, age thirty-seven, to get together all the things I needed to get together. If I wasn't quite in love with him, I was falling that way. It was the oldest justification in the book.

The affair did not last long, though it might have if we hadn't been discovered. It's hard to give up feeling alive, even when the source of the feeling is a cheat.

I'd been walking across the Brooklyn Bridge the last time he'd called, three months after we'd met. It was May, and the fresh spring wind was whipping against my phone so that I had to stand in a sheltered corner under the soaring arch of one of the towers to hear him. "My wife knows," he said. An electric surge of relief came over me. He'd spent two months going back and forth, back and forth: "It's over, I just don't know how to get out of it." Or, "I can't stop thinking about you, but I also have this life that I am just not ready to blow up." It would end and start. I would cut things off, saying, "Go figure it out." And then a few weeks later it would start again. This, now, finally seemed definitive.

My relief was short-lived. He, it immediately became clear, was not relieved she'd found out. "I may not even have a home to go back to tonight," he said in the panicked voice of a child who'd only just realized there were consequences to actions. I looked out across the East River toward the Statue of Liberty, listening to him grasp reality, apparently for the first time, and was struck by the realization that this would make a terrific opening scene in a romantic comedy. As he went on about the need to go home, I became furious at myself for managing to be such a cliché in every way. I held the phone out for a moment and looked at it as though it were a person that I could glare into his senses. I wanted to say to him, *No fucking kidding you might not have a place to go home to.* Had this never crossed his mind? I wanted to say, *You are gross.* And *You are an idiot.* And then, *I am gross.* And *I am an idiot.* But I didn't. It didn't matter at that point. A few days later I received an email that read as though it had been written by a crisis management firm: he needed to return to his life "without confusion"; he hoped I could "understand and respect what he was saying," (translation: keep my mouth shut), and that was the end of it.

The shock and dismay I felt over the suddenness of this ending was almost immediately dulled by the presence of the actor. I now thought of him as 646, the area code of his phone number. On paper (or rather in our text message exchanges, which numbered somewhere in the thousands), it was by far the more appropriate of the two relationships. In reality it had been far the worse, and I'd come to think of it as the more shameful decision of the two.

I first met 646 while covering the 2008 Democratic National Convention in Denver. He'd been there to perform, I think. Those four days, which culminated in Barack Obama's acceptance speech, had felt like one long jubilant circus, and meeting 646 was par for the course in a week in which every day had been filled with exciting encounters. We'd exchanged emails and then promptly lost touch. Four and a half years later, a few months after I'd collided with the married man, I'd bumped into him at a springtime event in Washington, D.C. He remembered me immediately. I'd rounded a corner to the bar, he'd spotted me, exclaimed "Glynnis!" and crossed the floor to say hello. (There is perhaps nothing more seductive to a person unsure of her place in the world than someone crossing a floor to pursue her with determination.) Telephone numbers were exchanged. Another post-midnight text, this time starting with *Hi!* which felt charming and direct. Over the following weeks messages were received and responded to, and then more, and then more.

In the beginning, I didn't take it seriously. He lived in New York, but I didn't see him and didn't think much of our correspondence. The affair with the married man had not yet ended and was still consuming most of my attention. Plus my time in New York media had placed me adjacent to enough celebrities that I knew better than to put too much faith in their behavior. In the aftermath of the affair, however, 646's texts became a nice, gentle distraction. The slowness and distance of our correspondence felt safe and responsible compared to the whirlwind and drama and pain of the married man. At the end of that June, 646 moved to the other side of the country for work, but still the messages continued. Sometimes in addition to the texts I'd get little videos of him walking and making jokes for me; I began to think of them as sweet. "It's old-fashioned. Like how the Victorians exchanged love letters," a friend remarked to me once, when I told her I was beginning to wonder what this all meant. Another friend took one look at them and told me to get on a plane immediately. "He's crazy about you," she proclaimed.

It was easy to think so. I heard from him morning to night, a constant stream of bubbles on my phone. The messages were tame and funny and caring: pictures of what he was doing, the little videos, never anything risqué. There was nothing edgy or dirty here. If there had been, I'd have shut it down immediately; I'd had my fill of risqué behavior. Slowly our correspondence became part of my regular diet, as necessary and stimulating as morning coffee. *Goodnight, XO* he'd write. Or *Good morning! XO* or just *XOXOXO*. Once again, here was an accomplished, busy person taking time out of his day, multiple times a day, to check in with me, a person who at that moment was not entirely convinced she would be hard at work or accomplished ever again. I was intoxicated. My heart beat faster every time my phone vibrated. I began to imagine I could hear it vibrating when it wasn't. All the mental energy I'd been missing in my life was reawakened and channeled into waiting for the dots on my phone that let me know he was typing a message, and composing responses in anticipation of them. As that summer drew to a close, it was nearly impossible to think of our correspondence as anything but the beginnings of a long-distance romance. How else *could* I think of it? What other explanation was there? Why else would a person, always so hard at work, devote this much energy into keeping a connection alive? When doubts crept in I simply looked at my phone, and there it was. I had it all in writing.

But the doubts still crept in. Invites to come and visit were frequent, but no plane ticket ever materialized. Rachel and I were still in the early stages of starting our business, and I was far too broke to buy my own ticket and far too proud to admit it. I'd get weird messages that had no context and seemed to belong to another conversation. Once he texted to warn me about an incoming storm. I was walking to work over the bridge at the time and looked up at the clear bright sky overhead, puzzled. *Oops, wrong map!* he wrote a minute later. Once I mailed him a small book of pictures I'd thought he'd like. I waited for a response and eventually asked him if he'd received my package. *I need to check my mail!* And also *your face, I love it!!* Later that day he thanked me for the place settings. I didn't correct him, but I didn't text him back either. A few days later, as I was coming up from the train, my phone vibrated as I always hoped it would (I'd started to anticipate the buzz of my phone each time I returned aboveground from a subway ride). I looked down. *Reminder: I like you a lot*, said the bubble.

Exactly a year ago, on my thirty-ninth birthday he showed up in person. *Glynnis! I'm in NY for a day*, he wrote that morning. *Is this my surprise birthday present?* I wrote back. I hadn't mentioned to him that my birthday was coming up and figured this was the easiest way to do it. *Ha! Yes!* he replied. I met him at a restaurant in the city later that afternoon, wearing jeans and a silk pajama top. "You're not going to dress up even a bit?" asked Rachel with a sigh, as I left the office. 646 arrived with flowers and a box of chocolates and kissed me on the cheek. As we ate, the waitresses hovered around our table at a safe distance, whispering to one another and stealing glances in our direction. Afterward he walked me to the subway. "*When* are you coming to visit me?" he asked. I floated through the rest of my day.

A few days later I woke up to this: *WHEN are you coming here? I want to see you.*

I'll look at plane tickets, I replied, once again thrilled by the invite. Maybe I could squeeze a ticket onto a credit card if I really did some juggling. While I waited for my coffee to brew I scrolled through Instagram. Without putting much thought into it, I clicked on the button on his profile page that let me see pictures other people had tagged him in. Immediately, I spotted two pictures identical to ones he'd sent me; both were on another woman's account. I scrolled through her pictures; a few lines down there was a picture of him, apparently wearing a sweater she'd knitted for him. It had been posted on my birthday.

Even then, I didn't confront him. I wasn't sure I had the

right to. What was this we were doing anyway? It felt real, but what evidence did I have other than all these gray bubbles? Did I have the right to be angry? So many messages exchanged, and now we're going steady? Reach a certain number of *good mornings* and *good nights*, and now we're exclusive? We hadn't even slept together yet. One day I went so far as to look up the definition of *relationship* in the dictionary, unable to trust my own instincts.

I dropped the conversation about visiting him. I tried to step back. *Me no likey not hearing from you*, he wrote. I didn't like not hearing from him either. I consoled myself again with the thought that no one who sent me so many messages every day could possibly be doing the same with other women. And why hold on to me? Leaving aside how emotionally deformed a person would have to be to do that, I thought, Who had the time? Was he copying and pasting? Did he have a special app? A text generator for women that spammed numerous numbers with *Hi! Just saying hello.* Had I fallen for a bot? It was too ridiculous. More than anything it was this that reassured me: the inability to believe someone could put so much energy into something that didn't matter to him.

By the time he showed back up in the city in November I was excited to see him again. He took me out for dinner. Afterward, we marched back to his apartment, as though on assignment, and I stayed the night despite my growing uneasiness. Or at least half the night. At about 3:00 a.m. he agreed that maybe it would be better if I left. He was weird about his space. He said it in a way that made me think it was something a therapist had told him to say. By that point I just wanted to get away. I could barely connect this man I'd just slept with to the one who had infiltrated nearly every moment of my life for the previous five months. Who was this flesh-and-blood outsider in my midst? It was alarming. It was as if I'd picked up a stranger on the street. And yet on the cold subway ride home I had to resist the urge to text the reliable person who resided there to tell him about this bizarre encounter I'd just had.

It should have unraveled immediately after that, but it didn't. I stayed overnight with him again at Christmas, and then again in March. Each time I left with the same knot in my stomach—who *was* this person? And each time, despite my resolve not to, I returned to my phone for comfort. Or the illusion of comfort.

I did try to cut it off once. Over the winter, he moved back to New York, and all the things I had been using his distance to quietly excuse now became impossible to justify. *I think maybe we start checking in a little bit less*, I wrote him one day. He did not like that. *Requesting a cessation of messages*, he responded, *is cold*.

If I'd been slightly less hooked, I would have pointed out that he was describing himself. He never asked about my mother or expressed any curiosity about my well-being, but he also never went away, no matter how many sharply worded texts I sent, or how many times I erased him from my contacts or refused to respond to his messages. Over the following months, as my mother's health declined, those gray bubbles were a strange means of survival. Something I could reach out for when I was lying in bed with her trying to calm her down or sitting in hospital waiting rooms.

Over the past year, in addition to caring for my mother it had sometimes felt as if I'd been living in a room filled with doors marked BOYFRIENDS, MARRIAGE, BABIES, FAMILY, and everyone but me was exiting through them. I was constantly being left. And here was someone who insisted on walking back in, whom I literally carried around in my pocket.

Finally, in June, more than a year after we'd crossed paths in D.C., we had a nice spontaneous dinner in New York. I talked a bit about everything that was going on with my family, and he simply listened. Afterward I spent the night at his apartment. I left thinking perhaps there *was* something there to salvage: I could count the amount of times I'd seen him on one hand, but I needed to buy extra cloud space for my phone to hold all our messages. I was thirty-nine, the age at which women make do with what they have, take the parts and construct them into something usable. Perhaps I could do that with this. But there wasn't anything. Two days later I clicked his tag on Instagram again and saw a twenty-four-year-old posting photos of the two of them out and about. I resolved to be done with it. It was hard. I tried every trick I could think of. But in the end, the surest way was simply to get rid of my phone. I figured if I could just steer clear of it for long enough, I could kick the habit of him. And so, I slept with it away from me. I deleted the Instagram app. I didn't text him for over a month. Considering there had been many months when we hadn't gone more than twelve hours without touching base, this felt like a remarkable feat. The effort *not* to know was practically herculean.

But now, hours away from midnight, I felt especially determined. I was not going to be a forty-year-old woman addicted to a phantom relationship that was held together by emojis and strings of *X*s and *O*s.

I stood on the subway platform, buzzing phone now in my hand, but I refused to look at it. 646 had an uncanny habit of popping up just when I'd stopped looking for him. It was as if he had an internal sonar that let him know when I was almost out of reach, if not literally, then emotionally. I took a deep breath. I could see the lights of the shuttle train moving down the tracks. I didn't want him here with me. I resolved whatever was on my phone I would delete it, get on the train, and keep going. I turned it over and typed in my pass code.

4. Woman of a Certain Age

It was Rachel again. I stepped onto the train, flooded with a mixture of relief and disappointment.

> You're going to a hotel by yourself?? Where is the hotel? What is the number? What if I have to call the police?? WHAT IF THERE IS A MAN THERE WHO WANTS TO WATCH YOU SHOWER AND LIKES TAXIDERMY.

I'm turning my phone off, I wrote back, equal parts annoyed that I had to explain myself and amused that we were always able to speak in cultural references that we never had to spell out to each other. *I'll talk to you tomorrow.*

The phone vibrated again and I looked down in frustration. It was a picture of Tippi Hedren being attacked by birds. I rolled my eyes, and wrote back.

> Wrong movie. BIRDS is the one where the unmarried woman is

made insane by . . . birds. PSYCHO is the one where the unmarried
woman is on the run alone and gets murdered in a motel.

People were always amused at how opposite Rachel and I
were in nearly every way. We sometimes joked that the only
thing that was missing to fully complete the contrast was that
one of us wasn't blond. While I was always seeking out alone
time, she was a gifted networker, the world's greatest summer
camp counselor, forever organizing a group.

You're going to a motel! Alone! There are birds at this beach, aren't
there? PSYCHO BIRDS.

I sighed. The public editor of the *New York Times* had once
told Rachel that she "should give a course in persistence, one
of life's underrated great qualities" after being on the receiving end of a series of emails requesting a clarification in a
story. After a decade of friendship and now a business, I didn't
need a course in it—I knew that if I didn't give Rachel some
information before disappearing she would get anxious at
some point and not hesitate to call the NYPD until they came
to look for me, regardless of whether I wanted or needed to
be found.

I'm going to the Playland Motel. It's just in Queens. That is part of
New York.

I switched to airplane mode before she could respond and
put my phone back where it had been at the bottom of my bag. I
was determined to be away. If there was an emergency it would
have to wait till tomorrow. It was doubtful anyone else would
reach out anyway. Maddy knew me too well to worry, and Mauri
had been on too many whirlwind trips with me to think this was

strange. It was unlikely my mother was even aware that it was my birthday tomorrow.

The smell of the sea rushed at me when I exited the subway car two stops later. No one got off the train with me. The bang of the exit door echoed loudly behind me as I descended the flights of stairs to the street below. As I'd expected, it was empty out here. The motel was on the far corner, and as I made my way down the vacant block the only noise came from the international flights out of JFK that were taking off in their regular intervals overhead.

I'd been emailed a code when I'd paid online back in the office; the instructions said to use it to access the front door and also my room, and now I understood why: there was no reception desk or check-in person. There was no front door either. Just the entrance to a bar downstairs that was open but empty. Instead I followed signs down an alley to the back of the building; the only people there were the kitchen staff from the Chinese restaurant next door, smoking cigarettes and eyeing me as I walked past. The smell of fried fish mingled with the cigarette smoke hung heavily in the air; I glanced at the stack of garbage bags at the back door of the restaurant, alert for any movement of rats.

Incongruously cheerful signs on the wall above the garbage pointed me to a keypad. The code worked on the first try. Once inside, I climbed a flight of stairs. It was silent. Could I really be the only one here? I stopped and listened for the sound of any human movement but could hear only the faint noise of a city bus pulling away out on the street. Rachel was right. *Woman alone in an empty motel* did sound like the beginning of a story that did not bode well for the heroine. This would make an excellent opening to an old *Law & Order* episode, I thought. Except if this really were a *Law & Order* episode, the detectives would spend the entire hour trying to figure out why I'd come out here by myself. I looked at the door numbers; my room was at the far end

of the hall. I knew from the website that each room had been
designed by a well-known artist and had been given a name. The
site had made it look fresh and adventurous. But in the silence
the hall looked long and foreboding. I walked quickly, forcing
myself to punch the keypad beside my door calmly. I was in. I
promptly locked the door behind me, considering briefly the
lack of a dead bolt. I took in the room. Half of it was covered by
a green geometric shape painted on the wall that reached from
the ceiling down the walls at an angle and onto the floor, giving
it an odd, lopsided feel. My stomach grumbled. I crossed my
fingers there was a kitchen at the bar, thinking it was going to
be a long night if there wasn't, and headed back down.

The bar looked like the kind of bright white and airy surfer
place one might find somewhere on the coast of California, not
at the edges of New York City. Except for a handful of people,
all of whom were hunched over their drinks in a way that suggested they were regulars, and some kids in the corner, the
room was mostly empty. I ordered a gin and tonic, grabbed an
empanada from a tray, and took a table to myself. It was open
mic night, and a few locals had begun to line the walls, holding their instruments, waiting their turn. As I wolfed down the
empanada and sipped at my drink, two young black kids took
the stage. They were both in surfer shorts and sandals; their
hair grew high and wild above their heads. They couldn't have
been more than sixteen. "Hey there," one said into the mic,
waving at the room, before moving back and nodding to his
partner. After a few false starts they began to play a very faith-
ful version of "Twist and Shout."

When I'd first set foot in New York, age twenty-three, it had
been like one of those videos of captured animals being released
back into the wild. There'd been no transition. The world immediately, finally made sense. When I thought of those years
now, what I remembered most was the sensation that I was in

the exact center of the world, inside the best secret, one that I shared only with those around me. I felt lucky, which in those days I'd found more reassuring than professional accolades or words of encouragement. Who knew what was around the corner or through a door? Who knew what the night might bring? Anything was possible. It had been a long time since I'd felt that way—at any time a quick Google search immediately dispelled the notion I was either the first to discover something or at the center of anything. I didn't want to be a person who spent the rest of her life moaning about change; still I missed that sensation, the exhilaration of being entirely in one place. Now, as the two kids on stage shifted from the Beatles to Radiohead's "Karma Police," and their earnestness and unlikely music choice wove its way around me—*this is what you'll get when you mess with us*—mixing with the sea air that breezed in through the open doorway, I was suddenly overwhelmed by the perfectness of it all. The wholeness. The incongruity and unexpectedness of two surfer kids out here with electrified hair, singing their hearts out to Radiohead. This was how I'd wanted to feel. This was why I'd come. I needed to be reminded that life was not a done deal. I was not a done deal.

Presently the duo, my unlikely birthday saviors, got off and were replaced by two white surfer dudes who immediately began wailing out Tenacious D as though they were at a suburban college frat party. Ah well, the city giveth and the city taketh away. It didn't matter. It was enough. I put my empty glass on the bar, pushed the change the bartender handed me back to my twenty for a tip, and left.

The beach was a block away. I could hear the waves now. Apartment buildings rose up behind me, and I thought about the people who'd been trapped in them after Hurricane Sandy hit in 2012, and the power had been knocked out for days. Some had been too old to get down thirty flights of pitch-black staircases and had no electricity or phones or family to help. I'd delivered food and supplies all around here that month. You'd never know looking at it now that everything along here had been ravaged. It seemed impossibly recovered. *It's a luxury to worry about your age*, those high-rises seemed to be reminding me, *to worry about being alone when there are so many other not inevitable things to be concerned over.* I nodded, as though I were in an actual debate with them, which wasn't that strange; my life had felt like a debate with invisible voices telling me what to do, how to dress, hurry, hurry, hurry, lest happiness pass me by. But now, in the quiet night, alone, I also knew better. I was lucky, sure, but more important, I was also a relatively modern phenomenon: a woman in charge of her own life, who could do what she wanted. With that came a responsibility. There was no blueprint yet for this: I was going to have to create it for myself.

I reached the sand and walked up to the dark boardwalk. The beach was deserted in both directions; above me there was the faint glow of the moon behind the clouds. I could hear the waves breaking in a regular rhythm, but all I could see was a large, dark expanse that reached out and out, broken here and there by a ghostly whitecap. Lights from ships far out at sea flickered in the distance like tiny candles.

It was nearing midnight. I gazed at the dark water for a long time, thinking how it made the perfect metaphor for the uncharted waters of the decade ahead. I let myself be overwhelmed by the idea that I had no sense of what the coming years would contain and no clue how to navigate through them. So few of the cautionary tales that had been told to me had panned out: I hadn't become a tabloid headline, the career hadn't ended, the empty motel marked a new beginning, not my demise.

I was determined to do better from this point, leaving certain baggage behind me. So many bad decisions, bad habits, bad relationships. I also knew, now that I was finally here and there was no more time for last-minute swerve-offs, that there were other things I was going to be required to leave behind. I made myself list them in my head. There might never be a child. I might always be alone. More than that, I was going to have to figure out how to live well in a world that had given me little indication that was possible. I didn't know how I was going to do that, just that I had to try. If I had a birthday resolution for the year ahead, that was it.

I made myself say it out loud: *I might always be alone.* It sounded less overwhelming against the noise of the breaking waves. I laughed. *Fuck off*, I thought, *I am done feeling bad.* And then aloud: *I can do whatever I want.* Just then I remembered seeing Patti Smith, two summers before, reading an old poem at the Brooklyn Bridge Park, the city aflame behind her in the setting summer sun. *I'm gonna get out of here*, she said, as if she were once again that young girl who'd written those lines decades ago. She was going to *get on that train and go to New York City.* She was never going to return, *no never.* She was going to travel light. How I loved that. *Oh, watch me now*, she'd said. As if she was about to perform the world's greatest magic trick.

Oh, watch me now, I thought.

Then I turned around and went back to my hotel room.

•

I woke up feeling victorious.

This was unexpected.

Was this what it was like on the other side? I thought, staring up at the ceiling. I felt like I was in the final scene of *Thelma & Louise* if immediately after their car had plunged off the cliff it had sprouted wings, Harry Potter–style, and flown away. I felt like Dorothy opening the door into Oz. Everything was suddenly Technicolor. I'd killed the witch; let the adventure begin. Or was I the witch now? I wondered with a smile: smart, powerful, a force to be reckoned with, and untethered from all the expectations of who I was supposed to be at this point.

It helped that through the open window I could hear the whooshing pulse of the ocean, punctuated by the intermittent roar of an arriving subway and the ding of the train doors as they opened and closed. Through the slats in the blinds, I could see the pale blue of the early morning sky; the breeze that rattled in smelled like salt. The world outside felt wide and open.

"I feel great." I said this out loud, lest the dueling voices that had been in my head the day before were thinking of making a reappearance. And then for emphasis: "I feel fucking great."

I got out of bed and put my bathing suit on under my pajamas, grabbed my book and a towel, and walked down to the beach for a swim. It was a Friday morning, and apart from the morning joggers I was the only person around. The water was so calm and flat the ocean looked like a lake. A lake with oil slicks and a few floating plastic bottles, which were probably always there, but easier to miss when the surf was up. I took off my pajamas, wrapped them in my towel, put the straw panama hat I'd brought with me, even though the sun was still casting only weak morning light, on top of the pile, and walked to the water. I waded in, trying to skirt the slicks and debris, and walked out until I was deep enough that I could comfortably dunk myself under. The gently rippling water did not give me the crashing baptism into this new decade that I'd hoped for, but the salt water felt good as I floated there, letting the current carry me back to shore. Afterward I sat on the cold sand, my now wet pajamas pasted against my legs, and read my book. Every once in a while, I turned my phone on to field birthday messages and scroll through Facebook posts. Mostly though, I wondered about my sudden change in outlook, which felt like a gift from the universe. Would every day be like this now? Would this sense of lightness and expectation weave its way into my life the same way the heavy dread and shame had these last few years? I felt a little bit like I'd just fallen in love. That same sense of elation and possibility. Except I was alone. It was confusing.

A man slowly walked by along the water's edge, his pants rolled up to keep from getting wet. I kept my head down out of habit, knowing that to do otherwise would be to invite company. Women alone always seemed to be seen as an advertisement: *open space, please fill*.

Under downcast eyelids, I watched him change course and wander slowly up to me. Sure enough, he stopped a few feet away. Head down in my book, I pretended to be fully occupied, even as I shifted my legs underneath me in case I had to stand up quickly. Finally, he cleared his throat and said, "Excuse me." I looked up as slowly as I could. He was older, and heavyset, and had what sounded like a Russian accent. His white shirt was held together by its two middle buttons and fell open over his lower stomach, revealing a hairy belly. I couldn't tell if he was distraught or drunk. His clothes were rumpled, but he didn't appear to be homeless. I glanced behind me as discreetly as I could to see if anyone was around, but the joggers had left, and it seemed I was alone. I turned my eyes to him but didn't say anything, hoping to make clear with my silence that I had no interest in this conversation. He was undaunted. He cleared his throat. "Can I ask you, what does a woman mean when she says she needs space?" He put his hand to his chest. "I have lost my wife, she has left, and it hurts so deeply."

I stifled a laugh, not because I thought his pain (or inebriation, if that's what it was) was funny, but because it was too ridiculous. After all this, to be happily siting alone on a beach on my fortieth birthday and be called upon by a male stranger to answer for *his* aloneness. I shook my head and shrugged, thinking if I kept silent maybe he'd go away. The silence stretched. But he didn't move.

"I see you here, you wanted space from . . . something." He shook his head. "And so I thought I'd ask you. Why would my wife want to be alone? Maybe you have wisdom."

I sighed loudly and gazed at him directly with what I hoped was a look that conveyed my deep annoyance. It had no effect.

"I have no wisdom," I said finally, reaching for my phone as though answering a call. "Maybe she just needs time."

"Maybe time," he said, nodding slowly, his head dropping, "maybe time." He stood there for a minute more silently. Then he said, "Excuse me," and walked away.

I watched him shuffle along and felt a little bad that I'd been so cold, but how could I be expected to explain to him why a woman would want to be alone when I wasn't yet entirely sure how to explain it to myself? I had no idea what I was supposed to do next. I couldn't even think of a movie to go see, or a book to read, where I could be sure to find some sense of my life reflected back at me. I had arrived in a land without stories.

Finally, as the last rays of the sun were disappearing, turning the water from gold to its more usual slimy black, I boarded the train back to my life and into this new decade. It had just been a day after all. A mostly regular day. Short and sweet, and other than the discovery that it was possible to feel good after turning forty—I hadn't, as it turned out, lost my head—there wasn't all that much to say about it. Not yet.

As I sat down my phone vibrated again. Probably another birthday message; they were trickling in more slowly now, but still coming.

I looked down: 646.

Hey—are you in New York City?

Of course. Of fucking course.

5. Women Never Really Faint

Asking a single woman to give the toast at her best friend's wedding the same week she turns forty sounds like a bad punch line, or the tagline to a film I would only watch on cable reruns when I had the flu. In the movie version, of course, the main character would not be forty. She'd be much younger. In *My Best Friend's Wedding*, Julia Roberts's character is *twenty-seven*. According to the setup, she and her best (male) friend once made a promise that if they weren't married by twenty-eight they would marry each other. Instead he's marrying Cameron Diaz, whose character is twenty. Jealous hijinks ensue. Julia does not get her man. Instead, the story leaves her dancing in the arms of her gay best friend, Rupert Everett. "Maybe there won't be marriage," he says. "Maybe there won't be sex. But by God, there'll be dancing." In 1997, the year the film was released in theaters, this was admittedly a somewhat bold story line move and launched the *I'll just marry my gay best friend* film and TV franchise that was so popular in the late nineties. But behind the subverted happily-ever-after there was, of course, the assurance that Julia, aged twenty-seven, still had many years of potential love and life ahead of her before things would get really dire.

It's the same assurance Billy Crystal gives to Meg Ryan in *When Harry Met Sally* (1989) after she discovers her ex-boyfriend is getting married. "Why didn't he want to marry *me?*" she wails. "What's the matter with *me?*" And then: "No, no, no. I *drove* him away. And I'm going to be forty!" Here Billy Crystal swoops in. "In eight years," he says pragmatically. Translation: there's still time.

Which was literally what a nice older woman at Mauri's wedding party assured me of after she wished me happy birthday.

It was the Sunday afternoon after I'd made my mad dash to the Rockaways, and I was standing at a small table in a back- yard in New Jersey with Maddy, Ally, and Kara, three women I'd known since my early twenties, when we all, Mauri included, worked together at the Cedar Tavern in Greenwich Village. Mauri had married Ben a few days before my birthday at Man- hattan's City Hall, with only their immediate families and me in attendance. Now they were throwing a big party at Ben's parents' house near the Jersey Shore for everyone else.

It was approaching 5:00 p.m., and the party was in full swing around us. It looked like a picnic from Brooklyn's Prospect Park had simply been lifted up and transplanted into Jersey; the women were in sundresses, and most of the men sported beards. The sun blazed through the sweeping leafy green trees onto the lawn, where a dance floor had been placed. Mauri's now- husband, Ben, owned a wine bar in Brooklyn, and there were huge silver ice buckets along the walls of his parents' home, filled with bottles of champagne and rosé.

I'd been recounting the sudden reappearance of 646 on my fortieth birthday, a story which itself sounded like a question- able plotline for a romantic comedy. Just as I'd been making my way back into the city, feeling victorious, he'd texted me to warn me he was going to be in the gossip pages the following day because he'd been sleeping with a twenty-five-year-old who hadn't taken kindly to his treatment.

"Did he know it was your birthday?" asked Ally, frowning as though she had misheard me.

"He was texting to warn me and to apologize. But no, he didn't know it was my birthday." *Or he didn't remember*, I thought, thinking of his surprise appearance the year before.

"Well, that's bullshit," said Kara, practically spitting out the words. "What a motherfucker." Kara had the skin of a twenty-two-year-old and the mouth of a truck driver, and she taught special education and English to sixth graders in Brooklyn.

"That's really all he wanted to tell you?" asked Maddy skeptically.

I nodded.

"Well, that's nice, at least. The apology, I mean," offered Ally hopefully. "At least he's thinking about you." Ally lived in Los Angeles, and after some spots in commercials, now made a living as a successful voice actress.

That had been my initial reaction, too. As if I should be grateful he thought enough of me to let me know I was right in thinking he'd treated me badly. It had quickly worn off. "I suppose. I think he just likes apologizing. It's like a performance piece: something else he can get applause for. He also said that he's working on himself."

"Like fucking hell," said Kara.

"It would have been nice if he'd tried to imagine how you felt *before* he found out it was being published in the gossip pages," said Maddy flatly.

"I just don't get it," said Ally. "All that texting. What did he want? It's bizarre."

I had spent months wondering the same thing. Wondering, just like Meg Ryan's Sally: What was wrong with me? Wondering if I had a right to be upset. And then eventually wondering why I had let it go on. I had interviewed a professional matchmaker for a story once, and she had taken a long look at me and said, "People who are unavailable attract unavailable people." Only recently had I started wondering what was wrong with him.

"I think it was an emotional blow job," I said. "Getting off on knowing he still had me on the hook." It pained me to say it. It was easier to believe there was something wrong with me than admit someone whom I had held on to for so long had considered me so disposable.

"That is fucking sick," said Kara. Her fury made me feel better; I tossed it back as though she had handed me a shot. It was Kara who'd first trained me to be a waitress. She'd been "living" on a mattress in the corner of a yoga studio on St. Mark's Place and Third Ave., which she had to vacate every day between 7:00 a.m. and 10:00 p.m. so classes could be held there. She was always pissed off she couldn't convince our manager to put Bikini Kill on the jukebox, an anger lost on me at the time since I had no idea who Bikini Kill was.

"I guess. But I was in it, too. Maybe I'm the star fucker." I said this not because I really thought it was true, but because I was hoping it wasn't. As much as I trusted them to tell me the truth, I also counted on them to be kinder to me than I was able to be to myself.

"You're not a star fucker," said Maddy so calmly it was as if she were giving the temperature. It was comforting to hear her say it, but I also knew it would take way more than this for Maddy to think I'd done something wrong or behaved stupidly. Maddy was the native New Yorker among us. She'd had the sort of chaotic, traumatic upbringing that in the movies is trotted out as a courtroom defense for major felonies. We'd met seventy-two hours after I'd landed in New York, at a coffee shop in SoHo where we both worked; I was just past twenty-three; she was twenty-one—a year and a half younger, but decades older in experience. By the time we'd met, she was living with her much older boyfriend, whom she'd moved in with when she was sixteen, and co-owned her own vintage clothing store in the city. She had both a cell phone and a pager, which in 1997 was exotic. She schooled me on the importance of maintaining good credit in order to be able to sign a lease. That was years and years ago. She was married now, and living in a house in Brooklyn with her husband and daughter, doing school runs and scheduling play dates. The fact that she had managed to construct outward markings of a conventional life always struck me as the most wildly unconventional outcome of her story. Nonetheless, it was nearly impossible to shock or offend her.

"It's pretty intoxicating to have someone shower that much attention on you," Ally said kindly.

"He's a fucking psychopath," said Kara.

It was at this point that one of Mauri's relatives, an older woman with short fluffy hair and heavily lined lips, came to the table and Mauri introduced her around before floating back away.

"You must be Glynnis," the woman said, her Southern accent floating through the New Jersey backyard like a heavily scented perfume. Mauri was from a small town in Tennessee, where most of her family still lived. "I've heard so much about you. You're the person Mauri always travels with. The pictures of y'all's trips are so incredible. What adventures you two have. I hear you just had a birthday."

"I did," I said, smiling at the *y'all*.

"Well, my goodness, you'd never know it. You look wonderful."

No one I knew looked their age anymore, or looked how women past a *certain* age were supposed to look. Decades of drinking eight glasses of water a day and slathering on sunblock had apparently paid off. But I took the compliment in the spirit it was meant.

"Thank you," I said.

She leaned in and placed her hand reassuringly on mine. "And don't worry, dear," she said conspiratorially. "I know it will still happen for you. There's still time."

There it was. I could feel the reaction of the table without turning, as though it were the shadow of a villain in cartoon movies, growing ominously behind me. They weren't affronted on their own behalf. All three of them were married; Maddy's and Kara's children were playing together on the still-empty dance floor. They were offended on my behalf, at the idea that anyone could think of my life as lacking. Too much of my life was their life, too. When we talked about ourselves we tended to use the first-person plural.

I didn't have many practical skills, but I did have a genius for friendship. I didn't have a best friend; I had best friends. I didn't have a group of close friends; I had groups of close friends. These women were the inner core. No doubt, if I'd landed in an office after I left school, I would have collected a similar group of friends, people I could return to over the years to talk about our shared foundation. But there was something particular about the bond formed sprinting to and fro across a floor, food and drink and cash in hand, for hours on end. Hours that became years. There was a strange carnal connection between us, too, borne of the fact that we had waited tables together for so long, and, in the case of Maddy and Mauri, had lived together.

There was no infrastructure to our jobs. No human resources to complain to, or sick leave, or benefits, or mentors. We became those things for one another. When a customer got handsy or physical or abusive, we passed them off and then cut them off, and on the rare occasions that didn't work, the baseball bat might come out from behind the bar and they'd be physically removed by the bartender and the line of regulars who emerged behind him.

We had no parents who stepped in to supplement the rent. Or college networks, or Ivy League connections; I would be well into my media career before I realized the latter even existed. We were those things to one another, too. For most of our twenties we'd lived in the racing, relentless now. In shared physical space. We knew without looking how the other person moved and when; we stepped around one another like choreographed dancers, forever keeping our drink trays from landing on the floor. The service station had space for only one plate of food when we got hungry, and one shared pint glass of soda, which one of us surreptitiously poured half a bottle of wine into partway through our eleven-hour-shifts-with-no-breaks. To this day, when we had dinner together, the unspoken assumption was that we were ordering as a group. We knew each other's horoscopes, crushes, boyfriends, one-night stands, birth control preferences, sleep habits. There were no secrets; our shifts were too long, and too intense; secrets didn't stand a chance. Our social lives were inextricably intertwined. Our after-work drinks took place at 4:00 a.m. once the gate had been pulled down. Sometime around 6:00 a.m. we'd bike home over the bridge to our apartments.

All of this had woven a decade of our lives together so tightly that our formative years seemed nearly indistinguishable from one another's. It was more than ten years since that job had ended, and we still had the ability to start conversations as if we'd just seen one another the day before.

I never had to explain myself to these women. Even if they thought I was being stupid, I knew they were still on my side.

But much to my surprise, I didn't need to lean on my collective self to navigate around this nice woman who thought she was providing me comfort by assuring me that, despite my age, I appeared to be someone to whom things could still happen. That, despite all available evidence, there was probably someone out there still who would be willing to fill up the vacant space that was so evident inside me. For a minute I felt all the old defense mechanisms go up, like metal toward a magnet. I took a deep breath and prepared to deliver my well-rehearsed responses: to throw up my hands in defeat and remark on how the good ones were taken, or check my wrist dramatically and say, *I hope they hurry up!* Or just simply nod my gratitude and implicitly offer up my apology that I was *still* alone. All the things I was used to saying to get out of this conversation and make the other person feel more comfortable. Instead, I found myself resisting the urge to laugh. Not at her. At the suddenly absurd idea that I was running out of time. I was no longer running, I realized. I was off the clock.

"I have to tell you," I said, making sure there was not one ounce of defensiveness in my voice, "I think it's going to be pretty great even if it doesn't happen."

I could see confusion flicker across her face like a shadow over the sun, and then she smiled and excused herself, and I promptly felt guilty. I knew her comment had been meant kindly; it had likely never occurred to her I could be feeling anything *but* bad. It hadn't really started to occur to me until a few days ago.

"Yeah, don't worry, Glynnis," said Maddy flatly, refilling my wine. "I'm pretty sure it's not over yet."

"Yeah, what the fuck does that mean?" said Kara. "Like you need a fucking man for things to happen to you?"

Mauri glided by the table on her rounds and took a large swig out of my glass of rosé. It would never have crossed her mind that asking me to give a toast this week might have been considered by some to be loaded; she never saw me as lacking.

"Whew, this is a lot," she said, gesturing to the party crowd who all wanted their moment with her. She'd put the white slip dress she'd been married in back on and pinned the white netting back on her sleek bob. She looked like a vintage photograph someone would put on their wedding inspiration board.

"I'm still working on my wedding toast," I said. "I should warn you, I might end up getting up there and reciting the old restaurant beer list."

Ally rolled her eyes. "You haven't written it yet?"

Maddy, with relief: "Oh good, you can speak for all of us."

Mauri laughed. "I'm sure whatever you do will be fine."

She meant it, too. This was the glue of our friendship, for better or worse.

Mauri was eight years younger than me, but unlike most people I knew, had managed to slide through her twenties un-encumbered by self-doubt or anxiety about getting things done by a certain point. The first time I'd met her, on her first or second waitress training shift, I'd asked her if she was on drugs because she seemed inexplicably cheerful. She'd always thought this was hysterical, even though I'd been dead serious. She'd ar-rived in New York to be a dancer, and eventually after touring with a small company, opened a home goods store in Brooklyn.

Mauri was also the person I most often traveled with, always willing to jump aboard my latest whim. *I've just watched the episode of* Mad Men *where Don disappears to Palm Springs. Let's go.* I'd writ-ten her one night shortly after midnight a few years earlier. I'd been working twelve hours a day, seven days a week for more than a year and had finally finagled a week off. The idea of dis-appearing was making me drool; did she want to fly to Vegas with me and rent a car and drive around the desert for a week? *I'm in!!! How do we make this happen?* came the response the next morning. The following year, when I was planning my first-ever paid vacation, I texted her again: *Plane tickets to Barcelona just* *dropped below $500, feel like a Spanish road trip?* An hour later: *Ok I'm in! Want to book these tonight or in the morning?*

It was always *I'm in.* It had been like that even when we were waiting tables, and our trips had been limited to days at Jacob Riis beach in Queens or house-sitting gigs an hour upstate. Or merely a last-minute drink at Bemelmans, where we'd "dress for the day we wanted" and skip dinner so as to afford the martini, counting on the fact that the bow-tied server would continually restock the free snack bowl of chips and nuts. She was my partner in my favorite version of my life. And now she was officially not. She was in with someone else.

I'd been thinking for the past few days about what I should say in my toast. I wanted to avoid the usual jokes and saccharine reminiscences and figure out how to recognize that it wasn't just Mauri's life that was dramatically shifting, but also what that meant to those around her. Particularly our friendship. When I'd watched her exchange her vows in a little corner room at City Hall, I felt myself beat back the familiar sensation brought on by the knowledge that I was about to be called upon to rearrange my life again. It was a mix of panic and resentment. I'd been through this before, many times. It sometimes felt like my thirties were an updated version of the old children's game Ten Little Indians (which no doubt goes by a different name these days); every year someone exited to marriage or babies, until now at age forty, there were none.

For a while this disappearing act had been literal. I'd lived with Maddy and Mauri for many years; they were a support system I'd relied on for more than a decade. And then in very short order they had all moved out and in with husbands or boyfriends.

We had all survived that with our friendships intact. But as I had watched Mauri and Ben exchange vows, I could feel myself steeling against the knowledge I was about to have my foundation knocked out again, and there was nothing I could do to stop it. I struggled to figure out how to articulate these emotions without sounding envious. There was no way to talk about any of this being hard without casting myself squarely in the role of the bitter, jealous friend.

I wasn't envious of Mauri. If anything, I was envious of our past lives together, and I was mourning a life I was losing. The resentment, I'd realized, was rooted in the fact that I never had any control over this upending of my life. It had never occurred to me that I was allowed to do anything but silently accept it. The fact that no one acknowledged that I had anything to be upset about made it all that much worse. It was hard work to root yourself so deeply in life that you could still love people and rely on them, knowing at any point they could make decisions that would leave you scrambling to find solid ground again. This was the better or worse of friendship, undeclared. What I wanted was for there to exist some way for me to say *I'm happy and sad and not jealous* all at the same time, and also *This is a loss and is still beautiful.* Maybe that was the wedding toast. *We are really the ones giving you away. And it's hard. And I will miss our life. And I am still so happy for your happiness. And so proud of you.*

Someone called to Mauri from across the dance floor, and she moved away from our table to continue her wedding rounds. Ally called her back. "Wait, we need a picture of all of us!" She handed her phone to one of Ben's wine bar employees who was at the table next to us, and we leaned in together.

"Do you think any of the regulars would have believed we'd come out so good?" Maddy asked as we marveled at the photo on the phone he handed back. We looked like a postcard for life: five smiling, well-dressed women secure in their lives. We exuded vitality and confidence. There was scant evidence of the chaos from which we'd all emerged. Certainly, very few people would have looked at a similar shot of us taken fifteen years earlier and leapt to the conclusion that any of those women, raging around New York, hanging on to one another tenuously, could possibly be headed for productive, stable lives. And yet here we all were.

Later that night, Ally and I found a diner that was still serving milk shakes. The party hadn't stopped for wedding toasts until long after the sun had set. By the time I got up to speak, we'd made our way through an entire bucket of champagne, and the dance floor turned into a sea of gin and rosé—then it started to rain. When we arrived at the diner, sometime after midnight, I'd already forgotten what I'd said during my wedding toast; I just had a blurry recollection of smiles and tears.

"I wish I'd recorded it," Ally said, as our plates of fries and mozzarella sticks arrived. "You said something about how we were the ones giving Mauri away, and that it was painful only because we loved her so much. But better than that. Not like a greeting card.

"I'm sorry about 646," she went on. "I don't think you're stupid, by the way. You'd have to be really fucked up yourself to realize what he was doing. I do think the question is, what do *you* want?"

A panicked look must have crossed my face because she quickly followed up.

"Look, I'm married and I don't know what I want. Do I want a baby, do I not want a baby? Do I want to go back to acting? I don't know!" She threw up her hands.

"*Do* you want a baby?" I asked. For as long as I'd known her, Ally had said she didn't want kids. Period. It was a running joke that whenever she got commercial acting jobs, it was always playing the suburban mother. But even after her marriage a few years ago: no kids. She was thirty-nine now.

"I don't know! Matt would be such a great dad. He's always said he's okay if we don't. But I don't know. And I have to make up my mind soon. But it's hard, I love our lives."

"This is why people have babies," I said, "because it's exhausting not to know what you're supposed to do next. A baby is basically a nonnegotiable map for the next two decades."

She laughed. "But, Jesus, a baby. It's so scary. What about you?"

I leaned my head back into the seat.

I didn't know. I had scrambled through the last few years, making the best of what I had, and then making sure other people got what they needed. I couldn't envision who the person might be that I did want. Did I want anyone? Had I just assumed the children would show up on their own, even as I watched so many friends battle to get and remain pregnant?

"Maybe I just like being alone," I said.

"Well, you're certainly really good at it," said Ally. Few people could have made that sound like a compliment, but she did. And something clicked.

For the first time it crossed my mind that being alone could be a good thing, and not evidence that I was defective. I had been beating myself up for so long about allowing myself to get involved with a married man, and I had been overcome with shame over keeping 646 in my life. Had I always actually just preferred to be on my own and not known that was something I could be without it being something I should feel ashamed about? Had I instead found men I could slip in without actually having to give up what I so cherished about my life? They were there, but not there at the same time.

"No more married men. No more fake text message relationships," I said.

"That seems like a good start," Ally said drily.

Goodbye to all that. I knew I could be alone, but what if I gave myself permission to prefer it? What would that be like?

"*I wonder if I've been changed in the night. Let me think. Was I the same when I got up this morning? I almost think I can remember feeling a little different. But if I'm not the same, the next question is 'Who in the world am I?' Ah, that's the great puzzle!*"

Alice in Wonderland

6. The Jet Set

The first time I got on a plane I was nineteen years old and alone. It was Halloween, and I was flying to London on a ticket I'd bought for myself using the money I'd earned working as a hot walker at Woodbine racetrack in Toronto (the job was far less salacious than it sounded: I walked hot racehorses in circles around a barn until they cooled down enough to return to their stalls). Over the summer, eager to put off university for a year, I'd signed up for a six-month work program in England. At the time six months sounded like a decade. My plan was to stay on after my job ended and backpack around Europe. Even though I'd been living on my own for almost a year at that point, I'd never been outside of Canada. When I complained about this growing up in our suburban house outside of Toronto, my father would helpfully point out that he'd once driven us across the border at Niagara Falls and then done a U-turn and driven us right back, so *technically* speaking I had, in fact, left the country. I was unmoved. Literally as well as figuratively. Unlike every other person I knew in Ontario, my family had not gone to Florida for winter vacation. We had not done the drive down I-95 to visit grandparents or go to Disney World. We didn't even make the trip to Buffalo to take advantage of the cheaper American prices at the mall outlets. The MacNicols stayed put. Travel was for other people.

I felt this keenly. Even as a very small child I liked to be on the move. I once sent my mother into a panic when, at age six, I decided to walk the mile home from school alone instead of waiting for the bus. One of my favorite childhood songs was "Carey" by Joni Mitchell (growing up in Canada meant that Joni Mitchell was not a late-teen discovery made during someone's dingy basement high school party, but an ever-present voice on the radio along with Neil Young, Anne Murray, and Gordon Lightfoot). It was the line *The wind is in from Africa* that reached out and held me with its promise: until I could go somewhere myself, somewhere would find its way to me. Even something as intangible as the wind could connect me in real life to a place that otherwise existed for me only in books.

Growing up, nearly everything existed for me only in books, which had the effect of making all travel seem automatically rife with adventure and exoticism, no matter the reality. When friends complained about the terrible monotony of being trapped during spring break in the back of their parents' car en route to Myrtle Beach, it fell on uncomprehending ears. To me, the concrete American Interstate held the same unknowable mystique as Paris. Perhaps it was less than surprising then that I cleaved on to the Little House books by Laura Ingalls Wilder the way I did: not only was she also an adventurous young girl, she was a real person; I could find the places she'd gone to on a map and know she'd actually been there, and that because she'd done it, perhaps I could do it, too.

Eventually I found my way to those dots in real life along

with many others, always slightly astounded that I had managed to manifest my own childhood imagination. After that first six-month stint in England when I was nineteen, where I learned to drive stick shift on the wrong side of the car on the wrong side of the road, I backpacked through Europe for three months with a girl named Ang, whom I'd met on the plane. It was during our time on the road that I picked up my habit of never arriving anywhere after dark—before the internet this self-imposed rule seemed less a practicality than a survival tactic for two teenage girls on their own in strange countries. I also learned never to hitchhike after a botched attempt to thumb a ride from Bari to Naples left us scurrying away from an aggressive truck driver who'd picked us up at a gas station and unceremoniously dropped us off hours later onto the shoulder of a Naples freeway at four o'clock on a Sunday morning, where we walked for hours till eventually we found our hostel. On this trip, I mastered the art of walking as if I knew exactly where I was going, quickly and decisively: a wrong turn was never a wrong turn, it was simply a different route I had *chosen*. This quickly resulted in Ang and me frequently being asked for directions, often by cute boys whom we'd allow to tag along until they got tiresome.

But my main takeaway on that first trip abroad was a lesson that would sustain me for the rest of my life: travel meant reinvention. On the road, time was measured by experience, not the hands of a clock. Motion could equal redemption.

During the years after I quit waiting tables, when I was trying to launch a writing career, I made too little money to even consider traveling. Being a freelancer meant that when I wanted to cover a story outside of New York, like the 2008 New Hampshire primaries, or even Barack Obama's inauguration, I had to pay for it out of my own pocket. Or now, out of Rachel and my joint pockets. We were both writers on the internet— Rachel had given me my first writing job, opening the door to a world I hungered after but had no access to—and we became well-practiced at pooling our money and resources and hacking our way to events we wanted to attend. Otherwise we stayed put.

My clearest memory of the months I'd spent burned out and unemployed were not the hours I sat on my apartment floor watching *The Golden Girls*, but of the mornings after my cable had been shut off, when I'd slink downstairs with an open laptop and pace the sidewalks under the stately trees of Brooklyn Heights searching for a free Wi-Fi signal. When I found one, I'd locate an empty stoop and take a seat as if I lived there and were just enjoying the sun. I always had my response ready in case I was spotted by acquaintances on their hurried, determined way to work: *Like my new office? My stupid Wi-Fi is down AGAIN*. Before returning to my internet-free apartment (my wish to be off the internet having been fulfilled with an ironic vengeance) I'd download a clip of Audrey Hepburn on her moped in *Roman Holiday*, or Grace Kelly in the convertible in *To Catch a Thief*, or even Keira Knightley languishing in that green dress in the humid English countryside in *Atonement*, to take back with me. Little crumbs of an adventurous life I desperately hoped one day to return to, even if at that point I had no idea how it might be accomplished.

Had I been able, on any one of those days, to gaze into a crystal ball and see myself two and a half years later, six weeks after my fortieth birthday, exiting a cab at JFK airport on a Friday night, dressed in a vintage fur chubby and asking for directions to the VIP check-in line, I would have ditched all those clips and simply watched my future self.

Four days earlier my friend Jo had emailed and asked me if I wanted to take a weekend trip to Iceland. She'd recently been hired as the deputy editor of a large travel website and was assigning stories; this was one of them. It was the sort of writing assignment you saw in the movies but never actually encountered in real life. (And it was almost definitely temporary: soon enough—two years or less was my bet—the company funding all this glitzy "content" would figure out there was no money in it and pull the plug.) Could I manage it on such short notice? Jo wanted to know. I nearly said no out of habit, before I realized I could! I could just leave. I thought of that bubble that had hovered over my head back when I was tied to my BlackBerry and Gchat windows; how badly I'd wanted just to get away. As I pulled my luggage toward the terminal door at JFK, I was dazzled by the sensation that I was occupying the life I'd yearned for for so long. And now I was doing just that. Calmly and chicly. I strode through the premium security line feeling that I was exactly where I wanted to be and who I wanted to be. And then.

SMACK.

I hit the floor so hard, and so loudly, that even in my dazed state I could make out passengers running toward me from fifty feet away. A sharply dressed man leapt to my aid and held my right elbow, helping me up. "Good thing you had the fur on to break your fall," he said, cautioning me to move slowly. I could see his polished shoes and was aware of his cashmere coat, but was too mortified to take a proper look at his face. "Thank you," I said, my head down. "I'm fine, I'm fine," I assured him, desperate to blend into the crowds and away from the smack that was still echoing in my ears.

What had I tripped over? I peered down to find the culprit and quickly realized I'd tangled my bootstraps together when I'd put them back on, probably because I'd been staring at the escalator the entire time, trying to make out where the business class lounge was. "Nothing broken?" asked the security guard, obviously concerned. I shook my head, hobbled over to a bench to remove my boots, and put them back on correctly. And then, as quickly as I could I limped away and up the escalator to the private lounge, eager to escape the scene. So much for my fantasy of being a glamorous international traveler.

This was my first trip alone, since getting on that plane to London all those years ago. Since then I'd always been one half of a pair: Rachel or Mauri; my university roommate Laura with whom I'd spent two weeks driving around France shortly after I turned thirty; Ang, my backpacking partner; my friend Lesley, a writer whom I'd accompanied to the far reaches of Kansas once for a story.

I reveled in the fact that I was being jetted away on someone else's dime and that I'd finally reached the point in my life where my career and, to some degree, finances had aligned to produce the life I'd fantasized about, though I couldn't help but lament the fact that I was likely going to be doing it alone. All my other halves now had their own other halves to travel with or young kids who made travel difficult. Just as my life was catapulting me into some great beyond, theirs were tying them down to routines and caregiving—decades of both. I would have to get used to the idea that if I wanted to travel, I had to be prepared to have adventures alone. Either that or I was going to be sitting at home hemmed in, not by my finances, but by my inability to see myself as a solo woman traveler.

This trip would be a good test. For the next few days, at least, my other half was my writing assignment. Being on the road with a purpose tended to cancel out all the questions the world liked to attach to women on their own. Certainly, no woman had ever been told it was a good idea to leave home alone for no reason.

I collapsed into my extra wide business class seat and pulled from my bag Beryl Markham's *West With the Night*, her memoir of life as an aviatrix in Africa in the 1930s and famed solo flight over the Atlantic. When I was flying I liked to reread the chapter of her precarious, middle-of-the-night transatlantic flight to calm myself down. The other reason travel was so otherworldly to me was that somewhere in my mid-twenties, I'd been gripped by a paralyzing fear of flying I couldn't shake. Every trip felt like an exercise in extended terror, during which I would cycle through all the scenarios that would result in our imminent death. Had all the screws in the plane been drilled in properly? Had any of the maintenance people had a bad day? Were they angry at their low paychecks? Untrained? Distracted? Had the pilot been fighting with his wife? (It never occurred to me the pilot might be a woman . . . they were never in plane crash stories.) Would something essential come untethered shortly after takeoff and send us nose-diving into the sea? Was it possible to water land in the ocean Sully-like? Remember that plane that exploded over the Rockaways and crushed those houses? Remember the TSA flight? Remember Air France? Did the pilots know to aim the plane down if the engine stalled, and not up as instinct would suggest?

I desperately wanted to be a person who enjoyed flying. Rachel was so blissfully oblivious to being on a plane she once slept through a series of alarming announcements warning us to buckle up because we were about to land on the edge of a tornado. Mauri fell asleep on takeoff. So far, however, I had failed. I never took medication on a plane; most of my flights were to Toronto and too short to knock myself out for (though they seemed endless in my head). Instead I relied on mind games. My friend Margeaux, whom I'd met two days after first arriving in New York and who'd been my last roommate before she too had left to get married, had the unlikely ability to make new agey adages and ideas that I would normally scoff at sound convincing. Among these was an unshakable, inexplicable (or if it was, I'd forgotten the explanation) faith in the number twenty-one. In moments of pure terror, which is what I experienced the second I stepped on a plane, I leaned on her faith in twenty-one as though it were a divine protectant. It was ridiculous (though perhaps no more so than any other acts of faith), but it kept me in my seat. And so the second I sat down I set about trying to make the seat number and the flight number and the date all add up into something approximating twenty-one.

The captain came on to let us know we were seventeenth in line for takeoff. I pulled out my phone. I hadn't yet kicked the habit of approaching it as if it held the possibility of dessert. But no texts. There was an email from my sister, Alexis, subject line: baby logistics. Her C-section had been scheduled for the last Tuesday in October, three and a half weeks from now. We'd agreed that I'd come home when the baby arrived to help with my five-year-old nephew and three-year-old niece. She was still going back and forth about whether she wanted me there for the delivery, or whether it was better for me to arrive home when she arrived home. I'd already booked a ticket that would get me there the day before the delivery, but I wanted to give her peace of mind. *I'll just book two tickets,* I wrote, *and cancel whatever I don't use. I have to be at the airport 90 minutes before the flight and can be at the hospital two hours after takeoff. You don't have to make up your mind until 5am that morning.*

I hit send and scrolled down. The plane rolled forward.

There was another email from the social worker I'd queried for information about setting up an appointment to view nursing homes for my mother. The process in Canada was sometimes years long, bureaucratic, and involved many boxes being checked. The exact opposite of my mother's decline, which was precipitous, continually shocking in its speed. For months, I'd been trapped in a feedback loop trying to figure out how to set up the help she needed; it felt like a video game I was trying to master: which doctor needed to sign off on what to get us to the next level. So far, no one had signed off on anything. We did not fit the picture of a family desperately in need of assistance. My father kept an obsessively clean house, something he liked to credit to his time spent in the seminary as a young man. When

I did manage to schedule a social worker to assess my mother in her home (level one), what they saw was a woman who was nicely dressed (my father insisted on it, even if she spent the day in bed, which was often the case), vacuumed carpets, and shiny counters. They only ever stayed ten minutes and then scurried away unworried, presumably to homes where dishes were not done, and beds were not made. My mother's great brain didn't help matters much either. There was, I discovered, a set list of questions doctors asked patients with dementia or Alzheimer's. Many of the results were gauged on vocabulary levels. My mother's vocabulary was legendary. She was a person, my cousin had once loudly joked at a family gathering when I was a teenager, who thought it normal to use the word *anthropomorphize* in a sentence, "As if ordinary people know what that means!" It had been the first time it'd occurred to me that not everyone spoke like this. "These tests are made for the average patient," a doctor had told my sister and me a few months earlier. "Your mother is quite above average." This after I'd expressed exasperation over her being sent away with yet another clean bill of health, only to arrive home and start raging that she didn't know who she was or who any of us were.

Like so much, it was all a matter of timing. I'd once had my heart broken by a man who'd said, "The timing is just bad." Every time the truth of this statement proved out it made me furious once again. In the weeks after our awful Christmas, I'd often wondered whether my conviction that my mother was worse in the evening was simply my being overdramatic, overkill in an effort to convince my father and the doctors that something was wrong. It was not. My mother was, I learned, *sundowning.* This was what happened to people with dementia or Alzheimer's patients when their confusion grew increasingly worse as the actual sun went down. It had something to do with circadian rhythms and explained the Dr. Jekyll and Mr. Hyde transformations I'd been witnessing for months. However, I could never manage to get it witnessed by anyone who could actually do anything about it. My parents lived more than an hour from all the specialists my mother was required to see, and my father, who liked to be in bed by early evening, made all their appointments for the morning. Between her vocabulary, and the unsteady clarity she sometimes had in the early hours, no one could understand my urgency. Half the energy I expended making phone calls and setting up appointments was devoted to not sounding like a hysterical overreacting daughter. I knew no one took hysterical women seriously. In the meantime, I was touring nursing homes every chance I got. I was required to make a list of our top five choices of homes and file it with the health care officials who oversaw senior care in the province of Ontario. When my mother's name reached the top of the list, a process I was told would likely take eighteen months—and that was only after I'd had someone sign off that she was eligible— she'd get the first available bed in any of those choices. If we turned it down, she'd go back to the bottom of the list. I felt as if I were playing Russian roulette with her life. Of the homes I'd seen already, I'd left only two not feeling physically ill at the thought of depositing my mother, my brilliant mother, in one of their dark and dingy rooms, amid the confused cries of other patients doing battle with their minds and bodies. So I kept making appointments, hoping to find better options. I made another for the end of October as the plane rolled forward.

I did another quick scan of my inbox. There was an email from the new accountant I had hired to reorganize the books of Rachel and my business; he needed me to dig up all the financials from the past eighteen months. And then there were more baby-related emails. Rachel had started spreading the word about her pregnancy, and people were coming to me for details. *Hey baby mama,* started one email, asking about what the registry plans were and where presents should be addressed. I swallowed a wave of annoyance. How many people could I be expected to be responsible for at the same time, and did responsibility for myself even count among that number? Then came the follow-up voice: *poor Glynnis, jetting off for a weekend abroad.*

I didn't like myself for being annoyed and sat there struggling to figure out why exactly the email bothered me. Yes, I was a little worn out from being on call for people, but I was also excited for Rachel. I knew she wanted this so much. And however hard they were—and they were *hard*—babies were exciting! They changed everything. It was amazing. I knew, too, that had our roles been reversed Rachel would have thrown me ten baby showers, probably with a musical theme and an original song written for the occasion. She was not the problem. The problem was the encroaching sense that I had somehow stepped outside of ritual and was always going to be a guest star, forever celebrating the milestones of others without ever starring in my own. What cultural markers were there for women other than weddings and babies? How else do women mark the progression of their lives? Would I forever be piggybacking on others? That was the depressing thought.

The pilot announced we were next in line for takeoff. I closed my email and shot Rachel a text as was our habit when either of us was about to take off: *Wheels up, Iceland.*

The plane began rocketing forward with the velocity that always turned my stomach cold. Nora Ephron once wrote that she'd ceased being scared of flying when her husband pointed out it was narcissistic to think *her* plane was the one that was going to go down. She said the thought had amused her and cured her of her fear. It had not cured me. But I thought of it often on bumpy flights. I always took turbulence personally, as if I were being punished for something I had or hadn't done. Maybe in this case it would help to think of myself as simply along for the ride. The turbulence could be someone else's responsibility. I put my phone down and leaned back. *If this plane goes down*, I thought with a jolt, *a lot of people are going to be fucked.* I was holding quite a few lives in my hand. I sat back and said a silent prayer of strength for everyone should I go pitching into the water off the Rockaways in the next three minutes, briefly forgetting my terror, unable to decide if I was being narcissistic or not.

7. Choose Your Own Rom-Com

We arrived at Keflavik International Airport at 5:45 a.m. Icelandic time after a brief five and a half hours in the air. This was one of the selling points of visiting Iceland—it's so close!—but it was confusingly short to my body; it felt as if I'd decided to take a nap at 2:00 a.m. The airport was small, clean, and mostly empty. Outside it was pitch-black, as if someone had hung blackout curtains on the windows. No famous midnight sun. I'd managed to visit during the time of year when Iceland's daylight hours were exactly the same as New York's.

After stumbling through customs, I found part of my press group. So far, it included me and a guy named Scott from California who had 200,000 Instagram followers. Scott was in his mid-twenties, had long hair and a long beard, and was carrying only a rucksack; I'd initially taken him for a backpacker. I would later discover he owned his own house in Portland but lived alternately out of his car and by hopping trains, Woody Guthrie–style, around the country. The rest of the group, which consisted of a morning television show from Denver, had been delayed two hours. This was the first press trip I'd ever taken, and I'd naively assumed we'd hit the hotel first and be given a chance to shower and rest before the day began. I quickly discovered this was not how press trips worked. The tour started *now*, our guide Michael explained with a smile that suggested my expecting anything else was the equivalent of asking him to stop the sun from rising till I'd had a chance to sleep. There was in fact a car outside ready to take us to our first stop; we were just waiting on the driver. Michael pointed to a tiny magazine store. If I wanted anything to eat or drink, I should get it there now. I promptly bought a hot chocolate from an automatic coffee machine tucked in beside the cashier counter, then thought better of it and returned for a second one. When I rejoined the group, a tall man who appeared to be in his late forties had materialized. It was as if, while I had been waiting for my drink to pour, Michael had called into Icelandic central casting and ordered up a tall, handsome, rugged guide, complete with the traditional wool sweater and mountain hiking boots.

Enter Viktor.

Almost immediately my bitter thoughts of missed sleep disappeared, and I became very aware that I'd neither showered nor changed clothes since the previous morning, and also that my outfit was now officially ridiculous. The vintage fox fur chubby, which had seemed reasonably practical when I'd scanned my closet for Icelandic apparel, now made me feel as if I'd walked out of a lost episode of *Absolutely Fabulous*. I also had on the same leather ankle boots that had nearly killed me earlier that night. Or now yesterday, I supposed. I shrugged it off, thrust out my hand, and introduced myself.

Viktor grasped it and smiled. Was that a spark? It had been so long since I'd sparked with anyone without knowing a single thing about him. It had been years since the married man had run toward me through the crowded room. 646 had largely been a long, habitual rush of adrenaline brought on by a vibrating phone; the physical component of that relationship had been sporadic, confusing, and forced. Meanwhile, I'd exchanged a total of five words with Viktor; whatever attraction I was feeling was purely physical and felt wonderfully uncomplicated. Then again, maybe I'd imagined it. I was tired, and presumably somewhat smelly, and he was a tour guide who was paid to be nice.

Viktor motioned for us to grab our bags. I downed my hot chocolate, and Scott and I dutifully followed him out of the airport and into the dark, cold, rainy parking lot. There waiting for us was an enormous SUV that looked as if it had driven out of one of those monster truck rallies my nephew liked to watch on TV. The wheels were enormous, practically as tall as I was. I looked at them skeptically while Viktor took my carry-on suitcase and tossed it way in the back—no hope of surreptitiously slipping into a better outfit now. Then he directed Scott to the back seat and opened the passenger door, took my arm, and helped my climb up into it. Perhaps I was not imagining.

A few minutes later, we roared out of the parking lot, crossed a two-lane highway, and drove onto a single lane road. Somewhere behind the dome of clouds we'd flown through the sun was rising, and the world had gone from pitch-black to a shade of gray. It looked like the moon. The land rose up from the road, pockmarked with boulders and craters. Everywhere jets of steam erupted. Some of the craters were filled with water and appeared to be bubbling like a witch's cauldron. I felt as if I'd driven into Mordor. I'd never been in the habit of calling my parents from the road, but thinking of the evenings my mother had sat by my bedside assuring me the Dark Riders were not coming down the street made me want to pick up my phone and call and tell her where I'd landed. Not that it would have meant anything to her. The last time I'd been home, I men-

tioned something about Narnia to her, books we'd read together
hundreds of times; she'd smiled pleasantly and apologized for
not knowing what they were.

We hadn't been in the car long before it became clear Viktor
was far from the strong silent type he appeared to be on first encounter. Twenty minutes into our ride, and he'd already caught
us up on Icelandic politics, Viking history, and his dislike of cit-
ies, or really anywhere with more than twenty people, it seemed.
In addition to being a tour guide (everyone in Iceland was apparently some sort of tour guide, according to him), he was also
a member of parliament and a mountaineer. As we jolted along,
my head began to pound. I couldn't tell whether I was dizzy from
all the information, from fatigue, or from the fact that Viktor
was addressing his monologue directly to me, turning and gazing
intently at me every minute or so, and not at the winding road
that was increasingly difficult to see as the rain became heavier.
Before we'd left the airport, Michael had told us where we were
going, but all I'd gathered was that there would be bread there. I
was hollow with hunger and had the feeling that all the clocks in
my body were running contra to each other. This travel writing
business was getting less decadent by the minute. Meanwhile,
no matter how welcome Viktor's gaze was, the rocking of the
car was putting me to sleep, and I began to wish he'd pay less
attention to me just so I could close my eyes for five seconds. I
turned my head to look out my window, or at least appear to do
so, and closed my eyes. Sweet relief. The car jerked violently, and
I flew into the door handle. Viktor had driven us off the road and
briefly up and onto the moonscape to avoid an oncoming car, and
then, without stopping or even slowing down, promptly jerked us
right back on it. That explained the wheels! I turned in alarm to
him, expecting to find the same expression on his face, but he
hadn't paused for breath. "The first Viking parliament is not far
from here," he said, pointing out and past me.

Our first stop was a geothermal spa. Inside a small empty cafeteria, we were served steaming slices of sweet rye that the owner had just pulled from the sand along the water as we'd arrived. "Iceland sits atop a volcano," Viktor explained as I inhaled piece after piece of the fresh bread slathered in Icelandic butter. ("It is the best butter," said Viktor. "The dairy is purer here, thanks to the clean glacial waters the animals drink.") The volcano was the reason why the country felt as though it were bursting and shifting and bubbling at every turn. It also meant the country was powered entirely on geothermal energy, resulting in an abundance of hot water. In the winter the sidewalks of Reykjavik were heated, farmers were encouraged to build their own mini power stations, and it was possible to bake bread in the beach, which was where ours had come from. The dough was placed in a covered pot and left overnight, its location marked with a small flag.

After we finished, we stripped down to our bathing suits (I'd stuffed mine in my purse on the way out of my apartment) and walked out into the snow and down a set of slippery stairs into a hot spring pool. The wind had quieted and the snow was falling softly. Everything was silent. We were on the edge of a large lake. Through the mist rising off the water, I could make out the shady outline of mountains in the distance. On the other side of the pool sat Viktor. Was this real? The jet lag was fading—fresh bread, fresh butter, and a geothermal pool were apparently just the combination to beat a red-eye flight. But the sense of disorientation had not. I felt as if I'd been dropped into another life. Or the poster for another life. My own, with all its responsibilities and anxiety, was weirdly distant.

When we eventually returned to the giant SUV an hour later, flushed from the heat of the baths, I offered Scott the front seat, thinking it might be a better vantage point for his pictures. But before he had a chance to answer, Viktor opened the door and took my arm. "You're good here, I think," he said, helping me up again. *Oh!* I thought, *I am definitely not imagining this.*

The rest of the day blended together in a mind-boggling array of waterfalls, rainbows, and geysers, as though I were perched on the edge of one of those flip books that animates when you release the pages. One morphed into the next as we sped from stop to stop.

Our final stop was river rafting. Back in my tiny, perfect, warm Brooklyn Heights studio I had read that line item on the itinerary Jo had sent me and thought it sounded fun. Now that I'd been awake for nearly thirty hours and spent the day in the rain and snow, I was significantly less excited. The pickup spot to board the raft was at an obscure corner of the Hvítá River. The rides went out every two hours, and we were to be the last one of the day. The wind had picked up again and the temperature had dropped, turning the rain into snow. As we sat in the SUV waiting for the river guide to return from his previous trip, I could barely see the river through the blowing snow.

"Will we go in this?" I asked Viktor skeptically. I was past the point of caring whether I sounded like an ignorant, spoiled city dweller.

He shook his head, leaning forward to gaze out the window. "I don't know, it's getting pretty bad."

I felt better knowing he thought it was bad, too. *Oh, please let it be canceled.* I was fighting off the sort of overwhelming sleepiness that comes when you have spent the entire day in the cold and are finally toasty warm and comfortable. *Please, please, please.* Two minutes later the previous trip showed up. I could just make them out through the swirling snow. A shadowy figure bounded over to our window and stuck his head in; he was dressed head to toe in a bright yellow slicker.

"We can go in ten minutes," he said in a tone that suggested it was Christmas morning and he was taking us to our presents. "Go in there and put your suits on." He waved out into the whiteness.

No, no, no, I thought. No way. I wouldn't get out of the car. I couldn't. No. Every molecule in my body was attempting to hurl itself into a horizontal position. Viktor got out, letting in a rush of cold air that practically made me whimper, and then walked around the front of the SUV and opened my door. I got out.

Ten minutes later I had struggled into what appeared to be a hazmat suit and shoved my feet into ungainly rubber boots. Three young women from Australia had joined us, and we were all crowded together in the hut we'd been directed to, trying to get our gear on in a rush; there was only an hour left of daylight. I reached up for a pair of goggles hanging on the wall and pulled them over my head. Viktor handed me a pair of enormous gloves. "Put these on—you'll need them." I shoved my hand into the first one but couldn't get the second on. He took it back and held it up so I could put my hand in smoothly. Then he did up the snaps at the base of both gloves. Then he reached back and took the hood attached to my coat and pulled it over my head and fastened the buttons under my chin. Such small gestures, and yet . . . I couldn't remember the last time anyone had taken care of me. Looked out for me. I was so in the habit of doing every single thing for myself, that his doing up my hood practically felt like a bodily caress.

"Follow me," he said, leading me through the group of Australian women, out the door and down the path to the river raft we would be riding in. There were three rows of seats in the boat. He directed me to the middle row. "Sit there," he said, pointing to the space farthest along. "It will be smoothest there." I clambered clumsily into the raft and sat down; he clambered in right after me and then turned and did up my seat belt for me. "Comfortable?" I nodded and smiled. I was freezing, and exhausted, and starving, but yes, very, very comfortable. Then he buckled himself next to me so that when everyone else arrived, which they did a few minutes later, they had to sit elsewhere. Only once the ride started, and we began racing down the choppy waters, did I realize he really should have been in the back row. That was the row that got the worst of the bumps and the water sprays. The Australian girls were now stuck back there and had already been soaked two or three times. The river was at the bottom of a canyon; rough walls of rock rose up on either side of us fifteen feet away. Our ride consisted of us careening down it at what felt like about 100 miles an hour. Every few minutes our guide would aim for one of the canyon walls and then slam on the brakes at the very last minute, spinning us around in a 360-degree turn with such velocity that we would be lifted from our seats and temporarily suspended in midair; it felt as if we were in astronaut training camp. The girl in the seat behind me started to cry and begged to be taken back. *Well*, I thought, as I gripped the plastic handles on the side of the raft and gritted my teeth, *I wanted to be away from the internet.* This was very away.

"Okay?" said Viktor to me. I nodded. He had put his arm around me on the first spin and had a tight grip on my shoulders. I leaned as far into him as I could, convinced we were all going to fly or bounce out of the boat.

"You'll be fine," shouted the guide cheerily to the crying girl. "Maybe move up a row where it's smoother." He slowed the boat, and after a minute Scott switched seats with her. Viktor hadn't moved. As soon as both were buckled in, we were off again, top speed toward a sheer rock face that appeared suddenly out of the gloom. The girl, now on Viktor's other side, cried harder, and he squeezed me tighter. The wind blew harder, turning the snow into small bullets and making me burrow down ever farther into my coat so that all that was exposed were my eyebrows. I leaned into Viktor harder and shut my eyes as we bucked and twisted and were hurled across the water. I didn't open them again until we finally pulled back into the dock thirty minutes later and Viktor unbuckled me.

Back in the SUV, I fell asleep before we'd even reached the main road. When we arrived at the hotel, Viktor shook me gently and then walked around for the final time to help me out and hand me my suitcase. Had it only been that morning he'd thrown it in there? It was hard to believe this had all been part of the same day. "Give me your email," he said, handing me a card to write on before taking me into a long hug and kissing me on the cheek. "Maybe I will see you tomorrow?" he asked, the hope clear in his voice.

I wasn't planning on seeing him again, though. I was booked into a full day at a spa, something I had specifically requested. Ten hours in a spa, all to myself; how many times in my life would I get that opportunity? had been my reasoning. Standing beside the SUV now, all I could think was that I would finally be warm again. I had visions of fur throws and burning fireplaces. Viktor, meanwhile, was spending the next day taking Scott on an eight-hour glacier hike.

"Maybe," I said, not wanting to say goodbye for good. "I'll have to check." I retreated into the hotel. I had just enough time before dinner to check in to my miniature hotel room—barely big enough to fit a double bed, it felt like an exercise in how many amenities could be squeezed in a space the size of Viktor's SUV—and take a shower and change. I resisted the urge to lie down and instead stood under the hot water for as long as I could, letting its warmth sink in and thinking about my day. Even through the fog of jet lag, the wildness of the country had taken hold and left me feeling exuberant. It wasn't just that I had boarded a plane and arrived somewhere new; I felt as though I had been flung out of my life into a place I hadn't

even known existed. It was thrilling and strange, but equally so
was the knowledge that it was possible, on a moment's notice,
to walk through a door and find myself in a different world. And
here, too, was this unfamilar man, who seemed (at least based on
the twelve hours I'd spent with him) to embody all this, who was
essentially my personal tour guide through this new place. Far
from invisible, I felt more seen than I had in ages. The warmer I
became the less enticing my day at the spa seemed to be.

Dinner was a multicourse meal at a low-ceilinged restaurant
on the harbor that had been getting attention in the food press.
It was filled with sharply dressed Icelanders. As we sat recounting
our day—after their late arrival, the television crew from Denver
had spent it whale watching—plate after plate of local Icelandic
fare was brought out to us, while our wineglasses were continually refilled. At some point the group at the table next to us, who
looked like extras from *The Sopranos*, also began to raise their
glasses to our unending meal. We later found out that the loudest
one of their group was a local bounty hunter. With each course my
jet lag was pushed down and then down again. I thought of Viktor
strapping me into my seat, arm wrapped tightly around me.

It was after midnight by the time we stepped back outside
and into the blustery wind. Our hotel was two hundred feet
to our left; downtown Reykjavik was half a mile to the right.
Iceland's nightlife is nearly as famous as its natural wonders,
and somehow we convinced ourselves that since it was Saturday
night and we were in Reykjavik, dancing was in order. The only
way to make this a reality was to continually keep walking away
from the hotel. I knew Viktor was picking up Scott at dawn, six
hours from now. The coldness I'd felt that day was beginning
to seep back in. Overhead the northern lights rippled through
the night sky. Eventually we ended up on the second floor of a
place called Kiki Bar, amid a crowd so fashionably dressed it
made New York look mundane. At 3:00 a.m., with the series of

vodka shots we'd just done racing through my body, I turned to Michael and shouted over the music that I wanted to cancel the spa. Could I go on the glacier hike instead?

•

When the phone rang at 6:15 the next morning, I was unsure what it was. The room felt as if it belonged on a spaceship. The white walls were covered in buttons that controlled everything from the lights, to the heat, to the hot water in the bathroom, to the toilet. I'd crawled into bed only three hours earlier. The buttons had proved too complicated for me to sort out at 3:00 a.m., and I'd merely stripped down in the dark and slipped under the covers. Now this ringing! What was it? I glanced around in the dim light of predawn and saw the phone. Maybe if I just ignored it. But it kept ringing.

"Hello," I croaked.

"Good morning. I'm downstairs. You are ready to go? Come now before the others so you can have the front seat."

It was Viktor. Michael must have told him I'd decided to come along. Our twelve-hour glacier tour started in fifteen minutes. Oh God. I gave what I hoped was an affirmative croak. It was not convincing.

"You are ready?" This time he sounded half alarmed, half annoyed. Also as if he were issuing an order.

I put my hand over the phone and cleared my throat. "Of course. I'm walking out the door right now."

"Good." He sounded relieved. "Okay. Goodbye."

I lay back down. My whole body was yelling at me. Getting out of bed was a terrible decision. And there was no need for me to do it. I could still switch back to the spa. I snuggled down even farther into the rough sheets, willing myself to focus on the hot steam and massages to come. Instead I recalled Viktor zipping me up. The absolute loveliness of being attracted to someone. No strings, no complications, no future, no texts, no thinking, purely pheromones. Five minutes later I was in the lobby. Viktor was standing at the hotel door looking every bit as rugged and masculine as he had the day before.

"There are two Chinese women coming with us today, too, so go get in the front seat now," he said, practically pushing me out the door.

"I just want to get a hot chocolate." If I could have attached a hot chocolate IV to myself, I would have.

"I'll get it for you."

I had been prepared for a lot of things entering into my forties. I thought I had been prepared for everything. But I had not been prepared for sweetness or for fun. Or, truthfully, for hot, attentive Icelandic tour guides. I had not been prepared to be the center of attention. And yet, that's what I was for the next twelve hours as I clumsily hiked up a glacier, and walked across a windy beach covered in black stones, and strolled up to the base of a fifty-foot waterfall. The front seat of the giant SUV became a wonderful little bubble—the rest of the world felt deliciously far away.

"You should stay longer," Viktor said when he finally dropped us back at the hotel. "I will drive you to the volcano that's exploding. We will camp."

I was struck by a vision of the two of us in a tent on the side of a mountain. Just the two of us pressed up against each other for warmth. Alone. In just two days the reality of my city life had fallen away with an ease that shocked me, and new paths suddenly sprang up in my line of sight as though a board had just been lit up. I was not married to my life as it was. It was not written in stone. It was like this country, hurling me around from extreme to extreme, and also like the glacier ice I had spent the day walking across, growing and moving in ways I couldn't see.

If my life were a romantic comedy about a three-day trip to a strange land, where I discovered things about myself and released the things that had been weighing me down, this is where the story would have ended. Off I would go, disappearing into the Icelandic wilderness with my hunky, capable guide, his arms wrapped reassuringly around my shoulders, my life neatly bound up—every romance must end with a woman safely tied to another person's life, after all, no loose ends. I could feel the impulse stirring from somewhere deep within me, an almost reflexive desire to start the usual calculations. For so long, considering an invite from a man felt like the equivalent of opening a door, gazing down a long road, and then gaming out whether this was a person I wanted to walk down that road with. Was he good for the long run? Interesting enough? Smart enough? Appropriate? Would my friends like him? Would he like *me* once he got to know me? Would he find me attractive? Was this the beginning of something? All these thoughts happened simultaneously, within seconds of even the most casual encounter. And started to again now.

But then, a realization: I actually had no interest in walking any farther down whatever road I was on here. Three days was just fine. I didn't need to know any more about this man (I knew next to nothing about him as it was; he might have been married for all I knew). I could just enjoy this for what it was. Not every encounter needed to be the first step in a permanent decision. Men, it occurred to me, perhaps for the first time in my life, did not need to be a goal.

I thanked Viktor, gave him a kiss on the cheek, and went back to the hotel. For now, I was going back to New York. I had never wanted to leave my life entirely, I realized. I'd only wanted to know that I had the ability to step out of it and into something new. Now I knew. And I could do it again and again, whenever I wanted. The knowledge I possessed that freedom made me feel more powerful than I could remember feeling for a very long time.

I don't know who you are or where you came from, but from now on you'll do as I tell you, okay?

Princess Leia

8. The Grown-Up

Perhaps you've seen some variation of this one, too: single, childless, glamorous-ish older sister agrees to fly home to help out her sister with children after arrival of third child. (Opening scene: NYC, brunch with blowouts.) Deeply inept and contemptuous of all things domestic, the older sister gets a crash course in how difficult and meaningful a life full of children can be, eventually shirking her shallow city ways (while also probably falling in love with the local mailman) having discovered the true meaning of happiness.

Or this: single, narcissistic older sister who can't quite get her life together arrives home to "help" her younger sister with the family. (Opening scene: running for the plane with half-packed luggage because the alarm in a nameless dude's apartment has failed to go off.) Over the course of the next few weeks it's the children who help her figure out how to be a kind, generous, finally ("Finally!" say the exhausted parents) responsible adult (who also probably falls in love with the mailman). Single women on the screen are almost always either inept or selfish.

In the real-life version, however, I was scheduled to fly home to help my sister because I wanted to, because I was needed, and because I could handle it.

●

The baby is coming!

TODAY!

My stomach dropped, and a cold jolt went through me as I read the text from my sister. It was Tuesday morning. I'd been back from Iceland for two weeks, and Alexis's C-section wasn't scheduled for another week. She'd been having complications for six weeks. Nothing serious, just serious enough. By now I'd come to expect complicated pregnancies.

For real?! I wrote back, hoping that if she was texting instead of calling it meant this was not a big deal. *How come?*

She told me she was feeling fine, but when she'd gone in for her regular checkup that morning her fluids had been low, and they'd decided it was best to go in early. *They're going to do the C-section this afternoon,* she wrote.

I had my two return tickets to Toronto; I'd purchased the second after I returned from Iceland, as I told my sister I would. One was supposed to get me home a few days after the original date of her scheduled C-section, to coincide with her arrival home from the hospital. One would get me there a few days before, so if she decided at the last minute she wanted me in the delivery room I'd be there, and if not, there'd be someone at home to look after the kids. But all that planning had been based on the originally scheduled day, which was still a week away. Thinking I wasn't leaving until the following week, I'd packed all my work meetings into the next few days, including one about a book I was possibly going to cowrite. I'd have to cancel them all if I was going to jump on a plane, and if she was going in this afternoon there was no chance I'd be able to make it for the actual delivery.

I wrote her back. *I'm set to fly in on Saturday, but I can see about getting a flight tonight or tomorrow.*

It's fine, she wrote back. The kids' other grandmother hadn't left for Florida yet and was going to stay with them for the next few days. My brother-in-law would be there for the delivery. I could just come on Saturday as planned.

I can't believe you're having a baby today! I wrote. Then I looked at my phone. It was October 21. It felt like a gift.

It's all going to be fine, I continued. *This is good. Today is the perfect day. It's PRINCESS LEIA'S birthday. This is the greatest birthday date of the entire year.*

This needed no explanation. My sister had spent our entire childhood in thrall to (some might say, held hostage by) my unflagging Princess Leia obsession. In my apartment was a framed copy of my favorite photo of us as kids, taken on Halloween the year I was eight. In it, Alexis and I are standing on our front porch with the three boys who lived next door. I'm dressed in a white sheet my mother has fashioned into a very passable version of Princess Leia's dress. The gold braided sash from our heavy living room drapes is tied around my waist as a belt. On my head is a pair of earmuffs with brown yarn glued on them to make it look like hair. My cheeks are heavily blushed, and my lips are glistening in my mother's red lipstick. Even now, decades later, the picture having faded and darkened, it's still clear that I am practically levitating with happiness. My sister is beside me, unrecognizable, swimming in a costume of leftover brown shag carpet my mother has sewn into a rough approximation of an Ewok.

It's possible you never love anything quite as fiercely as you do when you're eight. I loved Princess Leia with the intensity of a desert sun. She was proof to me that all the things I wanted in life existed: independence, adventure, taking charge. And she was beautiful to boot. Princess Leia was the antithesis of my mother's measured ways, a rejection of the skirts and white ankle socks she wanted me to wear to church and to holiday dinners. And she was everywhere. She was on lunch boxes, towels, sheets, pajamas. She was on the trading cards the boys in my neighborhood collected. She was on cereal boxes. She was on an enormous poster in my dentist's office. She was at the checkout of the grocery store, where I went every two weeks to spend my allowance on new Star Wars figures. I didn't ever need to look very far to find the reflection of the adult I wanted to be staring right back at me.

Somewhere along the line in my obsessive collection of all things Princess Leia, I'd picked up a trading card that had listed her birthday as October 21, the real-life birthday of Carrie Fisher. And now, if it all went well, of my nephew. I'd coveted that date the same way I'd coveted Laura Ingalls's birthday on February 7, real-life evidence my most cherished heroines had existed. In the midst of what had otherwise been only dark news from my family for months, it felt like a shaft of joy sent directly into our midst from our 1980s front porch.

I spent the rest of the day waiting for news and also dreading it. But sometimes life lives up to your eight-year-old goals: Connor arrived safe and sound later that afternoon. Four days later, I boarded a plane home.

•

My parents were waiting for me on the other side when I came through customs in Toronto. This was unusual. Until my mother's health had kept her from being able to drive, my father rarely made the trip. I had volunteered to take the bus, trying to avoid a scenario that would leave my mother home alone, but he had insisted on coming. They were standing off to the side together when I emerged, my father rigid in his black puffy winter coat and tweed hat, my mother floating along beside him, like an astronaut tethered to a space station. My mother was skin and bones.

People toss that sort of phrase about casually, the same way they say, "I'm losing my mind," or "This is driving me crazy"; remarks which now also felt like physical blows when I heard them. My mother literally *was* skin and bones. There was nothing else. Every time I saw her—and it had been only seven weeks since I was last home—there was less of her. Her frailness felt like a punch in the stomach. She was also literally losing her mind; I'd watched her grasping for it for months now, like a hand trying to retrieve a lost shoe under a bed, she vaguely knew it was there somewhere. Weight loss was a symptom of Parkinson's, I knew, but surely this was extreme.

In pictures from university and the first years of her marriage to my father, my mother had been slim and tall and inarguably beautiful (to everyone but herself. Whenever I or others remarked on her looks, she scoffed, entirely disbelieving). But for most of my life she'd been in some sort of battle with her weight. It was a battle largely fought in theory: she talked in detail about the diets she was planning to go on, though when she eventually did they usually lasted until bedtime; at some point after dinner, she'd pour herself a bowl of cheesy Doritos and declare she intended to start fresh "tomorrow."

Now, during the times she was lucid, she delighted in her newfound thinness. When I was visiting, she liked to go into her closet and emerge holding up a pair of pants. "Can you believe I need an extra small?" she'd say happily. When I tried to push bowls of ice cream on her, or slices of pizza, desperate to fatten

her up, she'd say, "Oh, I shouldn't, I don't want to get heavy."
Even as other things fell away from her mind, family histories
vanished, and relationships dissolved, the pleasure at having
finally achieved a certain appearance remained. And still the
weight disappeared. Walking down the ramp toward my waiting
parents, I could see my mother's collarbones showing through
her pastel top; her hip bones jutted visibly through the waist-
band of her pants. When I hugged her, her ribs felt like piano
keys under my fingers. She was so light when she walked it was
like watching a bird flit from branch to branch; I was never
quite sure she was touching the ground. It gave her a childlike
quality, as though she were skipping along, no longer beset by
the cares of the world. Her usual pleasant smile was still there,
though. That had persisted, at least in the more reliable morning hours.

That smile had infuriated me as a child. "Why are you always smiling at people? You don't *know* them," I would rage at
her in the grocery checkout line, at the mall, at the gas station.
I didn't know why exactly it made me so livid, but in those preteen years that pleasant smile would leave me vibrating with
anger. In hindsight, I'm not sure what I resented more: her
undying need to please people she'd never met or her inability
to just admit this was why she was doing it. I wanted a straight
answer. She never had one. Her answers were always long and
tangled up with big words and random associations until by the
end my anger would be worn down simply by trying to keep up
with her level-headed argument. "I like to analyze," she would
say, good-naturedly analyzing her analyzing while I stomped
around my adolescence trying to goad her into throwing a dish
or at least losing her temper enough to raise her voice. It rarely
worked. "You push and you push and you push," she'd say, exhausted by my persistence. But she almost never pushed back.
Sometimes I wondered whether one of the reasons I held on to

New York so tightly was because it was a place where people largely said exactly what they felt.

I could not seem to get a straight answer on her illness either. Every conversation with a doctor felt like it was weaving back in on itself. I kept a notebook beside me when I made phone calls now, recording names and specialties and extension numbers so I could reach the person I needed more quickly when I inevitably had to call back. Along the margins, I would doodle looping arrows from one to the other, directions to my future self. My mother's body was giving me a definitive answer, however. It might be making a long goodbye, but it was unmistakably a goodbye.

On our walk from the terminal to the car, my mother rolled into her usual chatter. She asked me about my friend who was the chef. My friend who had the baby. She told me she thought a long article I'd done about the "storm" was "just wonderful." Each new remark required some detective work on my end. What chef? (Answer: Maddy had years ago professed an interest in doing a cookbook.) Which baby? (Answer: fifteen years earlier, my manager at the Greenwich Village tavern had an infant daughter I would often babysit.) What storm? (This one was easier: I'd written a piece about Sandy two years earlier that had done well.) Figuring out what she was referring to meant patiently handing my mother different details, as though talking her through a treasure map, and then carefully sifting through her response until together we arrived at the thing she was looking for. By the time we made it to our level in the parking garage, I'd solved all her inquiries and was thinking with a drop of relief how she might be thinner, but at least her mind seemed as if it hadn't declined *too* much since I'd last been home in mid-August. The fact that it was taking only minimal prompting right now to keep her on a cheerful conversational track felt like a small gift of time. *There's still time.* I smiled to myself wryly, thinking of the woman at the wedding. Were our whole lives just a series of vainly constructed arguments to convince ourselves we had more time than we did?

As we reached the car, my mother turned to me brightly, her face lit up as though she'd just remembered something wonderful she wanted to tell me, and said, "Oh, honey, I'm so glad you're here." She wrapped me in her fragile embrace. I hugged her back gently, the way I hugged my niece and nephew. When I released her, she gazed at me with the same wondrous expression. "Oh, honey, I've been meaning to ask you, how is your friend who's the chef?" I clenched my jaw. I circled my emotions as though they were wagons preparing for an attack and took a breath. "Maddy is fine, Mom," I said as levelly as I could. "She has a daughter now."

My father was mostly silent during this exchange. Which was not unusual. My childhood had been populated by nonstop chatter from my mother, who considered it her responsibility to fill every empty moment, and long silences punctuated here and there with one-syllable responses from my father. It was never clear whether he was listening. When he was in the grip of deep depression, which as the years went by had been more often than not, he spent nearly as many hours of the day in bed as out of it. Sometimes more. Increasingly, he was like a main character in our family play who existed entirely offstage. Present in his absence. My mother's decline had forced him onto the stage, so to speak, but I was still figuring out how to navigate around his actually being there. Now that I had to, his habit of not answering had begun to make me crazy; I could sometimes hear my own voice return to demanding, dramatic teenage decibels, as though I were arguing for a later curfew and not simply trying to confirm specific doctor's appointments had been set up for my mother.

"Do you want me to drive?" I asked him, rolling my suitcase to the trunk.

No answer.

"Oh, honey, let me help you with that," said my mother, her hands fluttering toward my bag, a carry-on that probably weighed almost half as much as she did.

"It's fine, Mom. Why don't you just get in the car?" I tried not to let my teenage self bleed into my tone. Getting frustrated with her now only left me feeling guilty.

"Oh, but here, I can help."

"Just get in the car, Jean," said my father in his stern tone.

"All right," said my mother with a smile, clapping her hands together like a child who's just been promised extra dessert for good behavior.

"Do you want me to drive?" I asked again. I was not a nervous passenger; since I was a child I'd loved being in the car, but my father's driving unnerved me. Maybe this was normal; we spend our childhoods with full faith in our parents' decision-making, and our adulthoods second-guessing their every move, certain we know better. Yet, much as I was never convinced he was listening, I was never confident he was fully aware of his place on the road. On the rare occasions I traveled with him, I spent most of the ride alert and paralyzed, as though I were watching someone play a video game. Still, he almost always insisted on driving—I knew from the tone it was a point of pride, evidence he was still in control of something—but I asked anyway, always hopeful I might be spared.

He didn't answer. Instead he walked over to the passenger side and steered my mother into the front seat.

"Dad! Do you want me to drive?"

Silently he walked back around the car, handed me the keys, got in the back seat, and closed his eyes.

"I guess, yes," I said to the underground parking lot, fifteen years old again and filled with sarcasm. I got in the driver's seat.

"Oh, honey, how is your friend, the one with the baby?"

"She's fine, Mom."

I looked at the clock. It was a few minutes after noon. I pulled out my phone and texted my sister. *Leaving the airport now. I need a drink!*

I looked at the message, imagining her opening her phone while standing between two screaming children, holding a dirty diaper. I erased the drink part and sent the text.

When I was growing up, my mother would sometimes say, "Okay, everyone, let's gird our loins for the fray!" as we would leave the house. Like many things she said, I had no idea what it meant at the time; it was just another thing she did. It came back to me now; I could hear her gay voice in my head and taste the smell of that house. I knew what *gird* meant now. I girded for what was coming.

9. Having It All

My sister and I lived opposite lives. As opposite as two lives can be for people who have been raised in the same house. This had always been the case. Growing up, she was the cool one who went to rock concerts, the one with the boyfriends, the popular girl in school. We'd never had the intimate sisterly discussions some other siblings shared, but we'd also never been enemies the way some friends I had were with their brothers and sisters. We were on each other's side when called to be. However, children are very effective at bridging nearly all divides, and once hers arrived I made it a point to participate in her and their lives with regularity. Before my mother got sick I came home every three months like clockwork: for holidays, for birthdays, for baptisms, and eventually communions. It had been just the four of us growing up: my father didn't communicate with most of his family, and my mother's two brothers lived on either coast. Neither of my parents had a close circle of friends they saw frequently, and they rarely entertained. This lack of outside voices had often left me feeling as though our family lived in a separate reality from the people around us. I wanted my niece and nephew to know me as a regular person in their life, for them to have the outside family we had lacked.

My parents didn't stay when we reached the house. I wasn't entirely sure my mother understood my sister had even had a baby; she seemed to be confusing Connor with the other two kids. Still, when I kissed them goodbye, I explained to her one last time what was happening and why I was getting out and not coming with them. She nodded pleasantly. I could tell by the fluttering of her hands she was approaching the witching hour.

Alexis wasn't there when my parents dropped me off. She lived in a small town, and doors were never locked, though I thought it likely at least one of the neighbors had seen us pull in and was aware I was here. Whenever I ran into them on the street they never seemed surprised to see me. As I was walking to the door she texted *I'm out running errands with the kids, be back shortly.* She'd been out of the hospital exactly one day. The doctor had let her stay an extra night, mostly to give her a respite from the children waiting for her at home.

Inside the house was the aftermath of the constant storm known as small children, which also sometimes looked like the news reports you see from the aftermath of an actual storm: toys, socks, discarded t-shirts, shoes, puzzle pieces, books, and leftover breakfast dishes were everywhere. The air was heavy with the sickly-sweet smell of little children, the constant exhaust of breakfast cereal and milk and now new baby. I took a deep breath and began to tidy up.

The meeting I'd had a few days earlier about cowriting a book had gone well. My friend Naama ran a successful company that produced videos about puberty aimed at preteen girls. She'd been approached by publishers about writing a guide to puberty for them. I'd officially been brought on board as the cowriter. It was a terrific opportunity, a bigger project that would allow me to step out of the cycle of pitching article ideas to different editors, waiting for a response, and then chasing down payment. It was the next big step in the writing career I'd been slowly reestablishing for myself since burning out so badly. But we were on a tight schedule, and the first draft of the proposal was due to our agent in two weeks. I looked around again. I was going to have to figure out a way to lodge parts of my career into this maelstrom.

Before I'd made a dent in the chaos my nephew, Quinn, and niece, Zoe, exploded through the front door. They swept in like a summer storm, upending everything in their path. Up the stairs they rolled, not bothering to remove their coats or their boots, and hurled themselves into my arms, wrapping themselves around me with surprising strength. That was often the thing I was most unprepared for with small children—not the noise and the chaos and the unrelenting nature of it, but the boundless emotion, given and required.

Alexis slowly came up behind them, her right arm looped through a baby carrier.

"Are you supposed to be carrying that?" She was four days out from a C-section; picking up heavy things was, to the best of my knowledge, not allowed.

"I don't have much choice." She put the carrier on the floor slowly and stood back up stiffly.

Were there baby books for this? I wondered. What to expect when you're expecting to be alone? What to do when you can't avoid all the things you're supposed to avoid after childbirth? How to massage your own swollen feet. How to manage three children under the age of five. There should be a book called *How to Raise a Newborn When Your Hands Are Otherwise Occupied Making Lunches and Driving Children to Swimming Lessons*.

I gave Alexis a hug and looked down at my brand-new

nephew. Zoe and Quinn, ages three and a half and five, were such a complete unit it had been hard to envision an addition. But now as I gazed at Connor's scrunched-up face for the first time, it seemed he had always been here. Babies are like that. They appear, tear themselves a hole in the world, and somehow it becomes immediately impossible to remember a time when that space did not exist.

"You can pick him up," my sister said matter-of-factly, going into the kitchen.

I reached down and began to unbuckle him from his carrier. Babies are one thing. Newborns feel like another species; every part of him oozed vulnerability. At barely six pounds he was small, even for a newborn. Quinn reached over and roughly began pulling Connor's arms under his straps.

"I want to do it," Zoe yelled in her high-pitched three-year-old voice, and began pulling the strap in the other direction. My stomach dropped; they were going to break him.

"Everyone step back!"

I used my sternest military-commander-directing-an-evacuation voice. It stopped them just long enough to allow me to scoop up the carrier and put it on the dining room table out of their reach. By some miracle, the baby was still asleep. Was he breathing? Okay, yes. I slipped a hand under each shoulder, tried to get my fingers under his neck, and then, with the sort of deep breath, eyes closed, off-the-cliff-we-go mind-set, I lifted him up and put him on my shoulder. Had his neck flopped? The kids were hovering below me, hands reaching up for him like snakes from a pit.

"I want to hold him."

"No, I do."

I turned my back on them and lowered him into the crook of my elbow. He fit perfectly. He was the exact length of the space from my wrist to my elbow.

He cracked an eye open, then two, his brow furrowed, thoughtful and stern, as though he remained unconvinced that being on the outside was a good decision. Then he looked up at me and stared. This at least felt normal. For as long as I could remember babies had been fascinated by my face. All the contrast caught their attention: big eyes, pale skin, dark hair that exploded in curls around my head, as if I were a walking mobile. It was the same sort of look Drew Barrymore first gave to E.T., except without the screaming.

"Hello," I said, gently stroking his head. "You share a birthday with the most important person ever."

•

From the start, we agreed I would sleep in Alexis's room on the main floor with the kids, and she and Connor would take the spare room downstairs that I normally stayed in. This way she could try to keep her own sleep schedule with only the baby interrupting, and I could oversee Quinn and Zoe. I would also do breakfast and the school run. And take them to swimming lessons twice a week. Quinn was still young enough to go into the women's locker room, so I could change him, send him out, take Zoe upstairs to the viewing area, then back down, change her, and send her out as Quinn was coming back in. I'd do bath time, too. And bedtime snacks. And story time. Also, I'd finish my book proposal.

•

On the first morning, I set my alarm for 5:00 a.m. I sat up—it had to be done quickly or the odds of staying put doubled every minute—and reached under the bed for my computer, where I slipped it every night away from the kids. I hadn't slept well. One ear had stayed continually cocked through the night, listening for the movement of light feet. My dreams had been filled with the sounds of children calling my name and a vague sense of panic that I'd misplaced them. I'd fallen asleep in the chunky cardigan I'd borrowed from my sister, so I merely slid my feet into slippers and padded through the silent house to the kitchen. I listened at the top of the stairs for the baby crying, but heard nothing. The clock on the stove said 5:15. I'd wanted to be at the dining table by 5:05, and the lost ten minutes sent a cold shot of anxiety into my stomach. Already it felt as if I were losing the day. I opened my computer, and before I could look at anything I turned on the app that cut me off from the internet. Then I wrote. At home, the start of writing was a long, long ritual: Were the dishes done, the bathroom cleaned? Maybe I'd just quickly duck out and get another coffee, or do a quick grocery run, and drop off the laundry at the same time. Now I simply dove in, racing against the day that was chasing me down. I had fourteen days to research and write a forty-page book proposal that would hopefully result in us selling the book to a publisher.

Time sprouted wings and flew. My ninety minutes of allotted time whipped by in what felt like seconds. At 6:55, I closed my computer and placed it high atop the hutch. I retraced my steps down the hallway, stepped back out of my slippers, and slid back under the covers. I could have squeezed out a few more minutes of writing, but that would have meant giving up my few minutes of cuddle time in bed with the kids. No sooner had my head touched the pillow than I heard the shush of the door.

"Auntie Glynnis, I brought you coffee." It was Zoe holding a tiny plastic teacup from one of her toy sets. Since they'd started walking, I'd been encouraging them both to bring me pretend coffee so that when they were old enough to make actual coffee they would just bring it to me automatically. That was my plan, anyway. This was the first time it had actually worked. I felt a surge of joy, a sharp little jolt at the knowledge that I was a thread in this little mind that was continually knitting itself to-gether. I sipped the pretend coffee theatrically, as if it were the most magical thing I'd ever tasted, while Zoe clambered up, star-ing at me with wide, happy eyes. A second later Quinn arrived, doing a running leap at the bed and sending my head smacking into the headboard and the coffee cup flying. I picked Zoe up and put her on the opposite side of me and wrapped both of my arms around them tightly, hoping to keep them out of arm's reach of each other. The bed was practically vibrating with their energy. No quiet cuddle time today. I reached for my phone. I had about three minutes before the battle over the sheets would spin out of control and reach a pitch that would wake the baby.

"Let's take a selfie." I knew sooner or later (probably sooner) both of them would get tired of the phone and refuse to pose for it, like sulking teenagers on a family road trip, but for now it was a surefire way to get their attention for about ninety seconds. They leaned in, Zoe smiling as if she were auditioning for a real-ity show about toddler beauty schools, and Quinn with his fin-gers in his mouth pulling it in various directions while he stuck out his tongue and rolled his eyes around. I knew a woman in New York, a professor of gender studies, who swore gender char-acteristics were learned, not innate; if true, I could only marvel at what these two had absorbed in their short time on earth.

We returned to the kitchen like a herd of elephants. I had dined with enough newborns in New York to know it was pos-sible for babies to sleep through anything, including crowded restaurants and blaring fire trucks. Hopefully the one down-stairs could sleep through his siblings. I looked at the clock. It was 7:15. We had to be in the car and pulling out of the driveway in forty minutes. I went into military mode: there was no time for anything that didn't move us closer to our target. I opened the dishwasher to unload it. Time for negotiations.

"What do you want for breakfast?"

"Pancakes!"

"You can have cereal or toast."

"Why? Mommy makes us pancakes."

"Well, Auntie Glynnis can only make cereal or toast."

"Why?"

"Because I live in New York. Cereal or toast? You have thirty seconds."

"I want to see Mommy."

"Mommy needs to sleep. Cereal or toast?"

"What are you having?"

"Toast with peanut butter."

"I want toast with peanut butter, but with the crusts cut off and in four pieces that are a square and on my Anna plate."

I put the toast on; I poured cereal for Quinn. I swept in and out of the kitchen, back and forth from the dining room table to the dishwasher to the cupboards to the sink and back to the cupboards, dodging their little bodies as they wandered in and out. I was reminded of the old musicals I'd watched as a child with my mother. This felt like the choreography of life. Every five minutes I said, "Eat!" At 7:35 I sent them back to get dressed. Quinn, age five, was easy.

"Do you think you can get dressed AND brush your teeth in ninety seconds?" I said, dramatically pulling out my phone.

"Yes!"

"I'm not sure you can."

"I can!"

"Okay, I'm going to start the stopwatch. But you have to brush *all* your teeth. I'm going to look after."

"Wait! Okay, now."

"Go!"

He thundered down the hall.

Zoe, even at three and a half, was already superior to my ways. (Whatever these supposed learned gender traits were, there was never any doubt to me that girls were just smarter.) She sidled over to the hutch and, as I watched, opened the bottom drawer and pulled out an enormous container full of what appeared to be more than two hundred markers. She dropped it on the table with a bang.

"I'm going to draw you a special picture," she said sweetly, tilting her head.

"Not now, sweetheart, you have to get dressed. You can draw it in the car."

"No. *Now.*" Her shoulders hunched and she leaned over the construction paper that had suddenly appeared from who knows where, with the determination of a conqueror planting a flag.

"No, you have to get dressed."

"But I want to make you a picture." The note of whining in her voice was an early warning signal that if I wasn't careful, this would head south, and likely at a pitch that would wake my sister.

"Okay, as soon as you're dressed you can make me a picture."

She stared at me from across the room, her body perched somewhere between sadness and fury. I waited, wondering which way it was going to tip. Would this be one of those mornings I would be called on to carry a screaming, flailing toddler to the car and strap her in like a convict, or would she go on her own? She released herself from the table. Arms crossed, legs dragging, the slow, resentful march to the bedroom began. Quinn pounded past her and leapt onto the couch, his elbow barely missing my eye. He was fully clothed except for his shoes.

"I'm done! Was it ninety seconds?"

I'd forgotten to turn on the stopwatch. I glanced at my phone, mustering my most serious face. "Eighty-eight! Good job. I think that's a new world record. High five." He hauled back and slapped my hand as hard as he could.

"Can I play a game on your phone now?"

"No."

"But Auntie Glynnis."

Out of the corner of my eye I spotted movement. Alexis appeared on the stairs, babe in arms, and sat down wearily on the sofa. "Go put your shoes on," she said in a quiet voice, as though the phrase were emitted simply by routine, like a clock striking the quarter hour.

Zoe came out of her room dressed in what appeared to be a Halloween costume from the movie *Frozen*. I glanced at my sister. I felt as if I saw kids dressed in what appeared to be Halloween costumes on the streets of Brooklyn all the time. Maybe this was acceptable? I hoped it was acceptable; it was 7:45. We had ten minutes.

"You can't wear that to school," Alexis said in the same voice she'd used to tell Quinn to put shoes on. She was still on the couch, breastfeeding Connor. Quinn perched beside her, leaning as far in as he could over Connor's face. Zoe's face began its slow windup to a howl.

"Come on," I said, putting down the school bag I was packing, "Auntie Glynnis will be your salon stylist today." I rolled my eyes to myself even as I said it—a *salon stylist* for chrissake, and from someone who ran a feminist group for women. But we were running out of time. "Your Princess Leia salon stylist," I corrected myself, as if this one exchange was going to ruin or ensure her ability to negotiate pay raises on her own behalf twenty years from now.

We pulled out of the driveway at 7:51. I caught my reflection in the rearview mirror. My curly hair, so fascinating to infants, had not seen the shower since I arrived on Saturday and was now matted to the back of my head. I looked down to make sure I had my phone in case Alexis needed anything—we had only the one car—and saw that my pajama bottoms had coffee stains in awkward places, probably thanks to my jamming a cup between my legs because it wouldn't fit in the coffee cup holder.

Quinn went to one school a half-hour drive away. Zoe went to a half-day at the local school. I had to get him to his school and then turn around and get Zoe to hers before the stroke of nine o'clock. If I didn't, we'd be locked out and I'd have to go to the front office and sign some sort of slip explaining why we were late. I knew schools required lists of pre-approved adults when it came to picking kids up—my sister had had to submit one so I could get Quinn off the bus once—but I didn't know if the same applied to dropping them off. I didn't want to find out and be forced to call my sister from the school, especially since I was in the only car. Nope! We were going to make everything on time. Everything else went out of my head except that goal.

In the back seat the kids began arguing about watching a DVD.

"Auntie Glynnis!"

"I don't know how to work the DVD in the car."

"Why?"

"I live in New York. Look out the window."

"No fair," said Zoe, who'd been silent up until now. "Quinn has his iPad, and I don't."

"You can play with it on the way back."

"Nuh-uh," Quinn chanted in his most taunting older brother voice. "I'm going to hide it so you can't play."

"NO FAIR."

"Let's play 'who can keep from talking the longest.' Whoever wins gets to play one game on my phone after dinner tonight."

Silence. And then more silence.

Holy shit, I thought. It worked. I felt like a magician. How long was this going to last?

It lasted until I missed the turnoff to my nephew's school

and, looking at the clock, opted to do a U-turn in the middle of the suburban street instead of driving around the block.

"Auntie Glynnis, you're not supposed to do that!"

"Quinn spoke first! Quinn spoke first!"

"But it's not fair, you're not supposed to do that."

"I know," I said.

"But how come you did? How come, Auntie Glynnis? How come?"

"Because I'm a grown-up." Oh God, would every inane thing uttered by an adult in my childhood soon come out of my mouth?

I pulled into the parking lot, on the alert for small children. "Quick, quick!" I said, clapping my hands. I was on a mission. "Let's go. Bag and coat."

Quinn was now halfheartedly attempting to get his jacket on while finishing a game on his iPad. My niece was also unbuckling herself.

"No! Stay there," I said to her and reached for my nephew's iPad.

"Wait!" He pushed a button and dropped it on the car floor out of Zoe's reach and climbed out. I knew I should make him pick it up and apologize. Instead I twisted around and grabbed his hood with one hand to keep him from wandering in front of traffic, picked the iPad up, and handed it to Zoe. "Stay here."

I hit the button to shut the door automatically and briefly wondered if I was breaking a law by leaving Zoe in the car unattended while I dragged my nephew the twenty feet to the place where the crossing guard was standing. Could someone drive away with her? No, I had the keys. Still, I started jogging with the vague knowledge that the rules of my eighties childhood were no longer considered kosher, even though it was always unclear to me where the new borders of acceptability had shifted to.

"We have to go the other way, Auntie Glynnis." Quinn pulled

my hand toward a ramp whose only entry was at the other end of the parking lot. The crossing guard was ten feet ahead of us.

"Why?"

"We just do."

I knew he was right. Five-year-olds knew the rules better than most and still liked to follow them, but the clock was ticking and so I pulled him to the crossing guard anyway. I attempted to walk through.

"Hold up there, Mama." The crossing guard was a heavyset woman who appeared to be in her late forties, though I suspected there was a solid chance she was younger than me in reality. I recognized the tone of an absolute ruler—I'd encountered it before at customs, the DMV, and the social security office.

"She's my aunt!" Quinn yelled. I couldn't tell if he was coming to my defense or excusing himself from any responsibility in my misdemeanor. She nodded with *I've heard it all before* knowingness.

"You need to go up to the top of the ramp and take him down that way."

"I'm so sorry, it's my first day. I didn't realize," I said meekly, nudging Quinn toward the opening hoping he would take the encouragement and run through. No chance.

"I *told* you, Auntie Glynnis."

"That's no problem." The crossing guard used the exact same tone of *no chance* I had employed ten times already that day. "Just walk him up to the top. The kindergartners come down the ramp."

I was going to have to go up to the top of the ramp.

"See how fast you can run to the top of the ramp."

My nephew took off. I watched him reach the entry and come racing back down.

"So fast! Okay, have a good day. I love you." I gave him a kiss on the forehead over the railing and took off for the car.

Through the windows the car looked empty. Where was Zoe? My heart dropped into my foot. My life screeched to a halt. Every terrible story I'd grown up with about kidnapped girls exploded into my head, horrific details I hadn't thought about in years emerged from dark storage spaces. I flew across the lot and into the car.

"Auntie Glynnis, what is the password?" She was on the floor with the iPad. My ears vibrated with the sound of my pounding heart.

"The password for what?"

"For the iPad."

"I don't know it, sweetheart."

"But I need the password."

"I'm sorry, babe, I don't know it. Get into your seat."

"But I need the password."

I looked at the clock. My recent terror was quickly replaced by the need to be back on the road. "Into your seat now."

I pulled out of the parking lot as she was buckling up, waited till I heard the click of her belt, and hit the gas. It was a half-hour drive—we had twenty-five minutes. I was alive with purpose.

"BUT I NEED THE PASSWORD."

I didn't respond. I knew what was coming. The wails started. I just let them roll. I let them roll for a full five minutes, until they became a sort of white noise in the car. Toddler tantrums are different than baby fits, which I've often suspected we are genetically wired not to be able to tolerate. Finally she paused long enough to make words: "But I neeeed the password."

My stern voice took over again. "I don't have the password, and I won't have it for the rest of this ride. We can either sing or you can stare out the window."

"No."

"Fine, I'll just sing. *We're going on a lion hunt . . .*"

"I don't want to sing!"

It was now 8:57. If the next three lights stayed with me, I might make it. I stopped singing.

"We're going to play a game called the school bell Olympics, okay?" This worked.

"Yes! What is it?"

"It means as soon as I pull into the parking lot you undo your seat belt, and get your jacket and boots on, and then when I open the door you jump on my back and we see how fast we can run."

"Like you're the horsy and I'm riding you?" Zoe sounded very pleased with herself that she knew the game.

"Sure."

I thought about how much I'd loved my father's manic moods growing up and how much sense they had made. It was like being with an eight-year-old who'd been granted the powers of adulthood. In the morning, he would sometimes come barreling down the stairs, wildly chasing the dog until she, and sometimes we, ran hysterical circles around the house, much to my mother's dismay. If he was in a good mood on our way back from visiting my grandmother on the other side of town, my sister and I were often able to convince him to bypass our driveway and continue on to the cul-de-sac at the end of our street, where he would whip the car around the grassy knoll as fast as he could while we screamed with joy and counted off the rotations: one! two! five! Here was our very own amusement park ride! Sometimes we got as high as ten or twelve before he finally adhered to my mother's anxious calls for him to stop, and he slowed down and returned us home.

"But you have to be ready," I said in a serious tone, "so that means you have to put your coat and boots on now."

"But I can't reach my boots."

"You can undo your seat belt and get them as soon as I pull

into the parking lot." I paused. "But not before I pull into the parking lot."

I blazed through the next three lights, just making the left into the school as the last signal went red.

"Ready?"

I could hear the seat belt unbuckle, and I slowed down. This was likely the sort of thing that landed people in court cases that were covered on *Oprah* and launched a thousand hot takes. *Child was not wearing seat belt* . . . I looked at the clock. It was 8:59. I pulled into the first available spot.

"Ready?"

"Yesssss."

I jumped out of the front seat, opened the door, and turned my back. Zoe leapt on with the sort of abandon only a person who has never considered there might not be someone to catch them can possess.

"Go, horsy, go!" She kicked the side of my leg with her booted foot.

I'd forgotten that when we left the house I'd been unable to locate my shoes and was wearing my sister's Crocs, which were two sizes too small. I had a brief vision of both of us face-planting and getting bloody noses.

"Faster horsy!"

The school bell started ringing. The gate was twenty feet away, the school door behind it. There was a lineup by the door that was growing shorter with every step. Surely they would not close it if they saw me staggering across the parking lot. I picked up my pace. I focused with laser intensity on the gate. The bell stopped.

"I'm slipping!"

"Hold on!"

I twisted her around, grabbed her legs, and lifted her over the gate.

"Run!"

She ran. The woman at the door waved at me. "You must be the aunt. How is your sister?"

"I have a baby brother!" Zoe yelled. She had stopped running and was now taking her time walking to the door. She was on the other side of the fence, though, so this was officially no longer my problem.

"She's good," I called, wondering if I'd met this woman before. I sometimes had a hard time keeping all the kids' connections straight. "Baby is fine."

"Give her our best."

"Bye Auntie Glynnis!" Zoe stopped at the door and waved at me ferociously. I waved back just as energetically as her little figure, sporting an enormous pink backpack, disappeared through the door. What the hell did a three-and-a-half-year-old need with a backpack that big? I didn't stop waving until the door was shut. I returned to the car and collapsed back into the driver's seat. I thought of my mother, who, despite her near-suffocating concern over what other people thought, had never let how foolish she might look yoo-hooing at us through crowds stop her from doing it. I thought of how she'd spent my entire childhood in this routine, moving us from home to school to activity in an endless rotation. And now my sister was in nearly the same one, except hers was far more frantic; it was no longer acceptable to push your kids out of doors and tell them to come back when the street lamps came on. Still, this school run was the common ritual I knew was shared by nearly every woman with children. I could take my guest spot in it this morning if I wanted to, post a picture of my coffee mug perched precariously on the dashboard, include a summary of what I'd just done, and immediately be greeted with fanfare. I'd be part of the tradition of parenthood, if only for a day or a week. It was tempting. I did feel as if I deserved an award for making the bell. I felt fucking accomplished. I felt as accomplished as I did when I submitted a good story on deadline. I felt the old satisfaction of having achieved something tangible; it was the sensation I had most missed when I was writing meaningless posts for lots of money. It was nice. What if this was my life?

That was the question that continued to present itself to me as the week progressed. As showers became an increasingly distant memory, and my hair became even more matted to my head. My clothes filthier. As the nights got later, and the kids' unwillingness to go to sleep on time slammed up against my nonnegotiable writing routine. It was also there waiting for me when I woke up in the middle of the night to tiny scared voices at my bedside and warm bodies snuggled beside me. Or when I was asked intently by Quinn why Darth Vader wanted to kill his son. Didn't he love him? And again as I was humbly struck dumb one afternoon in the changing room when I took Zoe swimming and she pointed between my legs and said, "Mommy has fur down there, too." It was a good punch line to a story I'd later tell, but it was also an intimacy to which I wasn't accustomed.

Did I want this? I'd been given a gift, it seemed to me. This wasn't a fun afternoon with someone else's kids before I handed them back and went off to dinner. This was the deep end, and I was getting the chance to swim in all its messiness and glory for a while.

Parents, especially women, have a habit of talking about motherhood as though it were an exotic mystical land where everything is dazzling; as if they'd walked through a closet and the world has suddenly gone Technicolor. Or at least that's how it often felt, listening to them from the shores of childless land. With each breakfast rush and school run and nighttime snuggle, I was traveling further and further into that land, if only as a tourist. It did not feel mystical, unless you count the hallucinatory effect of having no sleep. But it *was* electrifying.

There was a charge in this I could not deny, a sense of propulsion and deep, absolute necessity. I'd be okay if this was my life, I thought. I could do this if I had to and probably enjoy it. This was not just fantasy theorizing on my part—I was written into the will. I could envision myself in this life with these kids if, God forbid, it came to that. And I'd probably love it.

Ambition is ambition; like running water it has to go somewhere, and this was a place I could understand it going. The truth was, there was some brief relief to that picture: on a very basic level I would know exactly what I was supposed to do every day, and it would always be important to someone. I'd never have to wonder over my own necessity or whether what I was doing was worthwhile. Like the images I'd found of Princess Leia everywhere in my youth to support my conclusion that she was the ideal of female adulthood, I didn't have to look far to find reinforcement that motherhood was the one true way. I vaguely knew it would look different from the inside, and that if I ever got there I would likely begin spending a great deal of my time anxious over all the ways I might be fucking up; at least half the world's economy ran on instilling the belief in women that they were always badly failing at something. But at least there would be a language for what I was doing, and an entire history of people doing it to fall back on for guidance and support.

However, the knowledge that I was good with children, and also that far from hating the idea, I could very much understand the appeal of having them in my life, was not, I understood, the same thing as *choosing* to have them. What was I choosing? Once I started digging around I realized this was the question that was lodged right behind all the *what if this were my life?* speculating I'd been doing. I didn't know the answer to that question. But, as it turned out, I was about to confront it head on.

10. The Showdown

My mother had an encyclopedic knowledge of movies made in the 1950s. In addition to detailed plotlines, she could recount the names of movie stars, their most famous lines, their marriage and relationship histories, and their many roles, as though reciting branches on her family tree. The fact that she would tell me these things in the same tone that she'd use to explain both the Latin root of a word, *and* how it had appeared in different contexts over time, left me with the impression that Hollywood was a thing to be taken seriously. When I was eleven, my father arrived home unannounced with a VCR. Almost immediately, my mother went to the video store and rented these movies from her childhood, reciting passages she still knew by heart more than three decades later. Gary Cooper westerns, Hitchcock mysteries, all the great musicals, everything Jimmy Stewart. She was a sucker for a good romance. She liked happy endings and hated too much violence. If the movie was too suspenseful, she would disappear to the kitchen, while we remained in front of the set absorbing this particular version of the outside world. Thanks to repeated viewings of films like *Rear Window* and *How to Marry a Millionaire*, my understanding of the outside world became synonymous with New York City.

When Quinn was born, I posted a picture on Facebook of Auntie Mame holding forth on her staircase, long cigarette holder in hand; I also posted a clip from the scene where her ten-year-old nephew is expertly mixing a martini. I, too, could be counted on for a similar education, I declared. I was thirty-four then. I liked the idea of being the independent, influential, chic (intermittently, in my case) aunt. A woman entirely in charge of her own life, a life that involved children but in less traditional ways. This was easier to do in my early thirties, when a conventional future (albeit one couched in dreams of a Beekman Place duplex) was still just as possible as an *un*conventional one.

But when I arrived at my sister's at age forty and seven weeks, it was not Auntie Mame who came to mind. As the days passed, I began to feel as if I had slipped into one of my mother's old western standbys, movies that had never interested me very much as a child because the women in them seemed to spend most of their time either cooking, washing, or wringing their hands. But now here I was, some sort of modern-day aging Gary Cooper, striding out to face his archnemesis in a final showdown. Except in my case, it was becoming clear, the nemesis was a week-old baby.

And not just any baby: a perfect baby. Connor wasn't fussy; he cried only when hungry; he was alert; he was sweet in a way people think babies are when they see them in pictures. He was what people who'd never spent time with a baby thought they would get when they said they wanted one. He was an advertisement for babies.

I had some knowledge in this department. People had been handing me their babies for nearly as long as I could remember. From age eleven (amazingly the legal babysitting age at the time) I'd been the top phone number taped to the suburban fridge, the person mothers raced one another to reach first, often calling weeks in advance. When I was twenty-three and new to New York, I cared for the infant daughter of my manager, a twenty-two-year-old single mother. I carried that baby around the New York City subway system, and streets, with what can fairly be described as aplomb (though it's just as likely I was simply too young to know enough to be anxious). I handled her with such confidence that everyone in the Spanish Harlem neighborhood where they lived assumed the baby was mine, which often proved handy, as it resulted in a lot of offers to carry things up and down sets of stairs, mostly from helpful young men who talked to me very differently when I was on my own. (The nannies and mothers at the Central Park playgrounds, however, only regarded me with silent hostile suspicion; white lady, dark baby was the inverse of the established norm there. It was weeks before I understood why I was getting such a cold shoulder, but it was an early lesson for me in how the Upper East Side operated.)

Since my friends had all started having children of their own, I'd come to be known as the "baby whisperer." I was a natural. Babies were neither a mystery, nor scary, nor something I idealized; they were a reality. They had always in some capacity been a regular part of my life.

And now Connor was my evening date. Every evening. Like our morning routine, we'd also developed an evening one. After the kids had been put to bed, and Alexis had fed the baby, she'd go downstairs hoping to slip into some rest of her own for a few hours. I would stay upstairs with him. It was heaven. Holding him in the dark, having him hold on to me, his little heart beating against my fingertips, made me feel as if I were in the middle of a birth announcement: so much love! My heart was discovering new pockets I didn't know existed, growing and melting at the same time.

It didn't take me long to realize how naïve I'd been to ever think I could slide into my forties without fully confronting the question of children. The first night after I'd met the married man, we'd been sitting in a crowded hotel bar having drinks, when he leaned over the table and said abruptly, "Do you want children?" I'd laughed. Women my age were always being accused of getting too serious too quickly, but in my experience, men were just as guilty of it, maybe even more so. I'd shrugged. "I don't *not* want them," I said. He'd shaken his head. "I want one so badly," he said emphatically. A month later, on a trip home from a writing assignment, I spent the four-hour flight with a strangely roiling stomach, wondering if he was going to get his wish; by the time I landed I had methodically planned out everything that would need to change in my life over the next eight months should the test come out positive. It turned out nothing needed changing; I had just been having normal period cramps. But I remembered how quickly I'd slipped into a new set of calculations about how I'd make it all work. I *could* make it all work if I had to.

"I don't *not* want them" felt like a feeble phrase now, sitting here with a babe trustingly asleep in my arms. A dodge. This was an enormous thing, far too big to leave up to chance. For years, I'd resented that my entire life had appeared to the world to be a clock, counting down, at every turn forced to confront the question: baby? And yet, how could it not be? It was still a question in need of answering. I thought back to the night on the beach, and my resolution that I would no longer behave as if I had something to apologize for. There were lots of ways to have children—though many of them enormously expensive, or largely out of reach for a single woman of modest means—but if I wanted to give birth to one, even just a little bit, I needed to own up to that now. Look it straight in the face, so to speak, which is exactly what I did. I uncrossed my legs and raised my knees and gently adjusted Connor so that he was reclined against them and facing me. And then I stared. I stared directly into the face of what I had been told my whole life was the thing that would define it and give it meaning.

Did I want this?

I stared and stared, inhaling the babyness of him. I stroked the curve of his cheek. I slipped my little finger in his hand and let him grasp it in his sleep. I made myself think only of all the good things. I thought of Zoe clinging to me for comfort, of the pride and joy I felt when Quinn had raced off the school bus one afternoon a few days earlier, waving a Star Wars comic book triumphantly in his hand and hollering, "There's a picture of Princess Leia in here, Auntie Glynnis!" And then for the first time I thought of the parts of me the children I wasn't having might be missing out on. All the things I could pass on to a child. I had been a recipient of all my mother's great knowledge. Where would that go?

There was also the thing I kept coming back to over and over. A baby was a clear path forward. If I went home and got pregnant, an entire infrastructure would materialize around my life. I would be seen; even if I was alone I would never be alone. I'd be a mother.

I waited in the quiet for the panic button to go off, or to hear the tick of my own internal clock. There was nowhere to go. No movement to quiet any second thoughts. I forced myself to lay down my emotional arms and be defenseless. I raised Connor up and put him on my chest and let him breathe softly into my ear. And I waited. I waited for regret to wash over me. To be drowned in the knowledge of all my bad relationship decisions, and bad life decisions, bad everything decisions that had led me to this seat, where I now sat alone, with someone else's baby. I waited for the panic, panic I'd seen overcome so many of my childless friends, to take me in its cruel grasp. *There's still time!* the woman's voice from the wedding floated into my head. A last chance bonus round if I wanted it.

Connor slept on, unaware of the awesome battle that was taking place in my mind, just inches away from him. He knew nothing. He was just a baby entirely reliant on me in this moment to protect him and comfort him. I began to hum softly, still waiting. But the panic I'd anticipated did not kick in.

I made myself walk further down the imaginary path I was on. It was so easy to speak of babies as if they were a concept. Like freedom, and peace. Rosy, ill-defined ideas. But I had seen enough of the reality, was currently living enough of the reality, to know firsthand the practicalities. Maybe I knew them too well. Maybe if I knew a little bit less about what was involved, I'd want it all a little bit more. For instance, if I wanted a baby, then the immediate next steps were clear: go back to New York and embark on the familiar odyssey of a forty-year-old woman chasing down her neglected fertility. I certainly knew what that looked like. Everyone in New York knew what that looked like. I could do it. I understood sitting here that if the switch I was waiting for to flip did, nothing would stop me from doing it.

But then, let's say I *was* successful. I'd be doing it alone. Or rather, I'd have to be very okay with the idea of doing it alone, since all evidence of my love life to date suggested this was my natural state of being. First off, my tiny apartment would have to go. I'd have to go back to a full-time job in an office with benefits, or promptly move back to Canada. I tried to picture myself living in Toronto. Yes, in theory the ability to move to Canada meant I was in possession of a universal lottery ticket of sorts, but I had a life in New York that I worked hard for and that I was not eager to give up. Then there was the life beyond the baby stage. I was living that now, too. Some people wanted babies the way they wanted weddings, but I knew what it meant to have children: a life of scheduling play dates and couriering someone to school and back, to after school and back, to sports practices, and managing summer vacations, and birthday parties, and homework, and everything else that sucked up time like a vacuum cleaner that never shut off. And how to *pay* for all that? I could if I had to, but did I *want* to have to? It would be brutal, for decades. My life for a long time would exist on the periphery. I would no longer be able to do what I wanted when I wanted. Those concerns would fade if a child ever arrived. But they were real now. And in my control.

That's what it came down to. The joys of parenthood, I knew, were deep, and often found in the small moments, rooted in a sustained current of unconditional love. However, I also knew without a doubt that the joy of my life was rooted in my ability to move when I wanted and how. I valued that ability to be in motion more than anything. I could hear the arguments in my head, the return of the magazine voices: *You're going to regret this in ten years. You don't know what you're missing.* Of course, I might regret it. I knew that. There were an endless number of things about my life I might end up regretting. Some I already did. But it seemed to me that going through life making decisions on what I might possibly feel in a future that may or may not come about was a bad way to live. I wasn't going to have a baby as an insurance policy against some future remorse I couldn't yet imagine. I had more respect for myself than that. The truth was, no one knows what they're missing in the end. You can only live your own life, and do your best with the outcome when you roll the dice.

I looked down at Connor again. He had gripped my finger in his sleep. Where the fuck was this biological alarm that was supposed to be going off? I thought of my mother. It would have made her sad, I suspected, to know my thinking on children. She had loved being a mother. I had not grown up with a woman who felt suffocated by motherhood. She had not struggled against its restraints or felt her great mind was going to waste, dulled by the mundane routines of caring for small children. In the early seventies, at the height of the feminist movement, she had quit her job and chosen to become a stay-at-home mother upon my arrival. I couldn't even say she gave it all up to stay at home, because there was never a hint from her that she felt she was giving anything up. She preferred her life at home, packing lunches and carting us to a carefully planned schedule of activities. Perhaps if she'd liked it a bit less I would have had an easier time relating to her, or valuing the choices she made; perhaps I would have been less fanatical about some of my own. As it was, starting at a very young age, I constantly pushed against the quiet, predictable framework of our suburban lives, loathing how mundane and stationary it all was. And now here I was, finally being forced to acknowledge the value of that life, simply by confronting whether it was something I could live without.

That was really the question. Would I be okay without a child?

Each night I sat with Connor and forced myself to go down the path of imaginary motherhood, suspicious of myself that this would be something that I would be willing to reject. Every night I expected to have a change of heart and come up with a different, more recognizable answer. But it never happened.

Instead, sitting in the dark and quiet, something quite unexpected occurred. My life, precisely as it was—the product of good and bad decisions—began to come into focus for me. Sitting there, I could see it for the first time as something I'd chosen. Something I'd built intentionally, and not simply a makeshift thing I'd constructed as a for-the-time-being existence until something came along that would make me a whole person in the eyes of the world. Once I began to see it as such, it dawned on me that I had no wish to escape from it. On the contrary: I wanted it. I was choosing my life. I was willing to risk it.

Eventually Connor would wake, and no amount of rocking or pacing could get him back to sleep. On cue my sister would appear on the staircase to reclaim him and feed him, and I would retreat down the hall to my bed, sticking my head in on the kids to make sure their blankets were pulled up, before sliding under my own, checking the alarm to make sure it was set to go off in a few hours.

11. On the Road

I was home alone when my sister messaged me. It was ten days into my stay. Quinn was at school, and Alexis had left the house for the first time alone with both Connor and Zoe, while I stayed back, ostensibly to write. It was two days after Halloween, and beside me was a growing pile of mini chocolate wrappers from the kids' stash that I'd been steadily plowing through. I'd seen almost nothing of my parents since they'd dropped me off. Normally, I split my time, often sleeping at their house, and in bed with my mother to get a sense of how she really was, but things had been far too chaotic with the new baby. Alexis had only one vehicle; any trip had to be coordinated around the kids' schedules, which didn't let up until late in the evening. Now I had a few hours to spare, my first time off, and the book proposal needed finishing.

Instead of diving in, however, I'd spent the last hour reading emails and relentlessly scanning Twitter. There was a string of messages from our business accountant requesting more paperwork. Rachel had just announced her pregnancy publicly in an article, and my in-box was full of congratulations from members of the network we ran. I'd also published a piece just before I left about burning out and was fielding many requests for a follow-up. Normally I'd have been in a frenzy to deal with all of it, but instead everything felt as if it were taking place in a different world, a universe away from where I was. As though it had nothing to do with me, a limb gone numb.

A green bubble popped up on my screen; I kept my phone off in Canada to save on international charges, but I had my text messages looped through my computer. It was my sister.

Can you call me from home phone? Issues with Mom.

My heart did a familiar drop. *What now?* I thought. I stared at the screen for a bit, taking deep, bracing breaths. Whatever it was would be bad, I knew. I waited, temporarily holding off the news of whatever was coming, as if I had the power to put my life on pause, even for just a few minutes. Then I went in search of the phone. I finally found it in the Barbie house in the basement and dialed my sister.

"What now?" I asked when she picked up.

The fire department was at my parents' house. Apparently, my father had left home without leaving a note, and when my mother woke up she'd been confused, as she often was after a nap, and thinking she was in the wrong house had called 911. No one knew where my father was. My sister had left a message on a cell phone he had, though neither of us was sure if it worked or whether he had it on him.

"They're calling to find out what we want to do," she said.

"Tell them I'm coming." I stood up and gazed out the window. It was pouring rain. "Oh shit. Wait. There's no car here."

"Fuuuck."

My sister's voice was a river of exhaustion. A few months earlier, Alexis had gone to visit my parents and coincidentally arrived at the house at the same time as the firemen who were responding to another of my mother's 911 calls. "They let the kids play on the truck," she told me when she'd called to catch me up. "They were both thrilled." Another time, the same thing had happened, but my father hadn't told us about it until later. He'd apparently gone to the hospital after being informed of her whereabouts, found my mother quietly sitting in the emergency room where the firemen had left her waiting to be seen by the doctors, and simply collected her and driven off without telling anyone. I was furious when I learned this. I thought of all the time I'd spent scheduling appointments in the hopes of getting my mother's condition formally recognized so I could start the process of getting help. Surely calling 911 in confusion and being deposited in the emergency room by the fire department merited some sort of intervention, but if it wasn't on the record, how could I argue it? My father was insistent that she was fine. "She exaggerates a lot of this behavior for attention." It wouldn't occur to me until much later that thinking this likely made the reality of what was actually happening to her bearable for him.

And now here we were again. I didn't allow myself to be sickened by the relief I felt at having another chance to get some official record of her condition. I simply knew I needed to get to the hospital before my father could pick her up and remove her.

"Where are you?" I asked my sister.

She was almost in the city. "I can be home in an hour if you want to take the car. Shit, wait, there's swimming lessons tonight. Maybe I can get one of the neighbors to lend you their car."

I walked to the window. All the driveways looked empty. The rain was turning to sleet.

"Hold on," said my sister. "Dad's on the other line."

"Tell him he has to come get me before he goes to the hospital." I walked to the bathroom and turned the shower on. I gave the kids baths at night, but couldn't remember the last time I'd showered myself. If I was going to the hospital I needed to look less crazy.

My sister came back on. "He's coming to get you. He says he'll be there in half an hour."

He'd apparently taken his desktop computer to the Apple store two hours away and had been en route home when my sister called.

"Hold on," my sister said again. A minute later she came back on. "That was the fire department again. They're taking Mom to the hospital. I said you'd meet them there with Dad."

By the time my father arrived twenty-five minutes later I'd showered, battled successfully with my hair, and fished out clean clothes from my suitcase, which still lay where I'd dropped it the day I'd arrived home. The first thing I noticed as I walked out the door was that my father was driving someone else's car.

I ran through what now felt like freezing rain to the driver's side and knocked on the window. "Want me to drive?"

"No."

"You sure?" I tried to keep the hopeful note out of my voice. He shook his head. "Whose car is this?" I asked, diving into the passenger seat.

"It's a rental."

I steeled myself. "Why do you have a rental?"

"I backed into a truck in the parking lot the other day. I was backing up, and he was just there."

I didn't ask for details. There was nothing I could do about it now. I just buckled up. The fire department had taken my mother to the nearest emergency room, which was a forty-five-minute drive northeast, mostly along a two-lane highway that wrapped around the northern shores of Lake Simcoe and was known for its unpredictable bursts of intense winter weather. It was only November, but up here it wasn't unusual to get blizzards. As we drove, the sleet turned back to rain and then back to sleet again. The car my father had rented was small and light; I could feel the wind shake it when we went through open stretches. Every time a truck passed us, the windshield would be covered in a splash of water and dirt, blinding us to the road. I breathed a quiet sigh of relief when we finally came up behind an enormous slow-moving truck and were forced to slow down. I pulled down the visor to apply lipstick, and just then my father gunned it to pass the truck. Between windshield wipes, which only briefly cleared the glass from the river of rain and dirt the truck was giving off, I could make out headlights in the distance coming in our direction. I felt the wheels of the car hydroplane across the groves of the opposite lane. *Would they make it?* came the voice in my head, as though narrating a cliffhanger scene.

For a second I was reminded of careening around Iceland with Viktor. Had that really been only a month ago? I felt as though I'd lived three lives since then. Funny now to think, or it would have been had I been able to muster a sense of humor, that I had approached my birthday gripped by the fear that my life would be a long boring slog from here on out. Instead it had felt like everything, good and bad, was happening to me all at once.

My father pulled back into our lane just in time, as the oncoming cars blared by us. I leaned into the seat, sliding back into myself, but only for a moment. Ahead of us were four more trucks nearly the same size; surely he wouldn't make a run past all of these. I turned to my father, took a deep breath, and spoke calmly. "When we get there, I want the doctors to give Mom a checkup."

I waited for a response, but none came. I went on in the same low voice. "We need official documentation to show how she's doing. And if she's confused enough to call 911 then that needs to be recorded. The lists for nursing homes are eighteen months long and she's not even on the list yet."

Again, silence. I wondered what the thought bubble above his head might say if there were one. I persisted. "Did you hear me?"

"Yes."

I felt the car gun up again as my father prepared to move out into the oncoming lane. I was suddenly flooded with anger. *I will be so pissed if this is how I die*, I thought, thinking how unfair it would be for my sister to have to deal with any other calamity. But we didn't get very far. The line of cars in the opposite lane stretched as far as the eye could see. My father pulled back into our lane and remained there.

We found my mother sitting alone in the brightly lit emergency waiting room with a pleasant smile on her face. She looked tiny and old under the harsh lights. Like a helpless child.

"We're here, Mom." I sat down beside her and put my arms around her, struck as always by how I was able to feel her bones through her clothes.

"Oh, how nice, yes," she said as if greeting a late-arriving friend for lunch. "Did your appointment go okay, Jack?" she asked, turning to my father. I sighed, my heart sinking—she knew who we were. It was entirely possible her confusion had passed since she'd been picked up, and she was actually thinking clearly, in which case the doctors would likely send us home after only a brief checkup. What I needed was for her to be at her worst, the way I'd seen her in the evenings on nearly every visit home since Christmas, so that I could get a doctor to sign off on her being eligible for the care I knew she required. I felt like a monster for wanting my mother to be worse than she was. The unpredictability of her dementia was almost as bad as the symptoms themselves. It was like living in a fun house; I never knew if what I was seeing was reliable.

I went to the nurse's window to make sure they were aware

my mother was there, and I was given a series of forms to fill out. Around us the waiting room was filled with all sorts of people, some injuries more apparent than others. Sometimes I couldn't tell which person in the group was the one waiting to be seen. Every few minutes my mother would try to get up and help someone, thinking she was back at her last job as a social worker in a center that was attached to a hospital, helping families figure out where and how to place their elderly relatives. That had been only two years ago.

After an hour and a half, we were called into an examination room and led through the swinging door that said DO NOT ENTER. On the other side was a long hallway; people were slumped in wheelchairs along the wall or lay on gurneys. One little boy in a cast was sleeping on his mother's lap. "Oh, can I get you anything?" my mother asked gently as we passed. We were put into a narrow, bright room with an examination table in the middle and nothing else.

"Do you want to lie down, sweetheart?" my mother asked, turning to me.

"That's for you, Mom," I said, trying to guide her toward the table.

"Oh, but I'm fine, why don't you take it?" This was the mother I had known all my life. Gentle, kind, and forever inquiring whether she could get something for someone else. But now I regarded it with a weary and defeated eye. There was no way anyone was going to be alarmed into action by this woman. My father sat down on the floor with his back to the wall and put his head in his hands. This wasn't unusual. In almost every specialist appointment I'd accompanied him on that required us to wait for anything, he'd usually sit down on the floor with his hands crossed over his chest.

"Is your back bothering you, Jack?" asked my mother. My father shook his head.

The doctor who eventually arrived was young and handsome, with a deep, gravelly voice that made me want to make him talk more. Before I even realized I was doing it, I tried to catch a glimpse of his left hand. Was he married? Could I live in Canada with a doctor? I blazed through my old mental questionnaire before I caught myself, stopped, and focused on what he was saying. He wasn't looking at me. He was addressing my father, who was now standing. Legally speaking, my father was in charge here. I stayed quiet, watching the doctor's face as I listened to my father explain my mother's symptoms in the friendly, conspiratorial tone he normally saved for the woman at the pharmacy who gave him his prescription pills. None of it sounded particularly alarming, neither did my mother currently appear alarming. I let him go for a few minutes before breaking in with my calmest, clearest, sharpest voice. I laid it all out, point by point and in detail, describing everything that happened, as if I were a professor standing at the front of the class with a pointer. I drained all the emotion out of my voice as I spoke, I made our world black and white.

I tried to mimic the tone of the nurses I'd dealt with when I described how in the evenings, after the cloud of rage had passed into confusion, my mother's body would suddenly go rigid, "as if struck by paralysis." I didn't say that no matter how many times it happened I was never prepared for it. That I'd lunge toward her, worried she was about to fall to the ground. How she would collapse into my arms instead, something that normally would have knocked me down, except she was so light now it was as though one of the kids had decided to take a flying leap. I didn't say that I wasn't quite strong enough to carry her up the stairs, though I often tried, leaning over and putting my arm under her legs. That when we finally reached her bed—minutes or an hour later, I never knew—I would gently lay her down, bending with her until I was sure the mattress could take her weight, and then try to remove her shoes. I did describe how her toes would curl too tightly for me to be able to get her shoes off, though, and how when I pulled at them she would cry in pain. It was a sound I'd never heard from her before, and it seemed to come from some deep place within her I didn't even know existed. And then when I stepped away she would whimper over and over, *Please don't hurt me.* It was the worst thing my mother ever said to me.

As I went on, the doctor methodically taking notes, my father slid back down the wall and put his head back in his hands. The doctor glanced at him and then turned back to me. I wondered how I appeared. The angry, overbearing daughter? The harried forty-year-old whose lipstick was now misplaced and obvious? Now and then I could feel my voice rising. *This is bad*, I wanted to scream. *I am not imagining this. I need someone to do something.* But I pushed back on myself, slowing down and taking a deep breath. I was a totally competent person. I imagined all the hysterical family members he must see every day. All the family drama that must play out in these back hallways, histories being sliced open and examined the same way bodies were. I was determined to separate myself from the fray, and the only way to do that was to sound the complete opposite of how I was feeling.

Every few sentences or so, my mother would interrupt with wide, shocked eyes. "Did I really do that? I'm sorry." I reached over and took her hand but didn't look at her. I hated saying all this in front of her even though I knew she wouldn't remember, but now that we were here I couldn't sugarcoat it. Finally, the doctor turned to my mother: "Jean, I'd like to ask you a few questions."

She nodded agreeably. Then he ran through the same basics I'd grown accustomed to hearing. What was today's date? What year were we in? Who was the prime minister? *For the love of Christ, why couldn't she answer wrong just once?* In high school my mother had won awards in both math and French but had dropped both subjects on graduation because she hadn't received a perfect score on her final exams.

"Oftentimes in the afternoon she doesn't know who I am or where she is," I interjected. I knew it was not part of my role as a calm, collected bystander to interrupt, but I couldn't help myself. The doctor just nodded and wrote something down on his clipboard. I breathed in and thought, *I will not scream, I will not scream, I will not scream.*

After a minute or so he looked up. "I think it would be in everyone's best interests," he said, glancing down at my father whose head was still in his hands, "if we admitted you overnight for observation."

"Does our insurance cover that?" I blurted out in a panic, not quite able to believe things were working out as I wanted them.

The doctor looked at me in confusion. I'd forgotten I was in Canada. Every once in a while, when I'd get especially frustrated with the bureaucracy of the Ontario health care system, I'd force myself to imagine my family's scenario if we'd all lived in the States as a way of calming myself down.

"Sorry, I live in New York . . . City." I tacked on the "city" part lest he think I meant I lived in Buffalo.

He nodded, deeply uninterested. No one is less impressed by America than Canadians. "The nurse will be back with all the papers. We don't currently have any extra beds, but Jean can stay here until something opens up."

I looked around at the tiny, sterile room and my mother sitting obediently on the hard examination table and was reminded of my only stay at a hospital. It had been to get my tonsils out when I was nine. My sister and I had gone in together, a sort of two-for-one deal that was apparently accepted practice in the early eighties. My mother had stayed in our room until the nurse had finally forced her to leave and then anxiously reappeared with the sun the next morning. I was suddenly struck by the reality that I was going to have to leave my mother here. Probably by herself. *What had I done?*

"I'll go home and get her things," I said to my father. "She'll need clothes and pajamas and toiletries." I turned to my mother. "Lie down, Mom, and have a nap."

"I think I'd rather go home," said my mother as though she were ordering from a menu.

"I know, but you're going to stay here for tonight. The doctors want to observe you."

"I'm sorry."

"It's not your fault, Mom." I'd gotten in the habit of explaining her disease to her, with some vague notion that the facts would balance out her anxiety and keep her tied to the ground and away from the terror that awaited her so many evenings when her mind untied itself.

"Dad is going to stay here with you."

"Oh, okay. And what about Medley?"

"I'll walk Medley when I get home."

"I'll come with you," my mother said, looking around for her coat.

"No, you have to stay here, Mom. They're going to keep you for observation overnight."

"Oh, okay. Will Jack know to pick me up here? We are going to a dance." Lately when her mind began to lurch, leaping through decades like a drunk time traveler, it landed on some version of the mid-sixties when my parents met, as if that were the tent pole from which the rest of her life hinged. Sometimes she referred to my father as her "first husband." "It's too bad that didn't work out," she'd say. "But don't tell your father I said that. I don't want him to get jealous."

There was some underlying truth to what she was saying. My father now was fundamentally different than the man I remembered from my childhood, when during his up periods he'd been exploding with energy and determination: making up milk shakes from scratch, officiating our swim meets. He had a black-and-white take on the world that from a child's perspective could make it seem very safe. Perhaps my mother, too, was remembering him from before and after his diagnosis. From before and after he'd lost his job, or they'd filed for bankruptcy. She seemed to have split him into two separate people in her head, which perhaps spoke to the cracks in their marriage better than anything else could. Sometimes it occurred to me that in my mother's untangling she had begun to tell more truths than she had the entire time I'd known her.

"Dad's right here," I said, gesturing to the hallway where my father now stood, signing paperwork. She smiled and nodded.

It was past 10:00 p.m. when I got on the road. There was no traffic; the weather had cleared up and the roads were now dry. The sky overhead as I sped along was pitch-black. It was the first time I'd been alone—without people, without children, without my computer—since I'd arrived. Ten days. It felt like a century. I turned on the radio. It was silent. I looked down and fiddled with the volume. And then into the void came the sound of an audience clapping and then piano. I'd caught the beginning of a song. Suddenly Bob Seger's voice slipped into the dark evening with me. *I know it's late, I know you're weary.* How many years had it been since I'd heard this song? I vaguely recalled it on the radio from childhood trips with my parents. I turned up the volume and let the gravelly singing loop its way around me in the darkness like a comforting arm. In the slow-motion tragedy of my mother's health, and the current chaos of my sister's home, there was only comfort to be given, and very little to be taken. But as I raced along, howling out the chorus to the empty night, the cold air rushing in the open windows, I felt comforted, if only for the duration of the music, and as the road rolled away beneath me and I sped through the darkness, I also felt very, very alive.

12. Be Careful What You Wish For

My mother stayed in the hospital for five days. After twenty-four hours she was moved to a room on one of the higher floors, which she shared with three other people. When I arrived on the second morning she was dozing. She was in the bed closest to the door, separated by a curtain. The only direct daylight came from a window at the other end of the room, and most of it was a secondary reflection off the shiny floor. This was a preview of what the rest of her life would be like if I didn't get her in a good home.

I stopped in my tracks when I saw her. She was lying on top of her covers, and over her pajamas she was wearing a bright orange vest, the type construction workers wear when they are working on busy roadways. I backed out of her room without waking her and inquired at the nurses' desk. They told me the evening before she'd become extremely agitated. "I barely recognized her," one nurse said with wide eyes. "She had been so gentle all day." Afterward, they told me, she'd gone wandering off and had ended up in an off-limits area of the hospital reserved for surgery staff. It had apparently taken them a while to realize she didn't work there.

"Is this all in her file?" I immediately asked. The nurse nodded, frowning slightly at my clinical reaction. I explained to her the problems I'd encountered and how badly I needed a record of this. She assured me it was all going into the file. "She is very bad." Again, she sounded amazed. I practically wept with relief that I wasn't crazy, and then felt so guilty for it I didn't want to go back into my mother's room. Instead I went to the coffee shop downstairs and purchased two double chocolate donuts. My pants had grown tighter in just the two weeks I'd been home. There'd been no time for exercise, and the brief amount of pleasure the kids' chocolate Halloween candy brought me felt like the only comfort I could currently rely on. I decided I wasn't going to feel bad about this, even if it meant saying goodbye to my wardrobe. I was going to take the small bits of consolation where I could get them. When I got back upstairs, my mother was awake and sitting on the side of her bed, bouncing. As I walked in she clapped her hands together. "Oh goody, you're here!"

"Hi, Mom," I said, watching her face to see if my calling her Mom would confuse her. But she just smiled. I leaned over, gave her a kiss, and asked her if she wanted some of a donut.

"No, no, I have work to do. I think they need me to admit some of the patients."

She tried to stand up.

"I think we should stay here for a bit." I didn't bother to explain that she didn't work here. She seemed so happy, what was the point?

"No! I don't want to sit down!" she said sharply. And then she grinned at me again. "Isn't this wonderful?" Her eyes were wide and alive. "It's just so nice to say whatever I want. It's such a relief."

I knew immediately this wasn't her illness talking. My mother was the direct product of a 1950s upbringing: assertiveness or thwarting convention was not allowed. She had never been able to overcome this. Whatever was dissolving in her brain, like a gel cap around medicine, was now releasing years, maybe decades, of unexpressed thoughts. We seemed to have moved into a phase, who knew for how long, where carefully contained, pleasant smiles and gentle accommodation were a thing of the past. It was the singular blessing of an otherwise relentlessly cruel disease, but all I was able to think of as I watched the gleeful look on her face was what a waste of time all the good behavior had been. Her whole life stretched behind me now, and from this vantage point it seemed so short. And these concerns about other people's opinions, which had dominated my mother's thinking, seemed so fruitless and unworthy. I was overwhelmed with sadness for her. At least she had no regrets; she couldn't remember anything long enough to have regret over it. Another tiny blessing I supposed.

•

When I wasn't at the hospital or running the kids around, I was on the phone. After much telephoning I had convinced the social worker in charge of my mother's case, a woman named Debbie whom I'd never met in person but who currently wielded an overwhelming amount of control over my mother's fate, to loop me in on the updates she was giving my father. Each time she called, before giving me any information, she reminded me that this was not how things were "usually done." Normally, only the person who held power of attorney could be directly contacted by an official. I'd nod silently, rolling my eyes; I had a New Yorker's respect for how things were usually done, which was to say, not a great deal. I operated under the assumption there was always a faster way around the system if you knew someone. But there was no point in voicing it here. I was not in New York; there was no skipping these lines in Canada.

But finally, finally, it seemed we were getting somewhere. A few days after my mother had been admitted, Debbie actually called me. "The social worker who did the assessment notes that your mother has experienced a significant decline in her functionality. She also noted in the file that your mother had been admitted to the emergency room."

I nodded my head vigorously but said nothing.

"She's recommending your mother be put in the queue for home care."

"What does that mean exactly?" I readied my pen, anticipating a new series of names and numbers.

"It means when she reaches the top of the list and a bed becomes available she will have the option to take it."

Oh, thank God. "How long will that take?"

"We don't have access to that list."

I closed my eyes and put my head down on my sister's bed, reminding myself yet again the sort of circumstances I'd be dealing with if we were in the States.

Debbie went on in her practiced voice. "But generally it's about nine to twelve months."

I took a deep breath. My mother needed help in nine days, not nine months. But so did everybody, I knew. "Is there any way to accelerate that?"

"If at her next assessment in three months something has significantly changed we may be able to move her onto the accelerated list. In the meantime, what I need from you, or actually from your father, is the list of your top five nursing home choices."

Three months. It was hard for me to imagine where we'd be in three days, let alone three months, but it was something.

I went over the nursing home list. I'd managed to get four of the good homes in; now it was just a matter of deciding on the least worst option for the fifth slot. Basic rooms were covered by the government. In the good nursing homes, the basic rooms were essentially like hotel rooms, airy, with sunlight and often a private bathroom. In what I had come to call the bad nursing homes, the basic rooms were narrow and dark, and bathrooms were shared. The private rooms in the bad places had shorter lists and made me feel less ill, but my parents' retirement income couldn't support the extra amount they'd need to pay for very long. I stared at the list for a while, and then filled in the last slot with the least worst bad place I'd seen, and marked the private option. I'd go back to the churn of an office writing job if I had to cover the difference. It would be easier to bear than the thought of my mother lying in a dark corner somewhere.

•

I went back to New York at the end of the two weeks as planned, and my mother returned home, while we waited for her number to come up. All the rigid competence that had fueled me since my arrival dissolved the second I stepped foot in the airport. My sister, now just over two weeks out from delivering a baby, dropped me off. The kids, eyes intent on the DVD screen, barely looked my way when I opened the back door to kiss them good-bye, but I felt as if I were being torn in two. My life in New York, which had been shimmering proudly in my vision all those quiet nights with my nephew, now became a distant point on the horizon in my mind, small and ever-retreating. As I walked away I felt poisoned by guilt. What was holding me in New York after all? Maybe I should ditch everything and come home and take care of everyone. Was I being selfish? Was I spoiled? Was I always going to feel the need to defend my life, even just to myself?

I got pulled into immigration as I was going through customs at the Toronto airport. I'd half expected this to happen; I'd flown in on one half of one ticket and was now returning on the other half of another. But I was still annoyed. Now that I was on my own and had only myself to look after, I could feel weeks of pent-up emotion starting to leak through the seams; I felt like a dam on the verge of breaking. Still, I kept my mouth shut when the immigration agent finally waved me over to his table and made me unzip my bag. Instead of noting the futility of this search, I silently redirected all my anger at him. *I dare you to ask me why I'm flying on two tickets.* I seethed in my head over and over as he began rifling through it. *I fucking dare you.* I wanted so badly to yell at someone. I wanted to scream about everything that I'd just been through. I wanted to say, *My mother is dying, and my sister is alone with three kids, and I am so fucking tired.* I wanted someone to acknowledge that it was a lot.

"Did you buy anything?" he asked, gingerly placing the pajama pants I had worn most of the week that were covered in . . . something—it was hard to tell at this point, but one leg was stiff as if it had been doused in starch—on the silver table in front of him.

"No."

He pulled out a toothbrush still in its packaging and held it up to me, eyebrows raised.

"I bought that." To my ears, my voice was devoid of emotion.

"Well, that's something, isn't it?"

Fuuuuuuuck you, I screamed at the top of my lungs in my head. But I knew better than to say anything out loud. I knew if I opened my mouth, even just a bit, all my anger would dissolve into tears, or worse. *Do not go over the edge in immigration*, cautioned a tiny rational voice in my mind, somehow managing to rise above the encroaching hysteria. *You are not that stupid.* I was not stupid. When you are your own emergency contact, you learn how not to get into an emergency if at all possible. I glanced up at the immigration official, pushed it all back down, gritted my teeth, and nodded in agreement; the toothbrush *was* something, my mistake. A few minutes later he let me go through.

After boarding the plane, I slumped into my seat, not bothering to figure out if any of the numbers added up to anything. For the first time in my life I was too tired to do my pre-takeoff mathematics. I would let other people on the flight worry about keeping it aloft. I texted Rachel that we were wheels up and didn't open my eyes again until we'd nearly reached New York.

As we came down the last stretch of the Hudson, swooping out over the Long Island Sound on the final turn to LaGuardia, the wind began buffeting the plane, making it buck and swoop with stomach-dropping intensity. Around me passengers gasped, and the flight attendants were forced to grip the seats as they struggled to the back of the plane to strap themselves in. But even then I barely moved. I was too drained to be scared. I waited till we began our final descent, circling Manhattan, and I sat up and smushed my face against the window. I gazed down at the city, sparkling below like a million glasses of champagne, the square of Central Park a dark oasis in the center. I pulled out my phone to snap a picture.

"Is this your first time here?" asked the man sitting next to me. I started laughing. It felt good to laugh. I shook my head. *Just your average New Yorker obsessed with her city*, I thought.

The plane dipped. Below I could see whitecaps on the water. Water, water, water, and then, boom, we hit the runway and the pilot slammed on the brakes and we all flew forward. Textbook landing at LaGuardia. I had the momentary sense of relief I got whenever returning to New York, of being back in a place that made complete sense.

As we waited to taxi to the gate, I scrolled through my back-logged email. People were still responding to Rachel's baby an-

nouncement. Someone had started a separate email chain for
a smaller group, cutting Rachel out, about a baby shower, and
was directing people to contact me for details since I'd "obviously" be the person organizing it. Another person in the thread
included a reminder that if it was going to be brunch it needed
to be "child friendly" because not everyone had time for fun
single lady brunches anymore. Smiley face.

Boom. The floodgates opened, and all my pent-up frustration and grief and exhaustion surged out. I was on fire with
rage. I was trembling in my seat. *I'll give you fucking brunch*, I
thought. *I'll shove it down your fucking throat. I'll give you so much
brunch you'll be shaped like a cosmopolitan for the rest of your fucking life.
You'll cry tears of mimosa.* I leaned my head into the seat in front of
me and took a deep breath, turning my face to the side to gaze
out the window at the skyline in the distance.

I was still struggling to see my life reflected back to me in
the world, and also struggling to live without that reflection, but
when others looked at me it seemed they often saw what the
Russian man on the beach had: half a person, empty spaces in
need of filling. There was a perverse truth to this. I'd learned
in the last year that being single past a certain age meant that
many of the most difficult things in my life were the direct result of overflow from other people's lives. You are the person
they call on to bike ninety blocks to the hospital because their
baby has no heartbeat and they are alone in the delivery room.
You are the person everyone turns to when your business partner gets pregnant, called on to organize everything around her
upcoming life as a single mother. And you're the person who
steps in when the marriage hits a rough patch or skids off the
rails. And this is how it should be. I wanted to be the good friend,
the good sister, the good daughter. The person who happily puts
together baby showers and organizes birthday parties. But I was
worn out, too. And once again I couldn't find a language for it.

What part of other people's stories did I have a right to? I found it difficult to talk about my own emotional exhaustion without sounding as if I were complaining. Or worse, appearing to be an emotional vampire borrowing other people's misfortune and challenges as my own. It wasn't my baby, my husband, my pregnancy, after all. And yet, some days I felt as if I were the sole doctor on call in a trauma unit, except no one berates a doctor for going out to brunch. It was hard work to do everyone else's emotional lifting when I was the only person responsible for my own. To have it implied that I was lazy or spoiled on top of it made my blood boil in ways I didn't know were possible.

My phone vibrated before I could shove it to the bottom of my bag. It was Maddy.

Hope you're still in one piece. Confirming Thanksgiving and here if you need a drink!

I smiled through my anger. E. B. White had once written, "No one should come to New York to live unless he is willing to be lucky." I had been very willing, and Maddy had been the lucky number that never stopped coming up.

13. The Family You Make

Maddy had cooked every American Thanksgiving dinner I'd ever eaten but one—sixteen by our count. Our first had taken place in the Stuyvesant Town apartment where she'd grown up not long after I'd arrived in the city. I'd shown up early, and she'd taught me to roast red peppers over the gas flame on her stove. But when we reminisced about our Thanksgivings together, it was the year she didn't cook it that we always ended up returning to most often.

That was the year her daughter Hannah had been born, and hands full with a six-week-old, Maddy had gone upstate to her mother's house for the holiday, leaving Mauri and me to fend for ourselves for the first time in thirteen years. We had not done so well. Accustomed to having a regular slate of duties starting at 5:00 p.m. on Wednesday evening, we found ourselves loose in the city and opted to fill the time by meeting for a drink in SoHo. We locked up our bikes on Prince Street in front of a Chinese restaurant and plunked down at the bar at Raoul's. The bartender

Franco was in the holiday spirit and plied us with drinks; as the hours went by the bar around us began to sway with New Yorkers returning home. We stumbled out the door at 11:00 p.m., laying a small pile of twenty-dollar bills on the bar for a tip, and went back across the street to retrieve our bikes, only to discover we'd mistakenly locked them up on the Chinese delivery bike rack and they'd been moved, along with the rack, and were behind the gate of the now closed restaurant. We stood at the bars staring at our confiscated transportation for a long while, not quite comprehending why we couldn't reach them.

Had we been a degree more sober, or facing a morning of errands, we likely would have gone straight home, bikes or not. Instead we wandered up toward University Place, where the tavern we'd worked at had been located (like homing pigeons we still tended to drift in that direction out of habit, even though it had closed in 2006) and into the still-open dive bar we'd sometimes gone to at 3:30 a.m. after our waitressing shift had ended. It had been five years since either of us had donned an apron but some of our old regulars were at the bar, and this time it was they who plied us with rounds of shots. I could sense in them something I was also experiencing that day for the very first time: the feeling that the city had temporarily become a stranger and I had no place in it. It was terrible; I'd never considered the city anything but a haven. Sometime after 4:00 a.m. we wandered onto a subway train and weaved our way back to Brooklyn. Mauri's boyfriend (and eventual husband) found her the next morning in the kitchen, still dressed, with her head in a bowl of potato chips. I awoke in my apartment on my living room floor with my shoes on. It would be 4:00 p.m. before I was able to sit up.

"We wandered the streets," we'd say to Maddy for years after that. "We wandered the streets forlorn and abandoned," as if having a newborn were not reason enough to not want to feed fifteen people. We were not alone in feeling untethered from our lives that day. Afterward we learned some people who had found themselves without a place to go had hiked out to Brooklyn assuming there'd be space at Maddy's table, only to find the door locked.

Growing up in Canada, Thanksgiving fell on a Monday in October, though most people celebrated it on the Sunday. As a child, I'd spent one confused and angry Thursday in November wondering why all my favorite television shows had been supplanted by football games. When I eventually came to the States, I was unprepared for the dramatic, all-encompassing screech-to-a-halt-ness of American Thanksgiving, but I was a quick convert.

During the years I waitressed, the night before Thanksgiving was my favorite shift of the year. I filled in for Maddy so she could prep for the following day. The night would start out slow and then swell up as New Yorkers returned home for the holiday; Frank Sinatra played on repeat for hours. The staff would start drinking early, and by 10:00 p.m. we'd drop our drink buyback requirement to two (normally a customer got a free round after every three drinks) and then toast their round with whatever we happened to have poured into our own glasses. The bar was closed on the holiday, and the owners adhered to the old routine of giving the staff their choice of a bottle or a bird. Everyone else took the bottle; I took the bird, which Maddy cooked for us to eat the next day.

At their height, our Thanksgivings became a November Mardi Gras for those lucky enough to stay in the city over the holiday. I, of course, had no family who was expecting me, the fourth Thursday in November being just a regular day for them. But eventually people, like Mauri, abandoned their trips home altogether in favor of celebrating at Maddy's. Why deal with crowded airports, family dynamics, and awkward conversations when you could come to us! For a few years this meant Maddy was cooking a three-course, sit-down dinner for twenty-five

people or more. She put enormous effort into the menu, pu-
reeing her own mango dressing for the arugula salad one year,
making turkey bibimbap the next. We made our own rituals.
Margeaux hand-painted invitations and constructed elaborate
piñatas (one year it was a mermaid, one year it was George
Bush's head), which we dragged out to the Brooklyn sidewalk
sometime around midnight, tied to a tree or a parking sign, and
wailed on until the candy (and "candy") tumbled out.

Before the meal was served we'd link hands around the table
and offer up things we were grateful for or people we wanted to
remember, and then Margeaux would lead us in a long *ommm*,
which everyone, regardless of how they felt about spirituality,
simply went along with. Guests assigned themselves dishwashing
shifts. There was an envelope in the bathroom to leave money to
cover the food expenses. Often in the retelling it was only possible
to separate one year from another by the decadence of Maddy's
food and the degrees of debauchery that followed it: there was the
year the busboy ended up in the hospital for mistaking the hash-
laced chocolate cake with the unlaced one versus the year everyone ended up nude in the bathroom doing lines off the medicine
cabinet mirror that someone had thoughtfully unscrewed.

Those days were long gone. Like everything else in our lives,
the day had calmed down and sobered up and streamlined. It
was no longer a dinner for twenty-five. People had married, had
family obligations. There was a kiddie table now. We'd stopped
being the best invite; none of the cakes were sending anyone to
the hospital. Still it was an annual highlight.

But in the days leading up to this year's holiday I found myself unable to get out of bed. At first I thought I was going to be
okay. The whiplash this time of returning to my life in the city
had been especially intense and given me the usual thrill. Less
than twenty-four hours after landing at LaGuardia, I'd been
sitting in the audience at Carnegie Hall in fur and silk, attend-

ing a magazine awards ceremony. I watched as Hollywood and
media stars traipsed across the stage making speeches and then
returned to their seats around me. I felt dazed, but also grateful. Not to be among celebrities—I knew better than that—but
to have a life that involved such extremes and be able to inhabit
both ends, painful and exhausting as parts of it currently were.

The high was short-lived. An emotional hangover slammed
into me forty-eight hours later—I inexplicably burst into tears
when the checkout clerk at Trader Joe's informed me my favorite
breakfast cereal had been discontinued—and had grown more
intense instead of fading away. I did not leave the apartment.
When I looked around, all I could see was a husband-shaped hole.
It was outlined by the dishes I'd left in the sink; the bottle of wine
I'd forgotten to buy; the food I found growing moldy in the fridge;
and the notice from my landlord that my rent would be past due
if not paid in twenty-four hours: all reminders that there was no
one else to help pick up the slack—even temporarily. After all of
the caretaking I had done, I was overcome with a bone-shaking
desire simply to have someone ask me if I was okay, to touch me.
Just to say, "I've got this." *This is why people get married*, I thought,
surveying my little square in the city. To hell with romance, and
men who ran across rooms to speak to you, or sent you a hundred
text messages a day. Fuck flowers. None of that really mattered.
You got married so that you wouldn't be in the trenches alone,
so that there was someone else to take the wheel from time to
time. So that you wouldn't have to ask for help; it would just be
there. At least that was the ideal.

I didn't ask for help. There are muscles that don't get exer-
cised when you live alone, and this was one. Instead, I continued to
hit reorder on the restaurant delivery app on my phone, thinking
if I ever did leave the apartment and somehow went missing, the
kid who brought me my milk shakes (without even a hint of sham-
ing side-eye, which brought me comfort if only because it meant

I was far from the only person whom he saw this regularly) would be the first to notice. Or the initial suspect in the ongoing, tabloid headline, *Law & Order* episode that played in the back of my head. *(Neighbors said they saw the delivery boy come and go on a regular basis.)*

Thanksgiving, which for so long had assured me I always had a place to go, felt like it was going to require more of me than I was able to give. I didn't *want* to go. Anywhere. And I had options. Each year I found myself inundated with more invites. The longer my friends were married, the more determined they seemed to inject fresh blood into their celebrations; it was as if I were a featured act they were trying to book in advance. But it never really occurred to me to go elsewhere. This was what I did. Like a once shocking music that was now considered elevator easy listening, it was too familiar to give up. We'd become our own family obligation.

This year, however, it was as if there were weights attached to my arms, and my tongue. I would skip, I thought. Maddy would understand; she understood everything. I would skip and lie in bed all day and not talk. Not speak or be spoken to.

I played chicken with the idea for a week: so I would do nothing on Thursday, what was the big deal? I could do what I wanted. But suddenly that reality was scary instead of liberating. It was a fine line between being free and floating away. And then, of course I got up Thursday morning and went. Propelled out the door at noon and onto my bike, primarily by the simple horror of thinking what it would mean to deviate from a ritual that had anchored my life for nearly twenty years.

Maddy and Ben lived in a three-story house in Red Hook, Brooklyn, that he had bought a decade earlier and rebuilt. Red Hook was like a little fishing village tacked onto the bottom of Brooklyn. It didn't have a subway stop, and even though it was just a ten-minute ride from my apartment and faced the Manhattan skyline, it felt a little dislocated from the city. As

I rode down the Columbia Street waterfront through empty streets, I could smell salt water in the air and immediately felt better. The solution to all my problems remained the same: I just needed to keep moving.

Maddy didn't even say hello when she opened the door. She just handed me a glass of wine and pointed me to the couch. Once when I was twenty-five and had just received especially upsetting family news, I had sat down and tried to tell her about it. We were at a coffee shop in Brooklyn, and I struggled to find the words; when they eventually came out, they were cold and flat. She was silent. When I looked up to see if she was listening, I saw that she was crying, as though she were crying for me when I couldn't manage to on my own.

Now I just lay on the couch, as if I were in my own living room. There was no expectation I do anything else. I didn't even need to explain why all I could do was lie on the couch. Every once in a while Maddy would bring over more cheese or refill my wineglass. Kara was also supposed to be there, but she had the flu and had sent along her husband and sons without her. Just before dinner was served Maddy's phone buzzed. She worked as a doula, and one of her clients had gone into labor. She had to go.

"We'll be fine," said Ben. "I have this under control."

Instead of setting the table we ate on the floor surrounding the TV: Ben's parents, Maddy's mom Viv and Viv's boyfriend, me and Hannah, and Kara's husband and kids. There was very little conversation. We ate and watched the parade, and when that ended, we switched to the Beatles movie *Yellow Submarine*. Eventually everyone left, and I went up to put Hannah to bed, reading to her from a copy of *Madeline* I'd given Maddy years ago for her birthday, trying to make up for a childhood she'd never had.

One year at Thanksgiving, Maddy's mother, Viv, had read us all our tarot cards. Viv's eyes, which Hannah had inherited, were such a deep brown they appeared nearly black, and her cheekbones were practically perpendicular to her jaw. Her long thick hair was streaked with gray, and she wore it down to her waist, sometimes plaiting it into two braids, making her look like an aged, ethereal Pocahontas. Maddy had faded Polaroids in her room of Viv roller-skating through Washington Square Park in the late sixties, same braids, only in hot pants.

The year of the tarot card reading nearly thirty people had shown up—it would go down in the books as the "biggest Thanksgiving." Maddy was then living in a huge ground floor loft in Williamsburg, on a dark deserted corner down by the bridge. When the cab dropped us off at 3:00 a.m. after a waitressing shift, I'd make the driver wait till she got through the foyer and I saw the inside light go on. Because the lease was in her name, Maddy had the big bedroom. The remainder of the loft was subdivided into quarters with curtains and shared by two kids who went to School of Visual Arts with Maddy and one of the bartenders we worked with. We'd taken down curtains that morning and moved the beds in the living room out to make space for the series of uneven tables we'd laid out lengthwise from one end of the apartment to the other.

I had never had my cards read. I'm not sure I'd ever even seen tarot cards before. When I was growing up, my mother had loved reading us all our horoscopes from the newspaper. "I'm a Taurus," she would say, "very stubborn!" But tarot cards were new, and I tried to comport myself with the same seriousness with which Viv dealt them out and interpreted their meaning. To my novice eye there was no difference between the gilded swords or the floating cups or the solemn figures; I simply waited while Viv stared at them intently for a long time as though they held the secret of the universe. Finally, she raised her black eyes to me.

"I think in a former life you were a servant girl, and Madeline was the baby daughter of the wealthy family you worked for. One night there was a fire, and you ran into the burning house to get her and saved her from dying."

I nodded and smiled. How else was one supposed to respond to that pronouncement? Viv had once declared she was from the star system Pleiades; I knew this sort of thing was something she took seriously. She flipped over another card and then looked up and took my hand. "Now you're back," she said, "and this time the roles are reversed."

Maddy and I laughed over that and made a show of extinguishing all the candles later that night, lest any fires get started. It was 1999; we were twenty-five. It was hard to see ourselves as people who needed saving in any dramatic sense. We filled in each other's phone numbers in the emergency contact line on forms and waited in cabs till inside lights went on—that was the sort of saving we were used to. After September 11, we rode bikes around the city instead of enduring the anxiety of the train in the tunnel or on the bridge, but that was it. It was only fifteen years later, lying in bed with Maddy's daughter asleep beside me, that I understood that sometimes saving someone simply means opening the door, letting them in for a deeply mundane holiday celebration, and asking absolutely nothing of them other than that they take up the space you've made for them. Which was what I was doing when Maddy got home at 2:00 a.m. and found me still there asleep next to Hannah.

14. The Long Goodbye Begins

The social worker called me first and left a voice mail. "Hi Glynnis, this is Debbie from the CCAC. A room has become available at the Roseview seniors complex. If you want to take it you have twenty-four hours to make up your mind, and twenty-four hours after that to move your mother in. I'm about to call your father but wanted to give you the heads-up. Please call me back at your earliest convenience."

I was sitting on my bed in Brooklyn. Outside the late December morning sun had just begun to feebly peek over the brownstones on the street behind me, casting weak shadows on the brick wall across from my window. I listened to the message and then held the phone out in front of me with shaky hands, staring at it, needing to confirm that it, and subsequently the message, were real. I was so flooded with relief I nearly wept.

But not yet. I needed to check my list to see which one Roseview was again. All the homes had nearly identical names: Lakeview, Southview, Greenfield—anodyne and pastoral, as though one were going on a nice holiday. I knew it was mostly for the family's sake. The less thinking about the reality of what this move signified, the better. *Please please please.* I said a silent prayer as I waited for my computer to turn on, *Let it not be the bad one.* My mother had continued to decline in the weeks since her hospital visit; her moments of lucidity were getting shorter and rarer. But even in this state of desperation I didn't think I could leave my mother in a narrow, dark room with a stranger, where the smell of deteriorating bodies was so strong that during my scouting visits I'd learned to breathe through my mouth. I dialed Debbie back even as I frantically scrolled through my email looking for the final list I'd sent a few weeks before. I couldn't quite believe this was happening, and so quickly. Doubt replaced relief. Had there been some sort of mistake? How had we gotten a room so quickly? It had been only three weeks since her last assessment; at the time, they'd told us it could be another nine to twelve months. Even the timing was extraordinary. It was the Friday before Christmas. I was set to fly home the next morning for the holiday. Oh, but where was this room?

I froze in my desk chair and then closed my eyes in a silent prayer of thanks. Roseview was my number one choice. It had been the hope against hope, the *I'm putting it at the top even though I'd been told by everyone that the waitlist was extra long, this probably won't happen, but at least it will keep the bad places off* choice. And we got it. The air around me felt as though it were wobbling, like someone had put time on pause. One thought flashed through my head: Sometimes things did work out. Sometimes timing was everything, and sometimes it was perfect.

•

I got the specifics from Debbie. Because the room had become available on a Friday we had an extra two days to get things ready. I flew home the next morning, and over the next forty-eight hours my sister and I scurried around in a mad dash against impending holiday hours, collecting all the paperwork we'd need to admit my mother. I was reminded of all the similar racing around I'd had to do to collect the paperwork necessary to get my apartment two years earlier. It hit me like a cold blast of air that this would be the first time in her life my mother had lived on her own; a private room with a bathroom and a window over the back garden, only slightly smaller than the little studio I lived in. I opened the car windows, letting actual cold air blast in and push the thought away. There would be time for thinking later.

Everywhere we went there were Christmas decorations and carols playing. While driving between offices to collect paperwork, I briefly let myself consider what Christmas would be like this year. Since the kids had been born I had spent it at my sister's in order to be there when they woke up and opened presents. My father had already signed us up for the Christmas dinner at the nursing home, but I couldn't quite envision it. It wasn't real yet. The only thing that was real was the folder of official paperwork I now had in my possession. Since speaking with Debbie I had asked no questions; after so much time spent racing down endless bureaucratic hallways trying to parse and translate the formal language of the health care system, I no longer cared how this had happened. Simply that it had.

•

At seventy-one, my mother was young for a nursing home. Even some of the medical staff I'd encountered in recent months, kind and sympathetic nurses accustomed to seeing nearly everything, remarked on it. I was also young to have a mother in a nursing home. I had a handful of friends who had lost their parents in car accidents or to heart attacks or early diagnoses of aggressive cancers, but none had yet moved into the era of elderly caretaking. I was years behind on every other commonly recognized metric for my age, but in this one instance I was way out ahead. Nearly all my friends had parents, many older than my own, who still took trips, worked, spent winters in warmer locations, still functioned as a reliable system of support, whether it be financial or emotional, or simply were able to live independently. People who were able to relate to my experience when I spoke of my mother's condition almost always made reference to their grandparents. I didn't have anyone I could talk to about this. Or who could prepare me for what it would be like.

As I prepared to put my mother in a place where she would spend the rest of her life, I was consumed by the knowledge that she was at the exact point in her life we talk about when we say things like, "I don't want to die alone." So many women I knew made decisions in fear of that outcome. As if not dying alone were anything but timing and luck.

At the same time, here I was having just tipped over into the second half (if I was lucky) of my life, and most of my fears and anxieties arose from long held assumptions about what it meant to be alone, *a woman alone*. My mother, meanwhile, was a manifestation of these fears. She would be dying alone no matter how many people were with her; her mind had cannibalized all of us, so that we were invisible to her. So many of the choices she'd made, that so many women made, had been toward the single goal of never being left alone, and now here she was, more alone than it was even possible for me to conceive.

I had grown up thinking of life as a series of linear decisions that if made properly would land me on some distant safe shore where I would finally enjoy the fruits of my labor. Now that I was getting a glimpse of that shore I was struck by the inanity of such an equation. My mother was never going to get another chance to do anything else. She did not have the capacity for regrets, nor was she even able to enjoy the comfort of nostalgia or fond memories—her mind had leaked away too imperceptibly to allow her the clarity to look back on her life and wish she had done things differently. As I continued to worry over what sort of future I was setting myself up for, she seemed a painful cautionary tale that life was not a savings plan, accrued now for enjoyment later. I was alive now. My responsibility was to live now as fully as possible.

•

My mother woke up happy and clearheaded on the morning we were scheduled to take her in. This was almost never the case anymore. Mornings and evenings were the worst times for her, and no matter what time it was she was always confused after sleeping. Some days she'd wander out of bed so early it was still dark outside. She'd float into the hall, greeting the dog—she was still never confused about Medley—calling my father's name in an uncertain voice, asking if it was time for dinner. Other times, she wouldn't get up at all, coming down at noon to announce she'd had a long day at work and was going to take a nap. Sometimes she'd appear out of nowhere, having silently awoken from a nap, and stare at me with frightened eyes, unsure of where she was or who I was. But on this particular morning she woke up completely herself. I woke, as I had nearly every morning for my entire growing up, to the sound of her voice cheerfully calling "Wakey wakey." In the moments between sleep and being awake it felt as though I had time-traveled, and the day ahead held school and swim practice and not the terrible tasks that awaited me.

My parents had gone out so few times when I was growing up that I could recount with detail the evenings my sister and I had been left home alone with a sitter. When I began babysitting, couples would often try to sneak out so that their children would not be upset by their absence, but even as a young child I was so thrilled at the idea of my parents being out in the world that I could still recall the sense of devastation that overwhelmed me when they canceled and stayed home.

Now suddenly I realized I had never woken up at home to a house that didn't contain my mother. Not once. So much of loss and grief is about shock and missed opportunities; *I had no idea it was our last conversation*, people say. But I did know. I knew this was the last time I would wake up in a house with my mother. The last time I would hear her voice sing out those words and know that her hand would be on my doorknob in moments, and that she'd be downstairs in the kitchen when I got there. But what does one do with the weight of that knowledge? There was nowhere to put it. I was deeply conscious of the fact that I was, at that second, inside what would become an intense memory, but that awareness did not help me understand it better. I just lay there and let it press down on me, as if by acknowledging the moment so directly I could freeze it. When the doorknob turned, I got out of bed and gave my mother a hug. There was no point in crying. I wasn't a crier and it would have upset her. She didn't know where she was going. We'd repeatedly told her what was happening in detail, but none of it stuck. When I came down for breakfast and said, "After this we'll go upstairs and pack," she looked at me in surprise. "Oh, sweetheart, do you have to leave already? It's so nice having you here."

•

Before we left the house, I lent her my lipstick. We had battled over lipstick for most of my teenage years. My mother didn't do anything without a coat of lipstick, including taking out the garbage. I, meanwhile, had wanted nothing to do with anything I connected to a quiet, acceptable suburban life. It didn't help matters that her preferred shades were brown and taupe pastels, completely unsuited to both my coloring and personality. It wasn't until after I moved to New York and was introduced to red lips as bold statement, a silent, powerful declaration (as opposed to my mother's lipstick, which always seemed to me to scream proper femininity, like the slips and purses she was always pushing on me) that I came around. It was the antithesis of her, but it had finally put an end to our conversations about makeup.

When I came downstairs, my father was already out in the car. I waited at the door for my mother while she flitted about, the same way she'd always done.

"Let's go, Mom." I could hear the old teenage annoyance in my voice. It had slipped in there out of habit, down well-worn grooves deepened over so many years of standing and waiting at the front door.

"I'm just looking for my purse."

"Dad has it in the car."

"Oh, wonderful." She bent down to pat the dog. "Goodbye, Medley, fret na lass, we'll see you in a little bit." She stood up and smiled at me. "What a lovely color you're wearing. I just need to find my lipstick and then we can go. Now, where did I put my purse?"

"Dad has it in the car," I said again.

I reached into my own purse and fished out my lipstick; I, too, was now never without it. "I'll put it on for you," I said. "Go like this." I stretched my lips out over my teeth the way she had shown me to do when I was a child playing in her bathroom and waited for her to do the same. I dabbed the red on as gently as I could so the color wouldn't overwhelm her face. When I was done, she glanced in the hallway mirror, a gesture as familiar to me as her voice. "Perfect," she said. "Now we're ready to face the world."

•

My sister and the kids were waiting for us at Roseview. I heard
Quinn and Zoe racing down the halls before I saw them. I immediately picked up Connor; he felt like an anchor. His contented
weight on my shoulder, holding me down so that the reality of
what was happening wouldn't blow me away, was simply proof
life moved forward.

Everything went down as smoothly as swallowing a pill. It
felt shocking how easy it was to flip my mother's life from what
it had been for decades to this new version that I had been
struggling toward like a prize. The walls of the nursing home
were decorated for Christmas: shiny red, green, and gold stars;
Santa and reindeer cutouts; fake green holly strung up over the
doors. Next to the sign about Christmas dinner being served for
families in the community room—presumably the one my father had signed us up for—was a reminder that an Elvis imper-
sonator would be performing in January. For some reason this
gave me great comfort, as if my mother were simply embarking
on a new, fun life, full of potential, different than the one she
was leaving in encouraging ways, and not a last tedious stop.

This respite was brief. The home was the best I'd seen, but it
was still a nursing home. Everywhere was evidence of where this
was all heading. Old people slumped into various chairs, mostly
expressionless; a few slowly walked the halls. Next to them my
mother, upright and beginning to bounce the way she did when
the sun began its slide toward the horizon, practically sparkled
with life. But she was one of them now. On the wall opposite the
public bathroom, beside the candy machine Quinn hopefully
dragged me to, was an In Memoriam frame with the pictures
of two women in it. Doreen and Gladys. Names that felt like
a wave rolling in from another era. In a few more decades it
would, no doubt, carry a series of Jennifers and Michelles. I
wondered whether it was Doreen or Gladys I had to thank for
my mother's room.

I sat in the office holding Connor and going over all my mother's paperwork with the staff. By the time I got to her room, my sister had unpacked and organized everything. In the scramble to prepare for the move I'd grabbed whatever I could to make the room more familiar, whether to her or me was unclear. I'd taken the photo album my sister had made for my parents' fortieth anniversary, the quilt my mother had sewn that had been on my bed for my entire childhood. I'd taken the nativity scene pyramid my grandmother had given them as a wedding present, the sort you lit candles underneath and which spun as the heat from the small flames rose. It was a ridiculous item to bring; my mother had neither a table nor, presumably, would be allowed access to candles. But it had been on our Christmas table my entire life, and somehow having it here made it seem less impossible that she would no longer be at the table at home. I'd also grabbed a silver framed photo of Medley, which I put in the little memory alcove in the hall beside her door. I reasoned that since the dog was the one thing she always seemed to remember, having the photo in her doorway might signify to her the room belonged to her. I looked up at the room number as I went back in. She was in room 121.

It was lunchtime by the time we left. We all walked my mother to her table in the dining room, which was already half full of residents who'd been wheeled in. "Oh, let me help," she said and immediately walked over to the kitchen area where the staff were setting up.

"No, it's being prepared for you," I said, taking her arm and leading her toward the table. "You don't have to do anything." And then to drive the point home, "We are *paying* them money to do it for you."

She smiled, surprise lighting up her face. "Really? Well, that's very generous of them."

Zoe insisted on climbing on my back on the way out. The

kids were growing impatient, but it was a relief to have their energy in the room; they felt like a crackling fire throwing warmth into a stone mausoleum. Their needs dragged us back into a world that was still full of possibility.

My mother's disease was so duplicitous. It had left me grieving for the disappearance of things felt, not seen, while furiously caring for what was in front of me. The person I loved, who had loved me and cared for me and filled my mind with all her big words, and learning, and gentleness, was almost gone. She'd been slipping away for months now, maybe years. A drop at a time. And with each part of her lost I'd had to ask myself whether I was imagining it. I could still hold her, after all, and hear her. And yet she was not there, too. Instead of marking the passing of these parts of her I'd never get back, I'd raced to save what remained. Her body. And now I was leaving that, also. But again not really. I was leaving it and saving it at the same time. In some ways, I'd already been forced to say goodbye to her, and in others I was nearly paralyzed at the idea that she would stay here while we left. It was the first time in my mother's life that she'd had a room of her own. The confusion over where I was supposed to put these different stages of grief left me with the sensation that I could see what was happening but couldn't feel it.

My mother always said she'd had a harder time leaving me at kindergarten the first time than I had had staying. "I was in tears but I don't think you looked back." And now I was the one who had to leave.

In the end, I turned back only once. I watched briefly as my mother thanked the woman who was serving her a plate of food. I wasn't sure if the enormity of leaving her dulled everything, as if I'd been crushed into numbness. Or if I was stunned by the fact that I had effected this great turn in my own mother's life, and now it was as simple as walking out.

15. Don't Forsake Those Duties Which Keep You Out of the Nuthouse

When I arrived back in New York ten days later, I immediately took myself out to dinner. I already knew my order: oysters, steak, and two gin martinis at the bar around the corner. I didn't shower or change, simply thrust my suitcase through my apartment door and turned around. I walked the two blocks down to the restaurant feeling empty. It wasn't the low, hopeless feeling that had so often dogged me after other recent trips home; I had, after all, succeeded in my goal and found a safe haven for my mother. It felt, instead, as if I'd emerged from a long battle: there was nothing left. The victory felt hollow; it brought relief but no joy.

"Don't forsake those duties which keep you out of the nuthouse," Katharine Hepburn once wrote. I'd thought about that line a lot over the past few years: the importance of knowing your limits, what keeps you from stepping dangerously over them, and how to pull yourself back when you had gone too far. I'd learned to get good at diagnosing myself, and just as good at prescribing the necessary medicine. There were times I worried my overdeveloped talent for self-sufficiency might be cutting me off from other equally valuable gifts, like the ability to tell others what I needed. If I was self-made, how would I know what I was forgetting to add to myself? But mostly I'd learned to follow my gut and not feel guilty when I gave myself what I knew I required. Eating alone was one of the inalienable rights New York bestowed on its residents. I'd been taking myself out for solo meals for nearly twenty years when I needed comforting. And I needed it now.

My wretched appearance must have struck a chord with the hostess, because even though the restaurant was packed with young, sleek, good-looking Brooklynites, she immediately gave me a seat at the bar. Likewise the bartender handed me my martini only seconds after I'd ordered it. It tasted like cold liquid velvet. For a while I simply sat and sipped my drink, watching the bartender go about his business. There was a language to bartending same as there was to almost anything else, if you paid enough attention. The Cedar bartenders had been the best in the city; the back-bar had been set up so that every bottle was precisely positioned based on how often it was poured and with what mix or glass. They had rarely looked at what they were reaching for. And always poured without measuring. I could always tell if a bartender knew his game simply by whether he had to turn to find a bottle. The guy behind the bar tonight was no more than twenty-five, had a carefully manicured handlebar mustache that reached all the way down to his jawline and tattoo sleeves up his arm, but he knew how to pour. It was satisfying to watch him line up the glasses, scoop his ice, stir his martinis, and pound the mint.

In my bag was a worn copy of *Middlemarch* I'd long ago plucked from my mother's bookshelves and returned to intermittently when I was between other books. On the inside flap her maiden name was written in her graceful cursive. Slipped into its pages, however, was evidence of me: receipts, business cards, and drink coasters from years of dinners and excursions just like this one. So many, in fact, that it was impossible to know what page I'd actually left off on, though it did alert me to the fact that I'd seen *Moulin Rouge* at the Ziegfeld on June 2, 2001. The idea of being a woman alone at a bar reading *Middlemarch* was nearly as satisfying to me as the martini I was drinking. And I knew the simple act of reading would give my mind a certain sort of peace nothing else could.

Instead I reached for my phone.

I would just have a quick scroll, I thought, and then return to practical, misguided Dorothea, whose beauty was thrown into relief by poor dress (unlike my own at the moment). I opened Instagram. I'd somehow forgotten it was New Year's Day. My feed was filled with shots from parties the night before and resolutions for the year to come. I'd spent New Year's Eve in a back room at the house of a friend of my sister's, cuddling Connor and watching television so that Alexis could have a break and let loose a bit. I hadn't yet thought of the year ahead.

I scrolled through the pictures, and I could feel a quickening of my pulse as I got to live vicariously in slivers of other people's lives. Half the posts on my feed were from New Year's Eve parties; everyone, it seemed, had had a fantastic night at a fantastic party. The other half were of babies and children. Some were a mix of the two.

I stared down at a particularly enviable picture of a woman I knew and her husband in a lush garden, their baby frolicking on the bright green grass in front of them. They were on some sunny island for the holiday. They were beautiful. I could feel my insides twist up as I mentally marked the things she never had to think about: health insurance for one, how to make the rent, whether she'd get to the end of her life and worry that not having children had been an enormous mistake.

Below that was a shot of a group of young up-and-coming writers on someone's terrace in Bedford Stuyvesant, Brooklyn, holding up champagne glasses and leaning into one another. They had navigated their careers early and well, had arrived when the digital world opened more doors much faster. They screamed brains, beauty, and potential.

Another was from a dinner party at the apartment of a svelte young illustrator who lived in Tribeca. The long table had been carefully set up with a row of candles and tall vases of white lilies. In the center was a roasted pig's head. When I clicked through on her tag I could see the progression of the party through the night.

Mixed into this was what seemed like an endless array of babies and children. There was one chubby creature staring intently at a champagne glass just out of reach, another wide awake on the chest of an already sleeping father. A toddler wearing matching New Year's paper glasses with the dog. There was a shot of a moist, red newborn, arriving in the world right at midnight. Just below that was a friend of a friend who'd been married as the clock struck twelve.

I knew I should join the chain of extravagant congratulations, but instead I scrolled on. I felt the familiar exhaustion of being required to bolster someone else's life—like! like! like!—even as I sat there feeling so depleted. I wondered, would anything in my life ever warrant the same excitement? I continued to scroll, refusing to like anything, feeling like an obstinate child. I began to feel as though all the color was being drained of my own life; nothing could be brighter than the pictures on my phone.

Taking in the tsunami of celebratory photos left me feeling as though I were standing just outside a very exclusive club that I was unable to enter. It reminded me of the society pages that used to run in the front section of *Vogue* magazine in the days

before the internet. Flattering photos of long, graceful creatures who inhabited a world where everything worked out and every dress fit perfectly. Like the fashions inside, but with a dose of reality—as if it were possible to achieve this if you were the right sort of person. I thought of my mother's lifelong love of gossip magazines. Before things had taken a turn for the worse, I'd often pulled up old photos of 1950s movie stars to show her; she remembered every one, and that fact comforted both her and me.

These were not movie stars I was looking at, though, even if we had all learned to pose just as expertly, mastering our best angles. These were friends. And yet their photos left me coveting their lives in ways I never did when I was actually with them. Nothing here comforted me; it seemed instead to capture, in carefully captioned and cropped shots, exactly what I could never have and never be. In my real life I felt as if I walked around with an empty space people felt obligated to fill up. But in the world captured on this screen, it seemed like there was no space—or place—for me at all.

The bartender put my tower of oysters in front of me.

I flipped the phone over. I shouldn't have looked. Now I was going to have to dig myself out of this emotional hole I'd allowed myself to fall into.

I stared at the decadent first course in front of me. I could take a picture of this. Angle the oysters against my martini glass, put on some red lips and catch those in the top of the frame, crop out the dirty clothes and unwashed hair. I'd be the envy. I'd envy myself in that picture even as I sat taking it. But what story would the picture tell? That I was a woman who knew how to sit comfortably alone at a bar and order oysters and gin martinis. I smiled to myself; actually, that wasn't a bad story. But like so many of the other photos I was looking at, it would have stripped away so much and been all veneer, no substance—an illusion, life through a filtered looking glass.

We're always drawn to the clearest articulation of what we think we lack. Whenever I encountered that husband-shaped hole in my apartment, I needed only to open my phone and I could find its cutout there, in exact proportions, in someone else's life. No doubt, my life, as broadcast, was the stuff of dreams to many. Even I, on my worst days, knew that to some degree it was very ideal. I could sometimes feel the eyes of sleep-deprived friends with small children gaze upon me with the crazed look of a hungry beast coveting my time like it was red meat. But I didn't want to make myself feel better by making others feel as if they were lacking. It was an easy fix. But it was ungenerous. It made me question my own obligation to the truth. If social media left me feeling bad, wasn't it up to me to do my best not to inflict that on others?

Oh, but there was such a thrill to voyeurism. Somewhere in an old journal I'd scrawled down Susan Sontag's quote that the modern age had turned us all into "image-junkies," and photographs were the "most irresistible form of mental pollution." And that was *long* before social media had become part of the air we breathed. I knew better than to allow myself to be thrown into a mental temper tantrum over Instagram. It just took effort. I had to lean on my knowledge of the real lives of the people in the photos, which were just as complicated and flawed as my own. I didn't have to imagine it; I had a front row seat to many of them. I knew all too well that behind the photo of the happy couple clinking champagne glasses was a life that required endless compromise in order to work. It had once compelled one friend to remark to me, "The only thing worse than having no one to complain to is having to not complain because the person at home is tired of hearing it."

I knew that behind another photo was a couple who slept in separate beds. And there was a friend who, every time I saw

her, was on the verge of hysteria from lack of sleep, a traveling husband, and three small children, but who only ever appeared in carefully choreographed shots taken at their country house. And those were the good marriages.

At least half the pictures I'd just scrolled through were of couples who I knew were "figuring it out." There was the husband who had a profile on the dating app Tinder and women who refused to share a cab with their husbands. There was the wife who had immediately become pregnant on discovering her husband's affair and who now posted a steady, enviable-looking stream of their child.

It was easy to turn to cynicism in moments like this, a quick and cheap balm. Being alone sometimes felt like being a solitary tree atop a very windy hill; there was nothing between the world and me to break its impact. I had to root myself very deeply in my belief about what was good about my life so as not to be tossed to and fro. Cynicism was a nice heavy armor that protected you. I'd known plenty of older cynical customers back when I'd been a waitress. They saw the worst in everything and scoffed at our naïve youthfulness. At the time I was mystified by the bitterness, but as I got older I understood the appeal. And the danger. It was a devil's bargain: keep everything out, even the possibility of joy, lest something gets in that hurts too much and too often.

I came back again to what I knew was true for everyone, even if my phone often forced me to take it on faith: life was hard and complicated. Once on a very punishing Saturday night waitressing shift, a twenty-two-year-old starlet had come into the Cedar. I could still recall how blond and glowing she'd been, especially against my black waitress uniform, which at that point was caked with splotches of dried mayonnaise from having delivered so many burger orders. "What a nice life," I'd said bitterly to my coworker Mary while standing at the kitchen window waiting for a plate of greasy chicken wings to come out. Mary was Irish, in her fifties; she lived with a roommate in a tenement on Second Avenue and was missing a number of her front teeth. She always had a cigarette going at the service station (this was in the days before the smoking ban) and was the kindest person on staff. Getting a shift with Mary was considered a lucky thing. "Oh no," she said, turning to me sternly, "don't you think that. She has plenty of her own problems which are just as terrible to her as yours are to you." "Do you think so?" I said skeptically. "Of course!" said Mary. I'd never forgotten that exchange, as much for the truth it contained as for the fact that Mary, who seemed to twenty-three-year-old me to have so little of value in her life, had continued to know it, too.

So often in the last year there had been no way to take any pictures of the life I was leading—the divide between the messy, painful reality and the screen had been so huge I'd felt unable to bridge it. Just as often, the pictures I looked at seemed to be an advertisement for the right kind of life, though I was never certain whether we were all trying to sell our lives to others or use others to sell our lives back to us. Sometimes I saw radical images, a wonderful reorganizing of what we considered beautiful and valuable, and I knew others were struggling to find a language for their lives, same as me, and I was grateful for their courage and resolve. But many of the pictures that sent me into a state of envy or despair were taken by women who I knew had been sold the same idea of life that I had, and it sometimes seemed to me they were willing to go to great lengths to pose in those roles, whether or not they had turned out to be real-life possibilities. As if they could fake it until they, and all the likes they accrued to help them, made it. My mother would have looked at some of these photos and, beneath the modernized fashion, recognized the same messages about how life *should* look that she had found in the saccharine gossip magazines of her youth. There were no more shades of gray in my feeds than there had been in those pages. Technicolor had been replaced by filters.

The bartender delivered my steak and a glass of red wine. "This one's on me," he said with a lingering smile. Between the martini, the oysters, and now this smile I was already feeling better; the emptiness of an hour ago was giving way to the enjoyment of being able to exert control over my own life. Was it always going to be like this? I wondered. This roller coaster of doubt and elation? Was this the price and the reward for not committing to some larger, more established idea of life? My mother had once told me she believed in the importance of marriage vows simply because they had been the thing that kept her from walking out the door early on. But how did one commit to the idea of not committing? Or was this it? A rolling interrogation of myself. Living in a constant state of reinvention.

The bartender's smile shook something loose in a dusty and neglected corner of my mind: I needed to have some fun. To go on some dates. A memory of Viktor popped into my head. The thrills of harmless flirtation and attraction. I was not looking for someone to go through life with. I wasn't entirely sure I was looking for anything. Buried beneath all the racing around and stress, there remained a part of me that was still relieved at having been let off the clock. But dating wasn't off the table, and with this different view of it, perhaps it might even be a good time.

I opened Tinder. I'd created an account ages ago and then never given it much attention. I hadn't looked at it since I'd sat by my friend's bedside in the hospital after she'd been told her baby had no heartbeat, letting her scroll through it for distraction while she and I waited for the epidural to kick in so they could induce. Her husband had left the room ("Few men can handle it," the nurse had remarked to me in a low voice). And as the two of us sat there together she clicked through the various profiles, eventually handing it back to me. "I think you should really make dates with some of these people," she said with a slightly admonishing smile. "It's so much better to go through life with someone than on your own." I'd put it away after that.

Now there were at least twenty-five messages waiting for me, most of them of the *hey* variety. Why not just write, *Please make this easy on me*, I thought. A few of them had written entire paragraphs; just seeing the text roll out was nearly as invigorating as the martini, but I was never going to get in a text relationship again. That I knew. Only real life. One man named Dan had written me five messages over five months, checking in with admirable persistence, each time asking for a date. I looked at his pictures. He was the same age as me, worked in film, and he hadn't included a single shot of himself with an exotic animal. His profile said, *Longtime New Yorker, I like Shakespeare, and wine, and good food. I'm honest and thoughtful. Not looking for a hookup. 6ft.* Good enough.

I decided to respond, short and sweet. *Hello. Would love to get coffee, let me know what works for you.*

Just as I put the phone down to reach for my book, it buzzed again. *That was fast*, I thought. But it was Maddy.

The apartment upstairs is empty. We only want you to move in. Interested?

Somewhere out there is a lady who I think will never be a nun.

The Baroness, *The Sound of Music*

16. Men of a Certain Age

In 1988 Cher won an Oscar for her role in *Moonstruck*. In the film she plays Loretta, a thirty-seven-year-old accountant who has given up on love and is preparing to marry Johnny, a practical man she can tolerate. At thirty-seven, she's in the clutches of middle age—it's either marry Johnny or live a life of loneliness as a sexless spinster. She is already halfway there; this much is clear. Her hair is graying. She wears black buttoned-up clothes. Comfortable shoes. No makeup. She lives with her parents (in an enormous, glorious brownstone that becomes a sort of silent family member). It's only when Johnny's mother falls sick, and he returns to Sicily to be by her side, tasking Loretta with the responsibility of making amends with his estranged brother Ronny (Nicolas Cage), that Loretta finds sex and then love. She and Ronny crash improbably, almost violently, into each other with wild, unlikely passion. Loretta promptly goes to the not-so-subtly named Cinderella Beauty Shop and sees a hairdresser who exclaims, "I've been wanting to do this for three years!" She

gets rid of the gray, finds a knockout dress, paints on some red
lipstick, and meets Ronny at the Met for the opera. *Bah boom*,
go the opening notes of *La bohème* as her sparkly red stilettos
appear from the yellow cab in front of the famous fountain.
Just in time!

This movie had been a favorite of both my mother and mine.
She loved the happy ending, and I loved the view of the New
York City skyline from the Brooklyn Heights Promenade. In
all my years in New York, I'd never once walked by the Met
fountain without thinking of the opera scene and hearing that
bah boom of the music. As a child, my other favorite scene was
the moment Cher emerges from the beauty salon, newly youthful with her glorious crown of hair—everything about it jibed
perfectly with my girlhood understanding of the world. Beauty
and youth equaled love and power (also I appreciated her curls).

The year I turned thirty-seven, the same age as Cher's Loretta, I had to move out of the apartment in Crown Heights
that Maddy, and Mauri, and then Margeaux and I had shared
for nearly a decade. One by one they had all left to live with
boyfriends, or in Margeaux's case, her new husband. I was still
in my media reporting job, financially stable for the first time
and able to find an apartment on my own and foot all the bills.

Pretty quickly I decided there was only one place to be:
Brooklyn Heights. For years I'd gone there to wander around
under the ancient leafy trees, gaze at the well-kept brownstones,
many of which still housed families that had been in them for
decades, and walk the Promenade with its staggering view of
the Manhattan skyline. It was the neighborhood I walked to
when I wanted to fall in love with the city again, or be reminded
why I'd fallen in love in the first place. It also represented the
city as I had known it as a child, decades before I ever set foot
here. It looked like the set of *Sesame Street*. It was where *The
Cosby Show* was set. It was where *Moonstruck* was set and filmed.

For three weeks, various brokers took me around, showing me apartments in my price range.

Some of the apartments I saw had obviously been carved out of once grand houses and had slanted floors and kitchens that were awkwardly shoved in corners. Other, slightly larger ones boasted intricate moldings, working fireplaces, and stunning shafts of light, but were so far out of my price range that I'd need a roommate to make the rent. Just for fun, I allowed one broker, an older woman, to show me a one-bedroom located on the street that overlooked the Promenade. I knew before I went that I couldn't take it; even if I ferociously budgeted and basically never ate or left the house I still would be hard-pressed to pay for it. But I'd walked by it so many times, looking up at the thirties art deco windows, I was dying to see the inside of the building and so I told her I was interested. It was a perfect apartment. Light and airy and spacious, with arched doorways. The bedroom had enormous paned windows facing both east and south, overlooking the trees below. If I moved in here, I thought, that would be it; I'd never leave. Fifty years from now, some concerned neighbor would check in on me and find me dead, probably under a stack of unread New Yorkers and New York Posts. The agent, sensing my interest, gave me a hard sell about how lovely the building superintendent was and how they'd be happy to sign me to a two-year lease. "And don't worry," she said, "you obviously won't be by yourself for long and there's plenty of room here for someone else." And then, seeing me hesitate at the price, she brightly suggested that perhaps my parents could help. I stifled a laugh.

Late one evening, a week or so later, as I was beginning to wonder whether I should take the sloped floor with the awkwardly shoved kitchen studio, I got a call from one broker who said that a place was opening up the next day and could I meet him at 7:00 a.m.? He was a young kid, new to New York, clearly tempted into the brokering profession by the promise of large cash commissions (which were about as easy to come by as a prewar, rent-controlled apartment), and now desperate for a deal. I said yes. I needed to secure something soon, and even though he wouldn't tell me the exact address for fear I'd try to end run him by reaching out to the management company directly, I knew the street he was talking about; it was two blocks from the Promenade, three blocks from five trains, and overarched by sweeping trees. It was lined with century-old brownstones and one art deco building with a red nautical front door that looked as if it belonged in a 1930s film set on an ocean liner where everyone wears silk and drinks martinis. I had often walked that street just to look at that door. When I arrived he was standing in front of it. The apartment we were seeing was behind the red door, three floors up. I handed all my paperwork over within five minutes of laying my eyes on its tiny dimensions lest I lose it to the next people through. Twenty-four hours later I was notified I'd been found reliable. Or close enough to it—I had to pay an extra half month's deposit, but I was approved and signed the lease the following day. The teeny, tiny apartment was now mine. At the age of thirty-six and three-quarters I finally had my own "room of one's own." Literally in this case. My new apartment was one room and a bathroom. It was 275 square feet altogether, for nearly twice what I'd paid to share three times the space. It was six blocks away from Cher's house in *Moonstruck*.

After I moved in, I rewatched the film, eager to match the streets I'd grown up dazzled by on the screen with the ones I was now walking daily. It held up. The makeover scene filled me with that same sense of contentment. But my ears caught something new this time. I rewound it and listened more closely. Then I did it again. There it was: Just as newly beautiful Cher is undergoing her final transformative touches, it's possible to overhear the hairdresser gossiping plaintively about another client, one who had sadly *not* seen the light in time: "*She* came in when she turned forty and her husband left her."

•

"Maddy wants me to take over the upstairs apartment in their house."

Mauri and I were sitting at her husband Ben's Brooklyn wine bar sharing a cheese plate. It was Saturday night at the end of January, and every table was full. Outside the streets were dull with the dirty barren cold that settles in when there's not enough snow. I'd ridden here on my bike, happy to be out in the night air, wrapped in an old white fur coat I'd purchased on eBay ten years ago for ten dollars that kept me warm in the cutting winter wind.

"That apartment is amazing!" exclaimed Mauri. "I love Red Hook."

I shrugged. I liked Red Hook, but I had grown to love Brooklyn Heights so much, even if the rent was ridiculous and would likely get more so when my lease renewed in June. "I've never seen the upstairs," I said, "but the rent is five hundred dollars less than I pay."

Mauri shook her head. "Seriously, I've been up there, and the apartment is incredible. And you'd be living with Maddy again."

It did strike me as rather wild our worlds might retwine again so intimately more than half a decade after they'd separated. "Maybe it's one of those instances where if you stay in New York long enough the city gives you a bonus and if you're too stupid to take it you have to leave forever," I said.

Ben leaned over the bar to peer at my phone, which was open to the Tinder profile of Dan, the guy I'd met for coffee a few days earlier. Within minutes of us sitting down he'd mentioned that he didn't want kids, and I realized he'd Googled me and read one of my recent articles. Of course, I'd Googled him, too, but I'd only found a scattering of professional details. It was strange to encounter someone who thought they had an inside line on me based on a personal essay. I let it go, though. I was determined to learn how to date. We'd had an easy conversation over cappuccinos. At the end of it, he'd said, "Well, now that we know neither of us is crazy, let's make a proper date. How about I take you to dinner? I mean, I obviously want to see you again." It was the "How about I take you to dinner?" part that hooked me. It felt reassuringly old-fashioned.

"Are you sure this guy is real? Or did you make him up?" asked Ben.

"I don't think so. He's a stunt coordinator, he's working on that new Met production everyone's talking about. He asked if we wanted tickets."

"He looks like a dancer." Mauri had come to New York to be a dancer.

"No idea. Maybe a gymnast? He said he once worked in the circus? He also works in film. He has a whole IMDb page."

She looked at his profile. "He definitely has a dancer's body."

Ben, who had seen all manner of disaster come through my phone, leaned over the bar and looked at the pictures.

"So, you went on Tinder and found a straight circus performer, who also does stunts, and knows Shakespeare." He shook his head. "It's about time."

I nodded, grinning. "I think so, too."

"And you liked him?" asked Mauri, cocking an eyebrow. I'd never known anyone less interested in what someone looked like on paper. This was especially remarkable considering that if Mauri had wanted, she easily could have been the sort of woman who arrived in New York and with very little effort, exclusively dated very wealthy, very powerful men. When I took her to media parties with me, this was the sort that immediately gravitated to her. With a flick of the wrist, it seemed to me, much of the city could have fallen right into her lap. But it never held any appeal for her.

"I mean it was just coffee." I shrugged. "But it was nice. He seemed nice. Honestly, it felt good to have someone excited about me, who also exists in real life." I laughed.

"Yes, it is, Glynnis MacNicol." Mauri had never been impressed by 646. "So, when are you seeing him again?"

"Dinner. Thursday at Franny's."

"Good."

•

Franny's was a Brooklyn institution. Famous for its pizza and locally sourced meats and cheeses, and always packed. It was a quintessential date spot.

Dan had emailed me three times since our coffee to confirm our date, including an email to wish me a happy weekend. (Mauri: "So sweet!") It felt a bit much, especially the fact that he'd already started calling me "G" and signing his emails "xod." But then again, maybe I was just used to so little, I had no sense of what was normal anymore. I let it go. I was in the sweet spot. My grandmother would have said I was being courted. It was nice.

Dan was already at Franny's when I arrived and waved at me from the bar as he made his way through the crowd. He had on the same baseball cap he'd been wearing when I'd seen him for coffee, and a crisp white shirt, and black pants. He *did* have an athlete's body, lean and muscular and completely under his control. He exuded physicality. And he was tall. I had on a black silk shirtdress over tights and a vintage brown and cream striped fur coat that went down to my knees. We looked exactly like two people who were on a first date at Franny's on a Thursday. On the wall, there was a flyer for Valentine's Day dinner the following Saturday.

"You look amazing." He leaned over and kissed my cheek as though we had known each other for much longer than three email exchanges and a thirty-minute cappuccino. I wondered how many of his friends he'd told about this date.

The waitress led us to a table in the corner a little out of the way from the madness of the dining room. I wondered if he'd reserved it especially. He took my coat. We slipped into conversation easily, and not the sort of conversation I had often found myself in with men on first dates, where it was mostly them talking and me nodding along, but actual conversation. He was good at getting information out of me, which, having spent so much time focused on others, felt a little jarring. Like zooming from understudy to starring role in my own life between appetizers and entrées. But I didn't want to dive into the deep end of my family just yet and so I steered us back to more familiar waters. I asked him where he lived. He said he had an apartment on "The Upper West Side, on Central Park West."

Right on the Park! *Movie work really must pay* I thought, imagining a sunny prewar with beamed ceilings.

"It's rent-controlled, I've been there a long time."

"Ah, the New Yorker's dream!" I nodded appreciatively. Rent-controls were not easy to come by ever, and they were practically an urban legend these days. "How long have you lived in New York?"

He'd taken off his baseball hat when we sat down and had revealed a perfectly round bald head. It didn't bother me. He looked a bit like Yul Brynner, the fifties Hollywood star my mother had always had a crush on. I wondered if he was self-conscious about it—it occurred to me that there'd been no pictures without a hat on his Tinder. There was a whole coded language to dating site pictures, I knew—men with animals, men with female friends.

Maybe he was just someone who wore a hat. He was handsome, and in better physical shape than nearly every man I knew, let alone for a forty-one-year-old. Even sitting he had that awareness about him that people whose livelihood is their bodies often have, a fluid way of moving and attention to the space around him. I wondered how that awareness would translate in bed. I was curious to find out. He was cutting up the entrée we'd ordered to share and carefully putting pieces on my plate. He'd already told me he loved to cook. I felt a bit like I'd summoned him from thin air during my night of martinis and steak at the bar.

He shrugged. "A long time."

"What is 'a long time'?" I was intrigued now. A rent-controlled apartment on the Park was the sort of thing New York real estate time-travel fantasies were made of. You'd have to go back a few decades to land one, or else have inherited it somehow. I was also curious to know where exactly we both stood on the New York City resident spectrum. In addition to everything else, could I have found myself an old-school New Yorker? For a brief period in my early thirties, I had routinely lied about my age, mostly for the fun of seeing what I could get away with. But I'd stopped doing it the moment it required me also to lie about how long I'd lived in New York. I could not be both twenty-eight and have been here for fifteen years, without some further detailed explanation about what high school I'd attended. My friend Kathleen, who had been born and raised in the city, had stopped lying about her age when doing so meant she couldn't claim the Beastie Boys opening for Madonna at MSG in 1984 had been her first concert. We all have nonnegotiable cornerstones on which we build our identity, and this one was mine.

"I moved here in 1986," he said.

"Oh, wow. With your parents?"

He shook his head in a way that made me wonder if I'd accidentally stumbled on a sensitive topic. An uncomfortable silence enveloped the table for the first time.

"There's something you should know," he finally said. "But I don't want to tell you. If I tell you, you won't want to date me anymore."

He was married. Obviously, that was it. All the energy of the evening seeped out of me like water down a drain. I was so tired of badly behaved married men; the older I got, the more they seemed to be everywhere. *Badly behaved married men:* the story of being a single woman. Sometimes it felt as if by not being married, I had been inadvertently tasked with the responsibility of keeping all married men from fucking up their lives. Say no and walk away; walk away from the constant drumbeat of flirtation, of flattery, of attention, of propositions, of direct messages and text messages, of admiration and adoration. I'd fallen down once; I never wanted to be that person again.

"What?" I said flatly.

Dan shook his head a second time and looked up at me with a nervous grin. The long tapered hands, that just moments before had been calmly and gracefully cutting up my meal for me, were now fidgeting nervously with the utensils, putting them down on the table and picking them back up again.

"I lied to you but I don't want to tell you about what."

What the fuck was this? "Well, if you don't tell me now, this will definitely be the last time we see each other." My voice was stern. Another minute and I'd be giving him the count of three. He shifted in his seat.

"The age on my Tinder profile is not my real age."

I smothered a relieved grin. "Oh. I don't actually remember what it said." This was not true: it had said forty-one; internally I shrugged. I wondered briefly if he was going to tell me he was actually younger, like thirty-four.

"It said I was forty-one. But I'm not."

I could feel the nerves coming off of him in waves. He looked scared.

"How old are you really?"

"I don't want to tell you."

"You have to now. No joke."

"Guess."

Oh for Christ's sake. "No."

He took a deep, visible breath. *Jesus,* I thought.

"I'm fifty-nine."

I was floored. And disbelieving. There was simply no way. "What year were you born in?"

"1955."

"When's your birthday?"

"I'll be sixty in two months."

SIXTY. Wow. Sixty. Sixty was not nothing. It was definitely not forty-one, or even forty-nine. Sixty was closer to seventy than it was to forty. I was on a date with a sixty-year-old man. I had to contain a laugh. There was always something. But still, he did not look *sixty.* I did some new calculations. I didn't want kids. He had a rent-controlled apartment. Did it have to be a big deal? I decided it did not have to be a big deal on this date. All this flew through my head with lightning speed born of years of practice.

"I know it's a lot. Sixty is old," he said apologetically, head down.

I shrugged, partly to myself and partly to let him know that it wasn't the end of the world. I smiled. "You definitely don't look sixty. Why'd you lie?"

"Some of my women friends said I'd never get a date if I put my real age. They said forty-one was the magic number. It's just, I'm not interested in casually dating, and I think this is going well, and I didn't want to lie to you."

Well, that was something. And maybe he had a point—

would I have gone on a date with a sixty-year-old? I might have. I had friends with boyfriends and husbands that age. I remembered the hotel drinks with the married man, when he'd eagerly asked me if I wanted children. And now here was this man, neurotically lying about his age. I'd spent a lot of my life being cautioned to avoid being a certain kind of woman: needy, desperate, hungry for commitment and babies, terrified of my age. Only now was it starting to occur to me that these female clichés had all been created by men, and perhaps, like many writers, they'd simply been describing themselves and projecting their worst characteristics.

"Thank you. I'm glad you told me." I handed him the bowl of salad and smiled.

"So, what have your past relationships been like? Who were you dating most recently?"

Oh geez. Here we go. How to explain the disaster of the last few years? Actually, I didn't want to explain the disaster of the last few years. This was a first date, and one revelation a meal was probably enough. I threw off a few casual answers about not dating anyone seriously and long-distance relationships. But he persisted.

"Where was he?"

"On the west coast mostly."

"Was he an actor?"

"I suppose. Do you work a lot in LA?" I attempted to change the subject.

"Was he famous?"

I shrugged and rolled my eyes. "I don't know. It's really not that interesting."

"He's famous. I knew it."

The waitress arrived to collect our plates and take a dessert order. After she left I steered the conversation back to his job and kept it there with questions about how one goes about choreographing. But I could tell we'd lost something. There was a strain to the conversation now, as though we'd snapped a string and were out of tune. Still, neither of us rushed; it was a perfectly nice conversation. When the check came, he insisted on paying, and when we finally made it out to the sidewalk, he offered to walk me down Flatbush Avenue instead of just jumping in a cab. The night had gotten cold, and we walked briskly toward Atlantic, his hand on my arm as though guiding me. At the subway station I turned, wondering what sort of good night kiss I might be in store for. I was not going home with him or taking him home, curious though I might be. I was going to force myself to take this slow. Mauri had suggested I go into it thinking of it as "just a practice session for you to figure out how to date a normal person." He was staring at me intently but making no move to kiss me. He reached into his bag. "I forgot I brought you this." He handed me a thick photography magazine that had the word *feminism* written across the top. Points for paying attention, I thought. I looked up smiling to thank him.

"So, who were you dating? Jon Hamm?" he blurted out.

"What?" I wondered for a moment if I'd misheard him, and glanced back down at the magazine, but it was just a vintage black and white picture of a topless woman wearing a mask.

"The actor. Jon Hamm. Were you dating him?" His tone reminded me of my nephew's when he thought he'd caught someone in the act of doing something they shouldn't.

"Was I dating Jon Hamm?" I thought he must be making a joke. But he wasn't. I looked at his face. He must have been thinking about this the entire time, I realized.

"Doesn't Jon Hamm . . ." I stopped. Who the fuck cared if Jon Hamm had a girlfriend? "I was not dating Jon Hamm," I said with finality, and then tried to laugh it off. Better if this was a fun joke.

"Okay," he said and leaned down to give me a quick cold

kiss on the cheek and a squeeze. "Have a good night." Then he turned and jogged across the four-lane intersection and disappeared into the subway entrance. I did not move. Had that actually just happened? I turned down Atlantic—it was too ridiculous. *Was I dating Jon Hamm?* I mean honestly. I went back over the evening in my head. It had been a nice evening, I thought. Had I been unkind about his age? I didn't think so. I mean, lying about your age by two decades is not nothing, but it hadn't bothered me that much. I had never been a dater the way some of my friends had, approaching it like sports practice that eventually led to the championship round. I preferred to jump into the deep end with as little thought as possible. Maybe this was what taking it slow meant?

When I got home, I sent him an email thanking him for dinner. The next morning, I got a four-word email response.

Thanks g, me too.

That was it.

I thought about responding. I knew enough to know that this could be saved. I could stroke what needed stroking. Inflate the deflated. Be apologetic. I also knew what else awaited me on Tinder. There was no end of messages, of *heys*. After I'd come home I'd slipped into bed and started chatting with a number of men, including one named Tiger who lived on the Lower East Side; all the old texting muscles had come alive. The familiar sense of allowing a person into an intimate space without ever having to share it with him. But I had no desire to actually see Tiger, who along the way had revealed that after accidentally sleeping with his ex-wife's therapist he was no longer using Tinder to date, just to chat. There was a lot of chatting going on here. I had three conversations running, and not a single one of these men had suggested meeting in real life. They simply wanted to tell me about themselves. Dan looked good against this. Good enough.

But the days went by and I never responded. Not in the playing-hard-to-get way, but merely because I couldn't see a way in which the amount of energy I'd have to put into making him comfortable with me was worth it.

People said things like, "You need to be willing to make room for others in your life." Suggesting there was something deeply wrong with me if I didn't. That I was a coward in some sense. But I made room for people in my life all the time; for a while my entire life had been nothing but a room for other people to occupy. Still, I had believed them. It had never once occurred to me that I might simply prefer to be alone, and that that was okay. These same people often talked about the compromise required by a relationship, as if that were the thing that gave it value. No doubt it did. But I was navigating the endless compromise of living without a relationship, and that was hard and valuable, too. And when it came to hard and valuable things, I preferred my version. Maybe this wouldn't always be the case. But I wasn't going to be performing acrobatics around a man who might be good enough, simply to keep someone in my life for the sake of having someone there.

Within the week, my irritation and disappointment had slipped away, a stark contrast to the years where I would hang on and on for scraps. It was Mauri who was deeply indignant on my behalf, when next I saw her. "That's it? That's all he wrote? That's bullshit."

Ben scrolled through the email. "Good riddance."

17. What Remains

At the end of February, we sold my parents' house for the asking price. I had no emotional attachment to the house. We'd moved every six years or so; the only home I still missed, which sometimes haunted my dreams, was the one I'd lived in from ages six to eleven. That was four houses ago. This place had simply provided affordable shelter. The sale was nearly as big a relief as my mother's nursing home assignment had been; it ensured my father would have enough to live on. I had come home for Zoe's birthday, and one night I sat at the kitchen table with my father and my uncle who was visiting, amid piles of paper, crunching numbers. My uncle was my mother's younger brother; he had helped my parents sort out their beleaguered finances many times. I'd cleared my plate since Christmas to focus on the sustainability of Rachel and my company and had grown accustomed to being surrounded by numbers. Still, I had only a vague understanding of all the things he was referring to—retirement benefits versus tax-free accounts, and so forth. The end result, laid out in cold numbers and organized spreadsheets, was comforting; it felt like an immovable stone column I could lean against and count on to remain standing.

Not long after we'd listed the house, the real estate agent arrived and remarked happily on how clean it was. "You could have a showing today!" Now when I looked around, I could see it was even sparser. I asked my father where everything was. He told me that in preparation for the move he'd begun getting rid of things. What things? My father was not sentimental; his manic desire for organization superseded any emotion he might feel toward an object. "It's just junk," he said about nearly everything. I began a frantic search trying to figure out what had gone missing since I'd been home a few weeks before. I rifled through closets and raced around the basement, scanning bookshelves to see if I could spot the titles I'd grown up staring at: *Tinker, Tailor, Soldier, Spy;* my mother's copies of Jane Austen from university, all signed on the inner cover in her flowing handwriting (all my life people had remarked on my mother's beautiful handwriting); our old Fisher-Price toys that my mother kept for when my niece and nephew visited. Medley faithfully followed me from room to room. Yes, my mother's wedding dress was still in the closet, and yes, the Christmas nativity scene centerpiece my grandmother had given us as children was still in a box downstairs.

The next day, I went out and bought a larger suitcase so I could collect things to bring back to New York with me. I packed what was left of a set of dishes we'd grown up with. They had a string of painted blue fishes around the rim; my mother had bought them shortly after she was married and we'd eaten nearly every meal off of them my entire childhood. I wrapped the eggcups carefully in my underwear, stuffed the teacups in socks. I took the goblets I recalled being used at dinner parties my parents had thrown when I was a child. I raced the Christmas decorations over to my sister's basement, along with boxes of records and books that wouldn't fit in my bag.

I felt as if I were on a rescue mission, packing up before an oncoming storm. What I couldn't take with me I organized carefully in a corner in the basement. I taped a piece of paper to it that said DO NOT TOUCH, walked my father downstairs, and pointed to it. "Do not throw any of these things out until I return," I said sternly. He laughed and threw up his hands. "I won't!"

I didn't think it was funny. I understood his rigid cleaning was his own way of implementing some order in a world that had very quickly dissolved around him. A frantic last-ditch effort to convince himself he had some control over what had befallen my mother. I knew he wasn't doing it to be malicious, but to me, it felt as though whatever beast had been eating up my mother's mind had stayed behind in the house and was now consuming it. Everything was shifting around me, and nothing could be counted on to be where I left it.

I spent one long afternoon sitting in the basement going through a big box that had been set aside for dumping. It was full of odds and ends, things my mother had obviously intended to organize in some fashion but never got around to. I pulled out the convocation flyer from her university graduation: a yellowing pamphlet plastered with the usual language of hope about the future prospects of the Class of '68. Paper clipped to it were blurry Polaroids of my mother in her graduation gown, standing with my grandparents. One looked like it had been burned by a cigarette ash. I found a postcard she'd sent them from a summer road trip to Prince Edward Island, her beautiful handwriting the same as it ever was. There was a photo album she'd carefully put together of the year she'd lived with her best friend Pat in Toronto while completing her master's degree in social work.

Slipped between two of the pages was an old matchbook from a bar in downtown Toronto. Each picture had a caption handwritten by her: "Jean locks herself out on the balcony"; "Jack enters the picture, December 1966." In some of the pictures she was wearing the bridesmaid dresses I'd later turn into Halloween costumes, or disassemble and wear to high school dances. So many bridesmaid outfits—it felt like the uniform of her early twenties. I hadn't been a bridesmaid for the first time till age thirty-two. Shoved in the box, too, were letters from me from the time I'd lived in England and a postcard from the time I'd visited Paris shortly after my thirtieth birthday. The postcard had a coffee ring on it, hers no doubt. My mother was never without a cup of coffee; growing up we'd find half-drunk cups in various locations around the house, where she'd left them before starting a fresh pot. I could easily imagine her at the kitchen table, reading my postcard, mug perched right beside her. I wanted to keep the card as much for the coffee ring as for the words it held. The matchbox as much as the pictures it was stuffed between. I wanted every remainder of her handwriting. It was all a strange sort of precious detritus generated by her life that let me know where she was, places she'd passed through, drinks she'd had in certain moments. Physical evidence of a life she could no longer remember, but I could now hold on to. A map of her past.

I thought about the thousands of text messages I'd exchanged with 646, and how no one would ever find them in a box. Or see any evidence at all of the time or effort or emotion that had gone into them. They were such cold, intangible proof of my lived life. What would any of us leave behind in this new digital age? What actual space would our lives take up in the world once we were gone?

I collected some of the cards and pictures and took them with me to the nursing home. My trips home now had a new rhythm; instead of hours spent on the phone with doctors, I triangulated between my sister's, my father's, and my mother. I thought there was a chance my mother might get some enjoyment looking at the old photos; for a long while her long-term memory had remained at least somewhat intact. And there were still flashes of it now and then. But none of it meant anything to her. She gazed at it all pleasantly and politely, the same way you look at someone else's child's artwork. "How nice," she said. All this history, hers and inevitably mine and my sister's, and one day my niece's and nephews', was no longer attached to her.

The same went for the bookcase my father moved into her room at my request. I filled it with all her copies of Georgette Heyer and Agatha Christie and Ellis Peters, carefully organizing them based on author and then color. I lined up all the Harry Potter books I'd given her on the bottom row. But when I returned two days later, there was a sheet over the bookcase; apparently other residents had been wandering in and taking the books. My mother hadn't noticed they were there, let alone missing. The stories meant nothing to her. She was herself now in a land with no stories. Except there was no way out of her new country, no map, no exploration, just the goal of keeping her safe and comfortable, and put.

But she did nothing but wander. It was as if some part of her knew she'd been released from everything that had kept her attached to her life. On the walls of the hallway leading to her room were taped up sheets of paper with the name JEAN written on them in all caps, and arrows underneath pointing back to her room. My mother, a woman who left the house only when required, now liked to go into other people's rooms and lie down in their beds, the old lady version of Goldilocks. She no longer even remembered the dog. The photo I'd put of Medley in the alcove beside the door to help guide her home was useless.

The things about my mother that stubbornly remained, however, were her knowledge of my father's name and her insistence on helping other people. When it came time to bring her to the dining hall for lunch, she'd insist on walking over to the food serving station, convinced she worked there. She always asked where my father was. I wondered sometimes what would remain for me if I ever reached this stage. What had been hammered so deeply into my psyche that even as everything else fell away, it would still stand, like ruins of a lost kingdom?

Eventually my father packed the books up and dropped them off at a secondhand bookstore; fortunately I'd already grabbed the copies of the Harry Potters that had my notes inscribed to her. *You'll love this*, I wrote on the inside of one flap, *it makes me feel as if we were back sitting on the couch*. I was, I now realized, the keeper of my history, and hers. All these pieces I'd been grabbing at so frantically were really just me trying to reconstruct her memory for her, in her absence.

•

A few weeks after I returned to New York, Rachel went into labor. The morning her water broke she texted me. *Are you up? It may be nothing, but I think my water may have just broken.* I sent her back a picture of Julie Andrews singing "I Have Confidence"— we'd named our company after a lyric from *The Sound of Music*— and then biked into the city and met her and her sister at Katz's Deli, where we ordered sandwiches and fries to take with us to the hospital. On the way out I asked the cashier if we could keep the ticket stub they normally took when you paid, as a memento. I pointed at Rachel, her protruding belly. "She's in labor." He handed it back, giving us a sideways look. "Good luck," he said, waving us out the door. Rachel's contractions were still too far apart for her to go to the hospital, so instead we stopped at a massage parlor in the East Village and got massages. "How far apart are the contractions now?" I called to her through the curtain between our tables, envisioning her delivering her baby in a massage parlor.

Ruby was not born in a massage parlor. She arrived healthy and round thirty hours later, at eight o'clock the next evening. I'd left Rachel at the hospital with her sister and Maddy, who was acting as Rachel's doula, at 4:00 a.m., when the doctor said it was unlikely the baby would arrive that night and Rachel needed rest. Second Avenue was empty, and I flew down it on my bike the way I'd done for so many years after long waitressing shifts, weaving back and forth along the avenue, relishing the feeling that I had the city to myself. This would probably be what remained if I ever suffered the same fate as my mother: the desire to be on my bike in the empty, predawn streets of New York. The air was fresh with spring, and overhead the low clouds were catching the light from the city, making the sky glow. There was construction down near the entrance to the Manhattan Bridge, and I stopped to let a truck go by. A worker in a reflective vest nodded at me. "You have a good night."

"My friend is having her first baby," I said.

"Well, congratulations," he called to me. "This is a great city to be born in."

Yes, I thought pedaling onto the still-dark bridge. No matter what she did or where she went for the rest of her life, Ruby would be able to say she was born in New York City, after a stop for takeout at Katz's and a detour to a massage parlor in the East Village. Talk about a great beginning to a story. The next evening Maddy texted me a picture of Rachel with Ruby shortly after her birth, somehow managing to capture with it the exact extraordinary moment when someone you know so well makes the transformation into motherhood.

Days later I woke to an email from my father saying he'd put Medley down. We had been given the move-out date, and I'd spent recent weeks scrolling through rental listings looking for an apartment for him that would fit his budget. He emailed to tell Alexis and me about Medley after the fact, claiming that she was getting old and wouldn't survive the move. I went white with rage when I read the email, furious with myself for not considering this possibility and whisking the dog away to my sister's or to my apartment for safekeeping along with the dishes and the books and the wine goblets.

I couldn't stay angry for long, though. I didn't have room for it. Things had settled down, my mother had a home, the babies had arrived safely, but my mind still felt like the bar on my phone that let me know how much storage space was left; there was only a sliver. I didn't know when the time would come when I could empty myself enough to recharge, but I knew until it did I simply needed to press on, until our family had been entirely dismantled and then rebuilt into whatever form it was about to take.

It was at this point that Jo intervened and insisted on sending me on a river cruise through the south of France. An only child, she had spent much of her life shouldering the responsibility of caring for a chronically ill, immobilized father and an alcoholic mother; I never needed to find the words to explain realities to her. Her offer—a week on a boat, with little internet connection, six time zones away—was the reset I needed.

18. The Other Woman

My friend Lesley was the only person I knew who shared my habit of pilgrimaging to places she'd long loved in books. Lesley was a journalist and a writer, and the difference between how we pursued our various obsessions was that Lesley turned her trips into feature stories for glossy magazines, whereas I merely aimed to satisfy my inner eight-year-old's desire to set actual foot in places I'd marked off on maps. When her stories involved travel, I'd often gone along with her.

One year, after attending the annual South by Southwest festival in Austin, I'd rented a car and driven to Kansas City (stopping briefly at Laura Ingalls Wilder's Mansfield, Missouri, house on the way), where I'd picked Lesley up at the airport. The next day we drove across the state, marveling at the straight roads and undulating landscape, all the way to the tiny town of Holcomb to research a story she was writing on the fiftieth anniversary of Truman Capote's *In Cold Blood*. Lesley was six months pregnant at the time, something she was not afraid to emphasize, theorizing it might make tight-lipped residents open up more easily. She was right. We soon found ourselves in quiet country kitchens, being fed sandwich meat on sliced white bread, listening to tales about the time Capote and his child-hood friend and then–research assistant Harper Lee (*To Kill a Mockingbird* was complete but wouldn't be published until the following year) had come to town. I was standing in front of the sink during one such visit, rinsing lunch plates under a framed needlepoint stitched saying, which read: I Am Woman, Hear Me Roar, when the woman who owned the house remarked that Lee was the more impressive of the two. "I wouldn't be sur-prised if she'd actually written the book."

The next afternoon I snapped a photo of Lesley in her chic black dress, sporting large black sunglasses, standing in front of the long driveway leading to the house where the murders had taken place. We sent it to her husband by way of a Wish You Were Here postcard.

Not long after that, Lesley convinced the journalist Sally Quinn to let us stay for a weekend at the Grey Gardens house in East Hampton, Long Island. Quinn and her husband, *Washington Post* executive editor Ben Bradlee, had purchased the home in the late seventies from Big and Little Edie Beale—the aunt and first cousin, respectively, of Jacqueline Kennedy Onassis—under the agreement they could not tear the house down. They'd then spent years carefully renovating it. The house and its former oc-cupants, the eccentric Beale duo, had been made famous after the release of the Maysles brothers' documentary *Grey Gardens,* which captured the mother and daughter, once members of high society, living in squalor with numerous cats and raccoons, though seemingly quite content with this reclusive world they'd created for themselves. The Edies, the house, and the film had long reached cult status, and when Lesley heard Grey Gardens would be empty for a weekend between renters, she went to work on getting permission to stay there. And so, one weekend in March the two of us drove out to East Hampton with Lesley's French pug, as well as her assistant, Alison, and took up residence in the twenty-eight-room estate a block from the beach. In the evening, before dinner we played records on the player while we each took baths in our own huge porcelain tubs with taloned feet. There was a full moon that weekend, and before bed I would walk down to the ocean by myself in the silver light and stand silently as the waves crashed. "My future self is so jealous of us right now," I said to Lesley when I got back to the house.

We'd been warned beforehand that the house was haunted, and Little Edie's room in particular was reported to be filled with ghosts; Ben Bradlee had once referred to Little Edie as a witch. In the movie she is seen performing an elaborate flag dance. Her presence was still very much apparent: there were framed pictures of her around the house wearing the turban and fur she was famous for. Her children's books were still in the library. In her youth she'd been a great beauty and dazzling debutante and liked to boast that famous, powerful men such as Howard Hughes and J. Paul Getty had proposed to her, which is easy to believe when you see pictures of her from that time. However, in her mid-thirties she'd returned to the estate to care for her mother, who'd slipped into financial ruin following a divorce from her father. She never left.

On our first night, Lesley and Alison insisted on sleeping with their doors open, worried about the spirits that might arrive in the dark. I was in the middle of extricating myself from the married man for the first time and offered to sleep in Little Edie's room, thinking if Little Edie did show up in the middle of the night, perhaps she could provide me with some guidance and if not, at least the distraction from my own problems would be welcome. I turned off all the lights, shut the door, and felt my way into the bed in the pitch-black. And then, after weeks of troubled insomnia, I collapsed immediately into the longest, deepest sleep I'd had in months. "Little Edie must have been looking out for you," Lesley said the next morning. "We're simpatico," I responded. Just two weirdos, I thought, adjusting the turban I'd plucked out of my suitcase and put on for breakfast.

•

Lesley was already set to be in Paris in late April for a magazine story connected to a book she was writing on Hemingway, when Jo swooped in and offered to send me on a river cruise in France for the same week. The cruise departed from Avignon and finished seven days later, up the Rhone in Lyon. It seemed improbable that Lesley and I would cross paths, but it pleased me nonetheless that we'd both be on French soil at the same time.

A few days later I was once again catapulted out of my life and across the ocean, and within hours of exiting the plane in Marseille, I found myself on the balcony of my gilded stateroom, overlooking the flowing Rhone River. When I leaned out the window to take a selfie against the scenery, it looked like I'd photoshopped myself into a van Gogh painting. Everything was decadent, from the light, to the trees lining the water's edge, to the cheese that oozed out on the china plates in the dining room.

Before coming on this trip I'd made jokes about the senior citizens' cruise I was embarking on. As it turned out, I *was* the youngest on board by about twenty years. But sitting here, rolling French vineyards visible through the windows, I was deeply struck by how these privileged men and women had seemingly excelled at later life. This was the lifestyle we were all encouraged to save up for: the reward. With my mother, I had seen the worst-case version of what we imagine growing old to be; here I was observing the best case. The difference was striking, especially coming back to back.

In the mornings, I watched as the women served careful portions of soft-boiled eggs and buttered toast to their husbands, while both sat in habitual silence. Perhaps that's what marriage became eventually: one long ritual of performed habits.

Over dinner one night I was invited to join a table of two couples. My solitariness stood out nearly as much as my age in this group, and since arriving I'd been on the receiving end of many curious stares, as if my being alone made *them* uncomfortable.

I picked up my plate and plunked down in the chair they'd pulled up for me. It soon became clear they didn't know each other, either. And as the first course arrived (dinner was at least four courses), they began well-honed introductory stories about themselves. The couple on my left had met as children in Afghanistan more than forty years ago. They'd had a clandestine (young people of the opposite sex were not allowed to even converse) relationship that continued into their teens. Afterward they managed to stay in touch when he was temporarily jailed during college for participating in protests.

"He wrote me notes on toilet paper," the wife said, placing her hand over his and smiling at me, "and then stuffed them into his pockets where his mother would retrieve them when she came to pick up his laundry."

After her family immigrated to Germany in the late seventies, they lost touch. A few years later, shortly after he was released from jail, he traveled to visit family in Germany. The very first person he ran into at the airport was her cousin. Inquiring after her whereabouts, he quickly traveled to meet her. Two years later they were married and immigrated to California.

"Thirty years and still we go strong," the husband said, smiling proudly.

The couple on the other side of me were two women, Judy and Joan, celebrating their sixth wedding anniversary and their sixty-fifth birthdays. At first glance I'd pegged them for a pair that had been together for decades, but I couldn't have been more wrong.

"We met on Match.com," Judy told me. Judy reminded me of Bea Arthur, tall and stooping, with a deep, commanding voice that suggested she was not in the habit of suffering the opinions of others. "My husband had died in a fire a few years before"— her breath caught with emotion—"and the second I met her I knew Joan was the one."

Joan looked like an older, heavier, taller version of Blanche Devereaux. I'd seen her being helped on board earlier, navigating the walkway with two canes.

"Same for me," said Joan. "I'd been divorced for five years, but I knew. My husband walked me down the aisle."

So much for thinking I had these people, or anything else, pegged. I could practically hear Katharine Hepburn's sharp voice ring out from *The Philadelphia Story*: "The time to make up your mind about people is never!" Here, I thought, were the stories that made marriage seem like a good idea. Something to be pursued, and something that could be sustained, but not moribund. Advertisements for marriage. Eventually talk turned to me, and I explained I was on board to write a story for a travel site.

"Do you ever come to California?" asked the man. "I'd like you to meet my son. He is very smart, and very handsome, but he needs to meet a good woman."

I laughed. "I'm sure he's too young for me," I said.

The man shook his head emphatically. "Oh no, he's twenty-eight."

I paused, but only briefly—I was learning to get a kick out of the response some people had to my actual age. "I'm forty," I said, and waited. The round of gasps and raised eyebrows I'd anticipated did not disappoint. After demanding I reveal what year I'd been born—much as I had done on my date with Dan the stunt guy—the man leaned back in his chair and looked at me with raised eyebrows. "And you are not married?"

"I'm not," I said, only realizing afterward the question had been entirely drained of its sting. Then again, perhaps it's hard to be stung when you have just stuffed yourself with a pound of stinky, gooey cheese and followed it up with a bowl of chocolate mousse.

His wife leaned forward. She'd been pleasant and smiling throughout the meal but now sounded a bit alarmed. "Oh, but I hope you're not ruling out marriage entirely?"

I looked around at all the wealth, and security, and pleasantness, and then back at this couple who had survived so much, and to the two women who'd found each other so late in life, and wondered at the idea that anyone could rule out anything other than death. I assured her I wasn't ruling anything out and then grinned. "But at this point it would take a lot of convincing." One of the reasons I was on this boat, after all, was because I never had to check in with anyone when I wanted to do something.

When I got back to my room, there was a message waiting for me from Lesley. Back in New York, I ate every Sunday night dinner with her and her husband, biking over the bridge to their West Village apartment, to feast on whatever recipe Lesley had plucked out of her cookbook that week. She would often text in the morning to inquire whether I was okay with her making beef bourguignon or ask how I felt about lobster pie. (I always felt just fine.) Now she was emailing to see if I could manage to meet her for dinner Thursday in Paris. Was there really no chance of making it work? She wanted to know. It had seemed unlikely to me when we'd discussed it in New York, but being on the road, or water, had pushed me back into that frame of mind where most things felt possible, and so I asked. It was absolutely fine, I was quickly informed. *I arrive at Gare de Lyon at 6PM!* I promptly wrote Lesley. *DARLING!!!!!!!!!* she wrote back.

The next day when we docked at a small town, one of the attendants on the boat walked me to the local train station and helped me buy a ticket to Paris. The boat would dock in Lyon the following afternoon; the plan was for me to meet them there. It was raining when I reached Paris later that day, a fine Parisian spring rain, but I decided to walk from the train station to Lesley's hotel in Montparnasse anyway. On the boulevards, the sycamores were in bloom, and the Luxembourg Gardens exploded in color. I stopped and stood in front of the Medici Fountain. The very first time I'd come to Paris, I'd been nineteen, and deeply unimpressed. I hadn't yet learned to like wine, or cheese (that didn't come presliced, anyway), and at the hostel I was staying in it was impossible to sleep thanks to all the American backpackers crowded around the television screaming at O. J. Simpson racing his white Bronco across the L.A. freeways. One morning on my walk to find a "normal" coffee, I'd stumbled on the Medici Fountain and thought I'd discovered a secret. It seemed otherworldly to me then, representing all the magic of the world I had been unable to touch growing up. It was still that for me now, more so even, cloaked in the mist of the afternoon. And standing there I thought about the girl I'd been the last time I was here and the woman I was now, and was pretty pleased with myself. But also pleased for the girl who had stood here all those years before not knowing but hoping for what her life might be about—namely adventure—and pleased, too, for the future I couldn't yet fully imagine that might bring me back here at some point yet again.

Later before dinner Lesley and I sat at Le Select, one of the hot spots of the Lost Generation, eating thick slices of brie and sipping champagne. "I'm jealous of us again," I said, looking at the picture the waiter had just snapped of us. Afterward we ate with Lesley's magazine team at Prunier, a famous seafood restaurant around the corner from the Arc de Triomphe that had been a favorite of Hemingway's. It was the last day for oysters until September, and they came out stacked on enormous trays, nestled in mounds of salt and ice. The oysters themselves were huge, "practically pornographic," said Lesley before we all dropped one in our mouths. We were joined at the table by

Valerie Hemingway. She had been Hemingway's research assistant when he wrote *A Moveable Feast*, his memoir about his early years in Paris. She later married one of his sons. She and Lesley were retracing Hemingway's steps through Paris for the story Lesley was writing.

As we ate Valerie told me about working for Hemingway. She'd been nineteen at the time. She said she thought that for Hemingway, returning to Paris to retrace his own youthful steps there had made him regretful that he'd left his first wife, Hadley. She told me how he'd signed over all the rights to *The Sun Also Rises* to Hadley before it was published. And that even afterward, when it was a huge hit, "he never went back on it."

Back in Lesley's hotel room that night we lay in the double bed as the rain continued its constant patter on the roof. Before we went to sleep Lesley called her husband and almost-two-year-old daughter to say good night. "You were with us at Grey Gardens, and Kansas, darling," Lesley said to her daughter. "And soon you'll get to come on adventures with us again."

I thought of Hemingway and all his wives. The series of women he'd married who, with the exception of Martha Gellhorn, another journalist heroine of both Lesley's and mine, had spent most of their lives making his life easier. He was the writer, whose adventurous lifestyle was so coveted as a definition of virility and masculinity. I had coveted it, too. Why else were we here, but to walk in similar footsteps? And yet the older I got, the more I thought about how his home life had been facilitated by his wives: reservations looked after, bags packed, meals cooked. No kidding he was adventurous; he didn't have to think about anything else. And yet here I was. In a hotel made possible by the friend who cooked extravagant meals for me on Sundays. On a trip organized by the friend who was intent on my benefiting from her job. Able to leave because I ran a business with another friend with whom I shared much of my career and finances. I had hurled myself into this year feeling alone, and prepared for more of it, but as I lay there under the Parisian eaves of our hotel room it occurred to me I'd managed to split many of the so-called duties of a partner between a circle of friends. I was the other woman in their lives, and together they combined to make the perfect husband in mine. They loved and supported me and understood me. For better or worse. Always.

When I returned to the boat the next day, Judy stopped me in the lobby. "We all heard you left and went to Paris for one night," she boomed. "Train to Paris, for the night. How chic!"

On my way to bed that night, the woman who had been so alarmed about my stance on marriage stopped me in the hall. "I am very envious of you," she said in a shy, hushed tone. "I got married so young and had children. I wish I'd done what you are doing. It is wonderful."

I was still thinking of her remark when I returned home to Toronto the following week to make the final move to my father's new apartment. It felt strange to be envied by a woman who had done "everything right" and was now enjoying the fruits of it, as if I were the lucky one and not her. I had been so determined not to live my mother's life, and now that I was as far away from it as I possibly could be, and confronting all the complications that had arisen from my decisions, I found myself curious to know why my mother had chosen what she had, and whether she had wanted it or had simply never considered there were other options. Or maybe I just wanted to know why she hadn't wanted what I thought she should have wanted. I had never thought to ask her these questions when she had been capable of answering them, and now the life I wanted to know about was no longer one she remembered.

•

In the end, I had to admit my father's manic cleaning had made the final move easier on all of us. We'd found a one-bedroom apartment for my father a few blocks away from the house where we'd lived when I was a teenager, around the corner from my old high school. When I arrived, he'd been there only twenty-four hours but had already set it up. As I drove over to see the apartment for the first time, through the same streets that I had walked and biked and bused and finally driven through as a teenager, I felt overwhelmed by the circularity of my father's move: after all this, simply to land right back in the same place we'd been all those years before. I felt as though if I glanced out the window at the right moment I'd catch a glimpse of my teenage self, marching down the block, resentfully planning her escape from these very streets.

This sense that I was continually meeting former versions of myself practically knocked me down when I moved into Maddy's at the end of May. In fact, it didn't feel so much like encountering my past as the sense that I'd managed to recapture all the best parts of it. Like when I dreamt we were back in the house we'd lived in when I was eight, or woke up from a dream I was once again waiting tables; it felt like some integral part of me that I'd once said goodbye to had been resurrected. It felt like I was coming home.

And what a home!

"Holy shit," said the mover, when he got to the top of the stairs and took a look around. The apartment was one big open room—the top floor of the house; Maddy and Ben had the first two floors. The ceiling rose up to eleven feet, and there were skylights over the kitchen and the bedroom, *and* there was a walk-in closet (there are three things New Yorkers fantasize about when it comes to apartments: dishwashers, a washer and dryer in the unit, and walk-in closets). The mover looked at me: "Well done." But for once I'd done nothing. I could take no credit. Maddy and I had simply hung on to each other, and then hung on, and then hung on. As though we'd made some implicit vow way, way back when she'd cooked lentils for us the summer we were too broke to buy any other groceries, and had kept it even when it seemed as though we'd both run in opposite directions. So often in the last years it had felt as if things were ending, but change wasn't the end; life came back around, and back around again if you let it. People leave, but they also come back.

As I rode my bike back and forth between my old apartment and new, transporting the last of my things, I recalled my move from the last place Maddy and I had lived together, and how filled with resentment and anger and fear I had been at the time. How my ability to get my own apartment—no small feat in New York, where signing a lease was nearly as complicated and expensive as getting a mortgage—had been drowned out by how tiny it was, and the knowledge I was committing to a life that felt as though it left no space for another person. Now I felt like I was in a place that allowed me to do anything. Not just because of the space, but because it felt safe, because it was affordable. I thought of all the times I'd bemoaned the husband-shaped hole in my life, the bills I had to foot on my own, the groceries and cooking, the unopened bottle of wine. That space was now filled, for the most part, in one way or another. Not the way I'd ever thought it would be, but is anything?

On the evening I moved in Maddy made a picnic for us in the backyard. We sat on a blanket on the ground, under the cherry tree that was just shaking the last of its spring blooms. The air around us was warm but still held the coolness of spring. It was one of those rare nights you sometimes get in New York before the season tips into the punishing heat of summer. When the breeze shifted, I could just catch a hint of the sea. Hannah, now four and a half, ran around the yard whooping and singing and scrambling up the climbing board her father had made for her and mounted against the fence. Eventually she sat down beside me and picked up a sandwich, staring at me evenly over the top of it as she ate.

"We are sleeping in bunk beds," she said. "The ceiling of my room is the bottom of your bed, and you're right above. Monsters can't get through to me that way."

I smiled and wrapped my arms around her, thinking of all the things I, too, was now protected from. "That works both ways," I said.

19. Women Are Well-Acquainted with Thirst

A funny thing began to happen after I moved in. Fairly quickly, as friends came over to visit, the apartment became a strange sort of confessional booth, as if people sensed I was so secure in my life that they could more freely confess their worst fears about theirs. It almost always began in the same way: a friend would arrive, take a look around, turn to me with a slightly awed face, and declare, "I'm so envious!" It became the most uttered phrase in my new home the first month I was there. The idea that I could be a source of envy was still something of a revelation. On paper at least—single, childless, forty—I continued to be the definition of the thing most women believe they should avoid at all costs. And, if it had been just one friend who'd mentioned it, I likely wouldn't have noticed. Objectively speaking, it *was* a great apartment. I was a New Yorker, after all; some people here aimed for apartments the way they aimed for careers. This was the equivalent of a corner office with great benefits. But when it kept happening over and over, I began to take note.

"I think they're just being nice," the mother of a friend of mine remarked when I noted in passing how strange I was finding it, after years of having it impressed on me that I was destined to remain an object of pity if my life remained on this trajectory, to suddenly find myself on the receiving end of the exact opposite.

The thought had never crossed my mind, but once the initial moment of shock wore off, I suppressed a laugh and sighed. I was increasingly frustrated that some people seemed incapable of believing me when I said I was happy with my life. My life, I was learning, was sometimes even more confusing for women a few decades older to comprehend than it was even for me. They had been forced to survive as well as they could in a world that had demanded they live a certain way, and they had internalized a certain version of feminism that had allowed them to succeed at this: it sometimes did not leave room for understanding, or celebrating, the choices I was making.

As far as I could tell, the men I knew had not given much thought to my choices as they pertained to me as a person. (When men gave thought to women's life choices, it was never the individual they seemed to have a problem with, just WOMEN, as if we were a great body of water to be sailed over.) Women, on the other hand, often responded to me in the exact opposite fashion. It was as if I were speaking for all women, and in the case of older women it sometimes felt as though they thought I was sitting in judgment on them, that my choices and circumstances were somehow a reflection on theirs, instead of a progression or alternative made possible by their own.

In this particular case, the idea that my friends were just telling me what I wanted to hear was laughable. I knew they were being sincere, and I could see my life from their point of view. It was as though by coming into my home they were being given the chance to walk a few steps down the path not taken (or avoided), and were discovering it wasn't as dark and thorny as they'd been taught. Or perhaps it was dawning on them that there was another path (it's not as though women are ever raised being overburdened with the sense that they have options).

"You make me want to be single again," said one friend who'd been married for more than a decade. "I mean, I love Sam and the kids, obviously, but this is incredible."

"So, this is your apartment," said another, a mother of two, grinning in a hungry sort of way. "Can I please come over and lie on your bed some afternoons and pretend I'm single?"

"I want your life," professed one woman I'd known for years, who had a much-desired two-year-old at home, before lying down on my bed and weeping. "I hate it sometimes," she said. "I obviously don't regret it, but sometimes I hate it. It's too hard."

"I wish I'd been braver about not getting married," said another friend of mine, newly divorced and a mother of two, who was visiting from out of town for the weekend. "I remember being thirty-two and in a state of near total panic at the idea I might be single at thirty-five."

Every woman I knew seemed to think she was failing in some way, had been raised to believe she was lacking, and was certain someone else was doing it better. Had been told never to trust her own instincts. Taught to think of life as a solution when "done right," when in reality we existed in a kaleidoscope made of shades of gray, able to be very happy and very sad all at the same time.

I knew the only reason I was hearing all this was because in me they seemed to have found the rare assurance of nonjudgment. I was not a participant in the mothering Olympics; it wasn't as though I was going to admonish someone for not breastfeeding (I was always thrilled when someone had switched to formula, because it meant I got to do the feeding). Nor did I get too frustrated by the fact that they could not hold a conversation for more than forty-five seconds at a time—I could see their own frustration at this. They were lonely, too. Which was painfully ironic, since I was certain more than one baby, not to mention a few marriages, had been conceived by women tired of being left out of every conversation her married with children friends were having.

"Don't ever have kids," said nearly all of them at some point.

"They don't mean that!" said a successful businesswoman I knew who was expecting her first grandchild. She seemed shocked and offended at the very idea. I wanted to suggest to her that she might change her tune had she had to do her small children mothering in the age of twenty-four-hour email and social media Greek-chorusing. I knew they didn't mean it, not really. What they meant was don't fall for the hype. They meant that this was harder than anyone had ever warned them. They meant that the longer they'd been able to rule their own lives, the harder it became not to. They meant that they had been promised things would get easier and better, not harder and more relentless. They meant they'd lost their own hard-won identity in ways they weren't prepared for, and were still trying to reconstruct it.

"I'm so tired of hearing women tell me how terrible it is to have children," said my friend Kim one afternoon when she'd come over to help me organize the closet. Kim was in her early thirties, had been married a few years, and I knew was starting to think seriously about kids. "The nonstop negativity is just exhausting."

This was the flip side, I supposed. I'd watched so many of my friends go into marriage starry-eyed and thrilled and then be bowled over by the realities of childcare that it never crossed my mind what it must be like to hear only the bad parts over and over and not know, as I did, that it came with plenty of good, too.

But who sits at a dinner party talking about the magic of a serene midnight feeding? You had to go to Instagram if you wanted that.

"I think they just feel like they were never warned," I said. "And they don't feel like they have the right to be unhappy. It's the same way people are constantly telling me what my life is missing, as if they can't believe I could be happy alone. I think they're told they aren't allowed to be unhappy when they have the only two things women are supposed to want."

Of course, not every woman came over and complained like this, and never my newly married or about-to-be-married friends, who were caught in the throes of romance and wedding planning. Nor did my single friends, some of whom had similar setups to me, nor my younger friends, who took my life in the way people in their twenties take every accomplishment of someone older: the promise of possibility.

But listening to these friends unleash their doubts and fears did make it that much easier to remind myself, on days that I needed reminding, that everything was just as good as it was bad, and not an either/or. The role reversal, however, was not lost on me. These were the same women who'd married when we were in our early thirties and spent a decade inquiring hopefully and encouragingly about my love life. Now it seemed that just as I had been released from my regrets, they were only now beginning to voice theirs.

The confessional trail through my apartment, fascinating though it was, was usually a one-way street. Some days I felt as desperate for someone to commiserate with as some of my friends did for sixty minutes of uninterrupted sleep. But how does one talk about the exhaustion of going it alone in the face of problems with a baby who has suddenly ceased sleeping through the night? It's a tricky line to walk, and I hadn't yet figured out how to do it. The result was that I often found relief talking to people I knew only casually.

This is what happened when I had lunch with an old book publishing acquaintance. She'd recently turned forty herself and was unmarried. I mentioned that it had been a wild year I'd not been prepared for. Was it just me? I wanted to know. Or did others also feel like it was better and harder than they'd anticipated?

"I have never been more relieved than on the morning of my fortieth birthday," she said. "It felt like I'd been released."

So I wasn't crazy! "I feel like we are the beneficiaries of extraordinary timing," I confessed. "We're the first generation that can make enough of our own money to live the way we want. I feel like we have a responsibility to figure out what this means."

"I guess." She nodded, now looking skeptical. "I mean, I understand that we're the first wave in this, and it's supposed to be exciting and we're lucky, but I've never wanted to be part of the vanguard of anything. It's never appealed to me. And yet here I am."

Perhaps the remark shouldn't have stopped me cold, but it did. In all my reckoning with my life in the past nine months, the thing that kept me buoyed was the idea that I had been hurled into an adventure. I thought often of Joseph Campbell's *The Hero's Journey* (even though, extraordinary man that he was, he didn't think it was available to women outside of motherhood) and even in my moments of doubt and uncertainty felt immeasurable gratitude that I hadn't been born too early, even by a few decades. That somehow the person I was capable of being was matched to the time I was living in. I hadn't stopped to consider that this might not be true of every woman living a similar life to mine.

A week later Jo came over. She was newly engaged to a man she'd met a few months earlier on one of her reporting trips, and in the early stages of planning her September wedding. She was here so we could plan our road trip; in mid-July we were driving her car, her things, and her dog across the country to San Francisco, where her fiancé, Nick, lived.

"This place is so much better than a wedding," said Jo, walking in, laughing.

•

In June, a publisher acquired the proposal for the puberty guide Naama and I had been working on. It was thrilling to think we'd be writing a book, and the book advance we would be paid meant that for the next little while I could stop the freelance frenzy of pitching articles and just focus on one big project.

A few weeks later, Alexis drove down to New York with a friend and a truckload full of the things I had put aside in my frantic clearing of my parents' house. She and her husband had reunited, and he was home with the kids while she took a few days away. Along with records, books, and phtotos, she also brought my parents' white living room couch, which now sat against the wall facing my bed.

I had said yes to the couch without giving it much thought beyond the fact that I now finally had room for a couch and this saved me from spending money. My mother had read to me on that couch nearly every night of my childhood. Those cushions had held my happiest moments, and now my happiest memories.

I spent a lot of time staring at it from my bed when it first arrived. I suddenly had a lot of time. Just like that, it seemed, everything had let up. My father was moved and settled. My mother was being cared for. Rachel was settling into motherhood. My sister and her husband had reunited. I had moved to a lovely new home and sold a book. As my mother might have said, "giddy Fortune's furious fickle wheel" had turned and taken with it many of the responsibilities and concerns that had dominated my last year and a half.

It all should have been a relief, but instead I felt conflicted by the shift. To suddenly find myself unnecessary on all fronts was jarring and made me feel strangely disposable. And what was I now supposed to do with all the freedom?

I'd started my fortieth year pondering what felt like an unmarked path ahead, but so much had happened that required my attention that for months the answer seemed to be that freedom means being at other people's disposal when they need you. Now I was at my own disposal. I felt like one of those families that had spent their lives below the poverty line and won the lottery, only to file for bankruptcy a few short years later; they'd never been taught how to have money, and the abundance of it seemed to do more harm than good. I had all this freedom—how to use it well?

Neither did I have friends to enjoy this with or lean on for solidarity. This was not my twenties being relived. Everyone around me was, and had been for quite some time, tied up in their lives. Our moments of connection were scheduled, consciously constructed bridges between two worlds that increasingly required sets of decisions that were unrecognizable to one another. I thought of the ledgers my mother had required of my sister and me to account for our allowance spending. I wished there'd been a similar way to teach me about how to budget freedom. Where to go when there's nowhere you have to be.

I was wide open. But before I could stop it, into that empty space, like an emotional squatter, crept all the grief and sadness I'd held at bay. The tears I'd choked back the day we'd left my mother in the nursing home, and all the days I'd left her since. The overwhelming loss of standing by while her mind evaporated. The dismantling of an entire life. Knowing the inevitable ending that was coming. For as long as I could remember my mother had read the last chapter of every book first; she didn't like surprises. She didn't want to invest emotionally in characters whose outcome she couldn't be sure of. And now I had seen the last chapter of hers. There was no comfort in this knowledge, just the awareness that there'd be no relief from it either. There was no flipping back to the beginning. I'd lived away from home for so long that if I didn't think about it too hard, it was sometimes easy to let my mind slip into the comforting groove that life at home was continuing as it always had. But I had only to open my eyes every morning and see that couch, the ground zero of everything good about my childhood, to be immediately reminded it was not. It was over.

Sometimes I felt like the couch was haunting me. As though I had been plunged into a ghost story, and the couch was possessed by the parts of my mother that had departed her. Sometimes I simply looked up and could see a shadowy version of us sitting there: me age eight, leaning into my mother as she scratched my back and read to me about Edmund and Turkish delight, or Anne promising to be as good as a boy, or Bilbo riddling in the dark. When that happened, I would get out of bed and go and sit on the exact same cushion I had sat on then, as if by doing so I could slip the grip of time and find myself there again.

THELMA: Good driving.

LOUISE: Thanks.

20. We Are Not on the Run

When Jo and I planned our route from New York to San Francisco, I dragged the blue line on our shared Google map document up and up so that it would send us straight across South Dakota, scene of the last four books in the Little House series.

"We can take whatever route you want," I'd said to her when we first began mapping our trip, "but it has to go through De Smet, South Dakota."

We set out at noon on a Friday in mid-July. The air was so thick with heat it was like walking through car exhaust and left a film of dirt on my skin. I gazed at Jo's tiny yellow Fiat with skepticism before wedging myself into the small area that had been cleared on the passenger seat. This would be our home for the next ten days. Behind me Jo's enormous dog, Lady, half Labrador, half Rhodesian ridgeback, was equally wedged between boxes and suitcases. The car was so small I had visions of us being sucked up into the underbelly of passing transport trucks on the interstate, like dust into a vacuum cleaner. Or lifted off the road by the summer storms of the Midwest, like Dorothy's clapboard house. I glanced at Lady, neurotic from years of New York City dog life, thinking she made for an interesting Toto.

"She would have eaten Toto," said Jo. "She doesn't like small dogs."

It was a faulty analogy anyway. Neither of us was looking for a brain or a heart or a home. We were grown women, long in the habit of navigating our own lives. Nor were we, despite the inescapable *Thelma & Louise* references, on the run from anything. Jo was on her way to a new life with her fiancé, Nick, and I was driving her there.

"It's like I'm walking you down the aisle," I said as we pulled out of Pittsburgh on our second morning under bright blue skies, "except the aisle is an interstate."

Later that afternoon we stopped for lunch at what was advertised as the largest Amish restaurant in Indiana. Jo planned to expense as much of the trip as possible and viewed every roadside sign, no matter how obscure, as a potential story.

The parking lot was the size of a city block, and on the grassy pockets sprinkled throughout, horses connected to shiny black buggies were grazing under sweeping, graceful trees. Overhead white fluffy clouds appeared painted on. The restaurant was a series of big connected rooms; the signs advertised twenty-nine different types of homemade pies.

At the hostess station a young pretty blond woman with round cheeks, wearing a bonnet, showed us to our table. I couldn't tell if the outfit was part of a theme uniform, or her actual clothes. The restaurant was crowded with families. It was Saturday, I realized, having already slipped out of the calendar. As Jo and I walked past a series of similarly dressed servers, all of whom pointedly glanced our way, it became clear from their sideways glances that something was amiss. Perhaps it was my pants. I was, in addition to my trucker hat, wearing a pair of high-waisted white silk pajama pants I often wore in the summer. We'd been in the car almost nonstop since leaving Manhattan, and I wasn't yet fully out of city mode. I thought of my mother, who always hated when I wore pajamas as clothing.

"Here you are," said the hostess, as she laid a number of menus down on a circular corner table big enough to seat six. She smiled and glanced behind her.

"Oh, but we're only two." The former waitress in me worried about taking up unnecessary space when it was clearly crowded.

She looked back at us, as though unsure of how to respond.

"Oh." She paused and glanced around the room. "Well, that's okay." She gestured at the table. "Someone will be with you shortly." And then she quickly stepped away.

"Ahh," I said to Jo as I slid into my seat, finally understanding the stares had had nothing to do with my outfit. "I think they kept looking at us like that because they were waiting for our husbands."

"Maybe they think we're a couple."

"I suspect that's a lot less interesting than the fact we just arrived in the middle of Indiana alone."

On the way out, a slim young boy in suspenders leapt out from the servers' area.

"I love your pants so much," he said. I recognized the look, a mixture of relief and joy at seeing evidence that a lifestyle you have spent so much time wanting to believe exists, does.

"We're on our way from NYC to San Francisco." I rarely volunteered information about myself while traveling, but saying so felt like code for *It's possible*.

"I want to go to New York someday," he said in a tone that begged to be taken seriously. To me it felt like we'd barely left the city, had not yet reached the real part of our trip, but I suspected to him, the city felt, and probably was, about as far away and unlikely as the moon. I remembered that feeling so well.

"You won't be disappointed," I said. "It's the greatest."

By the time we made it back to the car, the blue sky had turned an alarming shade of black, and the trees were beginning to bend in ways that seemed unnatural. My phone buzzed. *Tornado watch in effect.*

"I can't remember, is it the watch that's bad or the warning?" Jo asked, letting Lady out of the car for a run.

"I have no idea," I said. "I never knew there was a difference." This was part of my whole theory about New York versus America: New Yorkers are experts in human nature; the rest of the country are experts in Mother Nature. "All I know is, if the transport trucks pull over, to follow their lead, and if the sky turns green and it sounds like a lawn mower is coming, you are supposed to get out of the car and lie in the ditch."

As we pulled onto the highway the sky became even blacker. It looked as if we were driving into nighttime; off to my right the clouds began to form into strange shapes. My visions of the car sailing away returned. In the back, Lady began to whine. My phone lost service. I'd hit bad weather before on the road a few times. Once in my twenties, I'd driven through the edges of a tornado in eastern Texas an hour outside of Dallas. But that time I'd been in a large, heavy truck, on tour with my friend and her band of Israeli musicians, who thought it all great fun. It had become fun in the retelling, as most things do, but I'd forgotten the scary reality.

"Does that look like a funnel to you?"

"Did we actually drive into Kansas?" asked Jo with a shaking laugh, gripping the wheel. "Are we going to Oz?"

"L. Frank Baum only ever went to Kansas once," I said, leaning forward to get a better look at the alarming cloud rising up to our left. "He lived in South Dakota, not that far from Laura Ingalls, and based his description of the tornado in *The Wizard of Oz* on the ones he experienced there."

The rain arrived as if it had been dumped out of an enormous bucket, landing on us in blinding sheets that flooded the road. The little yellow car swayed from side to side in the gusts, as if being punched. Every few minutes we slid over the rivers of water that had filled the dips in the road. The cars ahead of us became shadows, the transport trucks dim beasts, now with flashing emergency lights like beacons to keep us on the road. The rain turned to hail. A feeling of panicked helplessness came over me. Ferocious bolts of lightning tore through the sky, as if out of a film about the revenge of Greek gods. Each strike seemed to run straight through my veins and alight on my heart. I could feel Lady shaking in the seat behind me. But there was nothing to do but keep going.

I was accustomed to exerting an extraordinary amount of control over my person. I'd never had any health issues. I'd never yet been held captive by my own body, as my mother had, nor as women I knew had, by babies or the desire to have one. Even with all the various emergencies that had been thrown my way, some of my own making, the decision of how to deal with them had been mine. Mine alone. For better or worse. I'd forgotten what it was like to feel utterly helpless. To be helpless against forces and powers beyond my control. Or perhaps I'd never fully known.

The cloud was not a funnel. The storm was not a tornado, though later we learned one had briefly touched down fifteen miles away. It took us no more than twenty minutes to get to the other side of the blackness and reach blue sky again, though during that time each second seemed elastic. But for the next few days I obsessively checked weather apps and stared anxiously at far-off clusters of clouds for any sign of darkening skies.

We drove in silence for long stretches, sometimes listening to the audiobook of Harper Lee's *Go Set a Watchman*. ("This book is really an extended lesson on the importance of a good editor," I remarked to Jo.) Every few hours we turned on the radio to catch the news. As the days went by, it was increasingly filled with stories about Sandra Bland, a black woman who'd been pulled over for failing to properly signal a lane change while driving home to Illinois having just signed on for a new job in Prairie View, Texas. She'd been placed under arrest after legally refusing to leave her car. Three days later she was found dead, hanging in her cell. Jo and I had left on our trip four days after that.

Bland's story, and fate, seemed to run alongside us as the miles rolled away and the country emptied out, the sky above us growing larger each day. I couldn't shake the sense that hers was the alternative version of the trip we were on: women driving off to a new life but toward opposite fates. A tale of two Americas.

I had run up against that other America before. Many times, in fact. I knew it was here beside me right now, but that it was like a disease I'd been vaccinated against: by my skin color, by my upbringing, by the fact I'd been given the benefit of the doubt my entire life. It was possible for me to travel safely through the other America as a spectator, or worse, completely oblivious. On the same trip with the Israeli musicians that had sent us perilously close to the Texas tornado, our van was pulled over on I-10 in Arizona by a border patrol agent; we were seventy miles from the Mexican border. It was April 2003, and the Iraq War was barely a month old. I was driving; my musician friend, a blond New Yorker, was riding beside me in the passenger seat; the Israelis were scattered behind us in the van. I watched in the rearview mirror as the patrol agent marched up to my door, my heart beating in much the same manner it had when we'd skirted the storm. His uniform was crisp, his walk as assured as any walk has ever been. He gestured for me to roll down the window, and once I had, he leaned far into the van and took a long, silent look at all of us, lingering long on the musicians with their dreadlocks and shaggy beards and darker skin.

Then he leaned back and said in a voice accustomed to being obeyed: "I will need to see everyone's ID in the back."

"I'm Canadian," I said, worried that not stating it might get me in trouble if everyone else was being required to pull out their passports; I had only my driver's license. "That's fine," he said, his eyes not leaving the back of the van. He wasn't interested in me. My identity was not in question. More than a decade later, I could still remember how nonchalantly he shrugged, casually lifting his shoulders, as if I'd remarked on the sky being blue. I had a million safe narratives connected to me that didn't require a passport to prove or disprove.

I'd spent the months since my birthday trying to figure out how to live a life that had no blueprint, struggling to know where I was supposed to go without any stories to lead me. It had been terrifying, and then exhausting, and then delightful. It would probably be all those things again, and again after that. But it hadn't been deadly.

Later that night, after many more hours of driving, Jo and I pulled into a motel in Madison, Wisconsin, just off I-90, the interstate that would take us all the way through to Wyoming. Once we were settled, and Lady had planted herself in front of the hotel door so neither of us could leave without her, I looked up Sandra Bland. I wanted to flesh out this person who was a name on the radio and a shadowy presence on our trip. I wanted to know more about where she came from, how old she was. The details on Wikipedia were still scant, but it listed her date of birth, which held my gaze like a magnet: February 7. The same birthday as Laura Ingalls. Sandra Bland was twenty-eight when she died. Laura Ingalls, I knew without looking it up, had lived to be ninety and three days.

I'd spent my life marking two birthdays—October 21 (Carrie "Princess Leia" Fisher) and February 7—as extensions of my own. As if by doing so I could hope to lay claim to the same freedoms and potential of those women. As if it were the dates themselves that held the power. But the numbers themselves held only the power I gave them. They weren't divine protectants or guarantees, or, in the case of my age, the death sentence I'd imagined back on my birthday. Like so much, they meant only as much as the beliefs we invested into them, the stories we attached to them. I was, by a rather extraordinary combination of timing and privilege, getting to tell my own story; to make it up as I went and live it. Sandra Bland had died as a result of the stories the world told about her, as much as the absence of stories that *might* have been told, but that we refused to allow space for.

•

We arrived in De Smet while the sun was still setting. It felt like the sun had been setting since we'd crossed the state line an hour ago. The enormous sky had rippled through pinks and purples as though the sunset were a symphony and the colors musical notes, and now an orange globe was hovering just above the horizon, shooting out a fluorescent pink band that made the clouds look like they were on fire.

"Imagine being Nellie Oleson," I said to Jo. "You're mean to some random girl in fifth grade, then her family moves away and you never see her again. Fifty years later you show up in a book and are forever known to history as the mean girl."

"The meanest girl," said Jo.

"It's a dangerous thing to be friends with a writer," I said.

By the time we pulled into the town's outer limits the windshield was nearly black with the dead insects that had descended in clouds with the setting sun. Each summer, over a series of weekends, the townspeople put on a pageant based on one of the books. This year it was *By the Shores of Silver Lake*, my favorite of the series, which recounts the Ingalls family's arrival on the seemingly limitless plains of what was then Dakota territory. But we were too late. As we arrived at the pageant location in the middle of a field adjacent to where the Ingalls homestead was, we were greeted with the sight of a thousand headlights pulling out and disappearing in a string down the two-lane highway onto the now-dark prairie.

"It looks like the final scene from *Field of Dreams*," said Jo.

The first time I'd come to De Smet was at the tail end of the same 2003 road trip. Most of the band had flown home from Seattle after the last show; my musician friend and I, and her bearded Israeli drummer who had lost his license and lacked the ID necessary to board a plane, were driving the empty van back to New York. In Wall Drug, the delightfully kitschy drugstore on the other side of the state, whose hand-painted signs advertising free water relentlessly lined the roads for hundreds of miles as far as two states away, my friend and I had purchased a picture of Wilder in her sixties and taped it to the rearview mirror. Later that afternoon we turned off I-90 and drove north to catch the state route that would take us to De Smet. From the depths of the van, the drummer, unsure why he was being dragged across the side roads of a desolate prairie state, removed his huge headphones and said: "Why are you following this old woman?"

I felt as if I'd been trying to answer that question ever since.

In the distance, I could make out the four cottonwood trees Pa had planted for his daughters the day they moved into their new home. Just as in Iceland, I was struck by a desire to call my mother and tell her where I was. That she had never gone herself to visit Laura Ingalls, who died the year she turned ten, was something I'd never been able to wrap my head around as a child.

"I can't believe all these people!" I said. "The last time I was here the woman who ran the little gift shop looked at me like I was insane." I paused, taking in the extraordinary scene. Laura had once told Rose that she wanted to write for "prestige rather than money." I wondered what she would make of this.

"What other woman do people drive across the country to visit?" I said to Jo. "Who inspires this level of devotion?"

Jo didn't miss a beat. "Carrie Bradshaw."

Two women famous for writing about their lives—one fictional, one not. It was amusing to consider and also a little sad—slim pickings. Here, too, was the answer to my question: the reason we were out here following Laura was that even after I reached adulthood I struggled to find anyone who could replace her. Hers was the only story of women on the road in America I could find that ended well.

I had missed the *Sex and the City* craze. I arrived in New York the year before it aired and didn't own a television until years later (I was never home long enough in those years to watch anything anyway). But I remembered clearly the scorn heaped on women who took Carrie Bradshaw as a role model, as if there were so many other single women over thirty to choose from.

In the Little House books, the only single, independent adult woman to make an extended appearance is Laura's sister-in-law Eliza Jane Wilder, who is portrayed as an object of great contempt. Some of the most dramatic scenes in the series involve showdowns between teenage Laura and her then-teacher in their tiny schoolhouse in South Dakota. These exchanges clearly stuck with Laura who, decades later (with the help of her daughter, Rose, who collaborated on the writing with her mother), made sure to unforgivingly cast Eliza as the adult Nellie Oleson, the villain to Laura's hero. Eliza Jane is a pioneer harpy; the bossy and overbearing older sister; an angry and lonely spinster who bullies her students, hates Laura, and in the end is felled by the heroic all-male school board.

It's entirely possible Eliza Jane Wilder *was* this terrible, but what was left out of the books, books that relentlessly celebrated

Laura's fight for and love of independence, was the fact that unmarried Eliza Jane, aged thirty-one, had come out West and taken her own claim, which she tended on her own while also teaching school. She was one of thousands of single women, largely unrecognized by history (and also by Laura, for that matter), who took advantage of the Homestead Act of 1863, which allowed women to claim land the same as men. Though, as was almost always the case, it was a claim made possible by the exploitation and suffering of yet another group; the same forward-thinking laws pertaining to women and power that briefly flourished in the West during the nineteenth-century land rush were directly aimed at further unsettling the native population.

Driving across the open land that was about to get even more open, I was struck yet again by who had actually built the country and who had received the credit and how both those things, including the fact that we used the word *build* in this context, were the direct result of who got to tell the stories and how they were told.

21. The Equality State

The following afternoon, we crossed into Wyoming. FOREVER WEST, said the sign.

We'd driven across the Buffalo Gap Grasslands the day before, spent the night in Wall. That morning we'd driven through the Badlands National Park and visited Mount Rushmore and the Crazy Horse Memorial, where a woman had asked me if her curly-haired daughter could touch my hair "so she can understand how cool it is."

The emptiness in Wyoming felt like another language. There were no houses. No hint of them, even. Every five or ten minutes we'd pass a pickup truck coming in the opposite direction, but that was the only evidence we were not alone. Both our phones had lost their signals shortly after we'd crossed the state line. It was a different sort of emptiness than South Dakota: uncivilized emptiness. If something happened to us we'd have to drive hours to reach a hospital or airport. It was as if the vastness of the ocean had rippled into land, undulating away in greens and golds as far as the eye could see. We were now in a place of no options. Even if we wanted to pull over and drop this whole thing, for whatever reason, we couldn't. It felt practically exotic. How many places was that even possible, after all?

We drove on in silence. Every ten minutes or so one of us would say, "It's just so empty," or "It looks like the moon." Lyrics from Bruce Springsteen's "Nebraska" flitted through my head: *Through to the badlands of Wyoming.* I'd been here once before, in 2008, when I'd driven with two fellow journalists from the Democratic National Convention in Denver to the Republican one in Saint Paul. The news about Sarah Palin had been announced shortly after we'd crossed the state line. I used the fact that Wyoming was both the first state to grant women the vote and to elect a female governor, Nellie Tayloe Ross in 1925, as the lede on a story I later filed.

A half hour later the empty land gave way to rows and rows of abandoned trailer parks. I picked up my phone intending to search "Wyoming and meth," reminded of the cautionary posters featuring people with rotting teeth that I'd seen at gas stations in Arizona, but I still had no signal.

Mountains appeared on the horizon. Mountains or a storm cloud, I wasn't sure. No, definitely mountains *and* possibly a storm cloud. A half hour later we pulled off the interstate into a place called Buffalo. It was quiet and the streets were empty. The large houses, on spacious yards with gracious sweeping trees, had lights on inside. The football stadium attached to the high school announced a rodeo for Saturday. I got that sense you can sometimes get passing through small towns in America, that time had collapsed. As if instead of across the country, we had driven back five or six decades. All it took was a trip into a gas station and a kid behind the counter playing games on his iPhone to dispel this, but from inside the car it was easy to get swept up in the nostalgia. As we drove through the center of town, my phone buzzed. I had a signal again.

"Look up the place we're going, before you lose it," said Jo.

I furiously typed it in. Jo had booked us into a dude ranch for the night, and it was located ahead of us somewhere in the Bighorn Mountains. Behind me Lady growled. I looked up. "Watch out!"

Ahead of us on the road three deer were calmly crossing. Bolts of lightning were illuminating the sky behind the mountains we were headed into.

"It's a half-hour drive from here. You're sure they know we're coming?" I said to Jo, thinking in my head that the little motel we'd just driven past didn't look half bad.

"I guess we'll find out." This mantra had attached itself to our trip like a slogan since our first day on the road, when we'd plunged into a series of lengthy Pennsylvania tunnels on I-76 with the gas gauge on empty. Jo accelerated as the road began to climb. I looked back down at my phone, hoping that if I zoomed in I'd see there was a road connecting the one we were on with the red pin that marked where we were headed, but it had lost the signal again.

Up we went into the Bighorns, the sky darkening, the flashes of lightning growing brighter, the road sharply curving as we zigzagged higher and higher. Even though I couldn't get a signal, the GPS on my phone was still working, and I could see our glowing blue dot moving along the map I had open, but it showed no road between us and the location of the ranch in the middle of a great green expanse. Finally, in the dying light, we saw a hand-painted sign directing us to take the next turn. Jo pulled off. We rolled over metal bars I would later learn were guards to keep the cattle from wandering off the property, and the paved road promptly turned to gravel. In the back seat, Lady was rigid and her hackles up. The road, if that's what you could call it, narrowed and twisted through tall pine trees that blocked out the sky. It started to rain. On and on we wound, the ground beneath us becoming rockier as we went. The car jolted back and forth as though we were at sea and made alarming scraping noises when the rocks jutted up and caught its belly. Suddenly, the trees parted and a huge shadow rose up ahead of us. I gasped and Jo slammed on the brakes. Lady whined. I leaned forward; we had come face-to-face with an enormous rock face protruding out in the road like a sentinel. We crept around it. The thunder sounded like someone was beating an enormous drum in the distance. On we went. Back out into the open, the lines of the hills were outlined in the lightning flashes. As the road climbed on and on, with no sign of human life, I did begin to wonder whether we'd be spending the night in the car. But finally, after winding up a steep hillside and then twisting back down an even rougher gravel road that took us back into the woods, we spotted lights in the distance. Ten minutes later we drove through a gate, past a paddock of horses, and into a cluster of what appeared to be small houses. From the largest one, closest to us, emanated the muted sounds of music, and I could make out moving figures through the glow of the windows. We stopped. It was pouring out.

Before we'd made up our minds what to do, someone pounded on the window and we both jumped. Lady launched into a series of deep growls. Jo rolled down the window and a thin, angular, grinning cowboy wearing an enormous hat stuck his head in. "You guys the writers?"

"Yes!"

"Welcome! Sit tight, I'll get someone to show you where to go. Or you can just come straight into the saloon; that's where everyone is." He disappeared back into the dark.

The saloon.

Five minutes later a pretty young woman with long, thick hair, who looked to be about twenty, ran out and directed us up a steep driveway to a parking spot and then down some steps into an empty log cabin. Inside we flicked on the lights and were immediately greeted by the head of an enormous steer mounted over a stone fireplace, the first of what would become an endless, and increasingly normal, stream of taxidermy. Everything was made out of logs, it seemed. I felt as if I'd walked into the cover of one of my Little House books.

•

I woke first. The window of my room backed directly into a hillside, but from the sliver of sky I could see, I knew the weather had passed and it was early dawn. I threw back the wool blanket covered in a 1950s cowboy print and walked out into the living room.

I gasped.

Outside the huge bay windows was a scene that did not seem like it could possibly be real. We were in a lush green valley. A stream separated the group of cabins from a pasture that gently rippled up and away into soaring green foothills, out of which fanned a curving rock face. Behind it, the rising sun was turning the sky mauve. I stepped out onto the porch. It was over ninety degrees in New York; here the air was so fresh and cool I needed a sweater. I heard a low rumble and turned to look. I gasped again; to my left, galloping down the pasture toward camp, were a hundred or so horses being urged on by riders in leather chaps and cowboy hats. I could hear one of the riders whooping. It was barely past 6:00 a.m.

I was at a dude ranch, which meant nothing to me beyond the fact that the entire scene left me speechless. Over breakfast I would learn that dude ranches had been popularized in the western states following the Second World War, catering to wealthy East Coasters looking for an "authentic" Western experience, but without any of the hardship. *Dude* was originally slang for Easterners who knew nothing, like the term *city slicker*, but more insulting. These days they were called guest ranches. I'd never heard of either. I had no idea they even existed. But apparently, plenty of other people did, because I learned the place we were at normally sold out the entire season six months in advance. Only because there had been a last-minute cancellation had they been able to slide us in for an overnight.

"Oh my God," said Jo behind me, walking into the living room in her pajamas.

Our plan, established only a few hours ago, when we'd finally climbed into bed at midnight after hot showers, had been to spend the morning here and leave in the early afternoon. We were scheduled to be somewhere in Yellowstone by supper, a fact that I'd been grateful for as we'd careened through the stormy darkness. But taking in the view we immediately began to reconsider. We'd see how the morning went.

An hour after breakfast, I put on a spare set of cowboy boots and climbed up on a horse named Cisco.

"Have you ridden before?" asked Garrett, the lead wrangler. Long and lean, with high cheekbones and a swagger, he appeared to have been born in his cowboy boots, summoned out of a historical fiction about the West one might find in an airport paperback stand. I was reminded of Tallulah Bankhead. "I came to town to fuck that divine Gary Cooper," she'd once said.

"Does riding my bike through New York City count?" I asked, only sort of joking.

"No."

Okay then. "Well, not in a really long time."

He put me on a test ride in the corral to see how I handled a horse. "Just move your hips in the saddle like you're making love," he said, before giving me the go-ahead.

Afterward I opted to do a "walking" ride, thinking perhaps in this case it was best to start slowly. All around me were young people moving about in cowboy hats and boots and Levi's jeans, and they really meant it. It was how much they meant it that made it all so surreal. Where were these young people from? They seemed so much a part of the landscape it was like they'd sprung up from the ground here, honest-to-goodness cowboys and -girls. Technically they were called wranglers, and they led the rides and took care of the horses. But I would learn that later. For now, I simply sat on my horse trying to get a better view of the wrangler off to my left who looked older than the others and had the kind of red handlebar mustache I thought existed only in old Warner Bros. cartoons.

While Jo went for a lope—what they called cantering here— I went for a walk with a wrangler named Ivy. I didn't have a cowboy hat so I wore my HONEY trucker hat and a long-sleeved silk pajama shirt, which was the only thing I had with me that would cover my arms but not be too hot. The ranch was at a seven-thousand-foot elevation, hot when the sun was out, chilly when it was not.

Ivy was in her early twenties, with long curly blond hair that fell down her back in a ponytail and a striking face it had been impossible to miss, even amid all the other strangeness of the morning. She led us directly up the side of a hill so thick with trees they kept rubbing up against the yoga leggings I was wearing, and so steep I practically had to lie on Cisco's neck so I wouldn't slide off the back of him.

Ivy, it turned out, was an Ivy League grad from Mississippi ("The bad state," she said). She wanted to be a writer, or she wanted to go to grad school, or she wanted to stay in Wyoming and ride horses. By the time we reached the top of the hill and came out of the trees, I'd launched into my well-rehearsed *so you are in your twenties* talk that boiled down to some version of "go out and have fun." Then I looked around. We were on top of the world. In every direction the land undulated away in great green and gold rolling hills, spotted by shadows of passing clouds.

"Incredible, isn't it?" said Ivy, looking at my face. "I never get tired of it."

I paused, struggling to put it into words. "It feels like the first time I came up from the subway in New York, the exact same intensity for the exact opposite reason."

"I'm dying to go to New York," said Ivy.

"I don't know," I said, for the first time in my life unsure of whether New York was the best decision a person could ever possibly make. "This is extraordinary."

•

"Are you sure we have to leave?" I asked Jo when I spotted her at lunch.

"Let's find out."

We did not. The cabin, it turned out, was empty until Saturday. It was Wednesday noon. We needed to be in San Francisco by Sunday in order for me to catch my flight back the next morning. I pulled out my phone. The camp had hacked up a wireless system so that it was possible to get online if you were standing within five feet of the dining hall.

"It's a nineteen-hour drive from here to San Francisco. If we leave Friday morning and skip the Tetons we can make it by Saturday night."

We stared at each other, eyebrows raised.

"I mean, really, who needs the Tetons anyway?" I finally said, grinning.

•

The next morning when the sun rose, I was twenty miles away from the ranch, sitting in a van with three bearded fishermen who were all singing along to Taylor Swift at the top of their lungs. We were going fly-fishing.

"You're not allowed to write about where we're going," drawled Dustin, the twenty-eight-year-old head fishing guide from Georgia whom I'd been directed to the previous evening during the weekly talent show.

"Is it a secret?"

"Yes."

I'd signed up to go fly-fishing, simply because I could. Because there'd been space, and because at what other point in my life was I going to get a chance to fly-fish? Also, Dustin was tall and handsome, with a scraggly beard; he had a deep voice with a strong Georgia accent I thought it would be nice to spend the day with. So far, though, he hadn't smiled once.

An hour outside of camp, we pulled into a gas station for coffee. "This is the last bathroom until the ride home," Dustin said. Inside, the walls were blanketed with taxidermy. Over the deli where they made egg sandwiches was the head of an enormous buck, with antlers that were at least six feet long. In another corner was a seven-foot grizzly bear standing on his hind legs. I poured myself a hot chocolate from the machine; it was only 8:00 a.m. and I was still freezing.

An hour later, the landscape had turned from the gently rolling grasses to jagged red cliffs. I felt as if I'd gotten on a rocket ship or walked through a wardrobe door. I opened the window, letting the air mingle with Taylor Swift's voice, and leaned back. *I feel good*, I thought. *I don't want to be anywhere else.* It was a strange sensation and made me realize how not good I'd felt for so long. I'd had hints of it here and there on the road, and in the past few months, but now it settled on me, or I settled in it. Like a bathtub I could climb into and lie down in.

The road got bumpier and narrower, until we had to slow to a crawl to ease our way into the deep potholes and back out again. Distance is as relative in Wyoming as it is in New York; our destination was just around the next bend, forty-five minutes away (in New York, the same would be true except the next bend would be three blocks and not thirty miles). Finally, we stopped. We were parked on the lip of a canyon. Five hundred feet below roared the river we'd be fishing in. For the next half hour, I gave my full attention to hiking down the rocky path without falling on my face, only stopping to give my burning thighs a break and gaze at the jagged canyon walls rising up above us.

We stopped on a slice of rocky beach at the bottom just long enough to change into water boots and gather up the fishing rods.

"Let's go," said Dustin, nodding his head in the direction of the river, which wound away from us. "You and I are fishing up this way."

"How far up that way?"

"A mile or so."

I looked for a path along the water but there was none. Dustin plunged into the river, against the current, I quickly discovered. He seemed deeply uninterested in whether or not I could keep up. For the next half hour I struggled against the water, over the slippery rocks as the water rushed by, sometimes as high as my waist. Around me small bluebirds bounced on the rocks as though connected to springs and then leapt off, zooming along the water like fighter jets. Finally I caught up to Dustin, who'd stopped at a curve in the river where a ten-foot waterfall emptied into a deep pocket of water.

"What would happen if someone got hurt down here?" I asked, staring up at the rock face towering above us. I'd lost my footing a number of times already, once on a sharp rock that I'd just missed landing on with my face. While pulling myself up, images of my own head cracked open and bleeding into the water went through my mind.

"Don't," said Dustin sternly.

"But why?" So far, this trip had been so untethered from reality, I'd not given much thought to, well, reality. But as I looked around, it seemed clear that should something bad happen here, we'd be pretty fucked.

"Well," said Dustin, his drawl now dripping contempt, "for one, we'd have to hike back to where our bags are. Then we'd have to use the satellite phone to call the forest service, then they'd have to get a helicopter, and then a few hours after that they'd airlift you out of here and send you a bill for a hundred thousand dollars."

In my purse back in our cabin at the ranch were eye drops that had cost me one hundred fifty dollars, because I did not have prescription coverage. The woman behind the counter who sold them to me had insisted on calling the insurance company herself to make sure I was correct, and she couldn't get them for me for cheaper. Still, there was something thrilling about the seriousness of this decision to be here. There were real-life ramifications to my every step.

It turned out I had very little interest in, or talent for, fishing. After a half hour of trying to teach me to cast a line and yelling one-word instructions with increasing frustration, Dustin took the rod back and I lay down on a smooth rock and watched him make graceful arcs as though his arm and the line were one, yanking huge fish out of the water and then releasing them. Eventually he lay down beside me. Overhead the clouds sailed gently by; below, the river streamed past in a continual series of whooshes and gurgles.

"I feel like I'm in one of those meditation, noise-canceling apps," I said.

"I was told I should try meditation."

"How come?"

That was all it took. Within minutes he unloosed his story, with a speed and defensiveness that suggested he'd spent a lot of time hoping for someone to show an interest and unhook whatever door was holding it back for him. He had a troubling relationship with his father. He lived with his mother, who was on disability. He was the first in his family to go to college and was there on a full engineering scholarship.

He told me all this without looking once in my direction.

"That's a lot," I said.

"I guess. I don't sleep much. I mean I have problems sleeping."

I'd had a yoga teacher once who'd advised us to envision ourselves lying in an open field and picture our thoughts as the clouds passing by overhead, separate from us and freely floating away. I told Dustin to do the same, except there was no need to visualize anything. It was all around us. We lay there for ten minutes in silence. *If our roles and ages were reversed, I'd probably be falling in love with him right now*, I thought. Ten years ago, I would have done acrobatics around him. Tied myself into a million knots over that silent non-smile, and stayed tangled for far too long. Looking at him now and thinking how much sway he might have held over me if the timing had been different felt like looking at an old picture of myself in an outfit I'd believed was the height of fashion when I'd put it on, but which now mostly just amusingly revealed my insecurities.

•

I tried hard to stay awake on the ride back to the ranch, not wanting to miss any part of the drive. The boys had cranked up Taylor Swift again. She was their dream girl, two of them told me. I dozed off anyway, despite the van plunging this way and that into deep pockets in the road. It was my vibrating phone that woke me. Like an air bubble in water, we'd caught a pocket of signal. It was my friend Rebecca, who ran a website about death and grief, asking me if I wanted to contribute something about my mother. We'd talked about the possibility before I left.

I don't, I wrote, even though thanks to all my years as a free-lancer, I almost never turned down a writing assignment. *I'm feeling so happy right now, I want to stay in this space for as long as I can.*

I looked out the window. It was true. I was happy. Not excited, not exhilarated—but deeply satisfied. It was as though the immensity of the empty space around me had absorbed everything else, my sadness, and anxiety, and emotional exhaustion, and left me in only this present moment, driving back to the ranch. I whispered it out loud to myself. A declaration. *I am happy.*

My phone buzzed again. I looked down expecting it to be Rebecca. It was 646.

Of course. *Of course.* I hadn't heard from him in months, hadn't thought about him in nearly as long, but who else in this moment of contentment could it be?

Hello! Sending you greetings and I hope everything is going great.

I looked at the screen for a while. And felt . . . nothing actually. He didn't belong here. I felt as though I had crossed over into someplace else and he was back on the edge of the cliff on the other side shouting. That was how I knew it was completely over. Whatever empty place I'd once leaned on him to fill up for me was full now. There was no space for him. All there was to do was wave politely and turn.

I'm actually the best I've been in a long while.

I hit send just as I lost the signal again. He was gone. It would be another two days before it occurred to me to check my messages again. By that time, Jo and I were racing through Nevada. We left the ranch Friday afternoon, as late as we possibly could. In our few days there, it had become a camp-wide game to map out the shortest route we could take to San Francisco, and then estimate how far we could push our departure.

It meant driving nineteen hours with only a few hours' break at a motel on the Wyoming state line. At a sprawling Flying J gas station outside of Reno, the kind that has showers for the truck drivers and a dark, cavernous casino, I picked a Corona out of the fridge to take with us with the intention of drinking it while I drove. We'd been in the car so long, I'd stopped thinking of it as a vehicle; it was simply where we lived. It took me a full minute to agree with Jo that I should put it back.

We pulled into San Francisco at dinnertime on Sunday, and the next morning I boarded a plane back to New York. I spent much of the flight gazing out the window, marking parts of the land below that we'd just spent two weeks driving across. I'd left Jo in her new life, and now I was returning to mine. It was August 1; the first draft of the puberty book I was cowriting was due in mid-September. All I had ahead of me was a month of writing.

The plane landed in the August heat. The city had that wonderful pressed-in, intense stillness that it gets only in August. Like a slow-motion explosion. Maddy had stacked up my mail and turned on the AC so the apartment wasn't a furnace when I walked in. A note on the fridge said there was a chocolate Popsicle waiting for me in the freezer. I lay down on my bed and looked up through the skylight. It was perfect.

I didn't want to be here.

I could still feel Wyoming as though it were both a mirage and a net I couldn't untangle myself from. I texted Jo.

I want to go back to Wyoming.

You should.

I texted Dustin.

I want to come back.

You should!

I could feel all the machinery in my head start to move the way it sometimes did when a fleeting idea, seemingly ridiculous, took hold. I lay still as my mind mapped out a way back. The owners of the ranch had mentioned they were eager for social media, some sort of internet presence, but they didn't know how to do it. It was the sort of job that in New York media circles was now being assigned to interns; I didn't really consider it a job. Perhaps I could do it for them in exchange for room and board. I could sleep in a bunk bed in the staff quarters, write the book in the morning, and spend the rest of the day creating this for them.

It sounded ridiculous even to me. I'd just landed. I couldn't just up and go back to Wyoming for the month in an entirely self-created position. It was bananas. Laughable. I thought about the open mesa top, the horses running in from the hills in the morning, the intense brightness of the Milky Way at night, the cowboys and their unironic hats. There was nothing keeping me in New York except my own idea that somehow I was expected to stay put. No one needed me. *Why not find out how ridiculous?* I thought. *All they can do is say no.*

I sent the owner an email the next morning laying out my plan. Took a breath, and hit send. Twelve hours later he wrote back asking me to let him know what time my plane landed so he could arrange for someone to pick me up.

22. "Balls," Said the Queen

The book I associate most closely with my mother is *The Lion, the Witch and the Wardrobe.* Despite her own inability to read without knowing the end of the story, she was adamant about sending me to bed at the end of each chapter. I think of this often when I read to my niece and nephew, and naturally find it completely understandable; she was tired. She wanted a few hours kids free. But as a child, it felt like a cruel rule written in stone. Lucy gets into Narnia, reaches the lamppost, and spots a very strange person carrying an umbrella, wearing a red scarf. He sees Lucy, gives a start, and the chapter ends. When I think of my mother and me on the white couch, Pauline Baynes's illustration of Tumnus the Faun on the last page of that chapter often comes to mind; it seemed to signify all the adventures life held in store, but that for the moment were just out of reach.

We read that book so many times that many years later I could nearly recite the opening chapter by heart. When I arrived back at the ranch a line from those pages, which Peter utters the first night they are in the Professor's house, having been sent away from London during the war because of the air raids, repeated itself in my mind: *We've fallen on our feet and no mistake.*

I had been given my own cabin. I'd proposed, and been expecting, to be shuffled into a bunk bed in the corner of the staff quarters, which I'd heard about but never seen. Instead, I had my own little house, huge by New York standards: a large living room, a stone fireplace, my own washer and dryer. As I sat on the couch, staring out the window at the same view that had taken my breath away just two weeks earlier, I remained stunned, not just that I'd pulled this off, but that I'd thought to do so in the first place. I'd followed my gut, because I could, and had wrenched myself out of my life into a place with no internet, no cacophony of voices, no lives that I recognized.

At first, no one knew what to do with me. I was neither guest nor employee. I was the woman alone. I could feel the side-eyes as people tried to sort out exactly where I belonged.

The staff fascinated me. Almost immediately I began attending their breakfast, served at 7:00 a.m., a half hour earlier than the guests, so that I could eat with them. Nearly everyone was under thirty, many of them still in college. There was a hierarchy that revealed itself most clearly at breakfast. The wranglers, ten of them, five women and five men, ate together at the center table. When they rolled in in their worn jeans and leather chaps, required plaid shirts, and cowboy boots, all I could think of was the Jets and the Sharks in *West Side Story*. Each morning they'd remove their cowboy hats and place them on the stone mantel before taking their seats or going to the buffet and dishing out large bowls of fruit for themselves.

At the tables on either side sat the housekeeping staff, girls from Kansas and Ohio, and on the other side, the office and childcare staff. I sat here with Laura, the pretty young woman with the thick hair who'd met Jo and me in the rain when we first arrived, and some of the kids' staff. Girls in their early twenties, just on the brink. I remembered myself at that age, so determined to hurl myself into the deep end of life. These girls seemed calmer, more assured and in control of where they were going. They had come up with the internet; the world was not a great unknown, but something that could be mastered and directed. No doubt some of their mothers were the same age as me, or close; many of them had grown up in small towns, with conservative religious upbringings. They'd been homeschooled up until college, and many of their friends were already married. Some expecting children. But they took me on as an older sister, and after the initial settling-in period, I could see their eyes light up when I spoke about my life.

By day two, I'd forgotten that cowboy boots could even be considered amusing. My leggings and the trucker hat I still donned when I went out walking in the hills now struck me as ridiculous, a sartorial punch line. But the camp seemed to take my appearance in stride, part and parcel with my arrival during a thunderstorm and reappearance ten days later.

By day three a routine began to take shape. I rose at 5:45 a.m., slipping out from under the many blankets I had piled on my bed, into the brisk August mountain air. I pulled on my thick winter leggings, my hiking boots, my wool sweater, and a down-filled vest, and stepped out into the predawn dark to watch the "morning jingle" come in. There were 190 horses in camp; each evening half of them, the ones being used by the guests, would be released into the hills for the night, thundering along the path from the barn to the pasture, driven by a gang of whooping wranglers and then fanning out over the hills like a flock of birds before reassembling into their various groups to graze. In the morning three wranglers would ride into the hills and round them up. This was called the "jingle," in reference to the bells that were attached to lead mares on the open range to alert riders to where they were; horses are pack animals and never stray far from one another.

As I walked down through the still-dark cabins and up the road, past the barn, to the fence that lined the driveway, I could hear the whoops of the wranglers in the hills. I reached the gate that separated the camp from the road to the barn so the horses couldn't wander in. One of the rules of the mountains was to "always, always leave a gate the way you found it." I was nervous I'd somehow not close it properly so I scrambled over, leaving handprints in the frost that had gathered on the wood. I scurried faster up the road. I needed to be on the other side of the fence before the horses came down, or else I risked getting hurt, or hurting them, or worse: throwing a wrench into the wranglers' long day. At the bottom of the driveway, just up the road past the barn, was the chapel. I climbed up the steep hillside toward it, and then perched atop the fence that surrounded it. I was just in time. A minute later I could hear a rush, like the wings of many birds taking flight, then it deepened and became a rumble, and then like water bursting through a canyon the horses came galloping down the road, all one hundred of them, in a sea of browns and grays and whites. A few attempted to dart away, running up the road to come alongside where I was alighted on the fence, before catching a glimpse of me and shooting straight back down with rolling eyes.

This was not like my job at the racetrack as a teenager, where the horses had been carefully monitored from stall to track and back again. This was primal. It spoke to some long-forgotten instinct I didn't know I possessed.

After they had passed and been put back in the corral for breakfast, I hiked up the steep slope behind the paddock—named the ski slope thanks to its nearly vertical angle—slipped once again through the gate at the top, and set off through the band of aspens that ringed the top of the valley. A black bear had been spotted in camp with her cub. There were no grizzly bears on this side of the state, nor, sadly, any wolves. But as I marched through the towering aspens I kept my eye out for any movements. There was no need; I was too loud and clumsy to come upon anyone, much less a wild animal, without them knowing. Still, when a young buck, his rack still new, burst out ahead of me on the path and then bounced away like an enormous rabbit, my heart nearly exploded.

By the time I reached the top, I was huffing and puffing with exertion, all my extra layers tied around my waist. I was on the mesa. The very top of the flaxen hills that surrounded the camp and undulated as far as the eye could see toward the Bighorn Mountain Range. I strode across it as the sun peeked over the lip to the east, turning the mesa gold and the mountains purple and casting my shadow in front of me until it was four times longer than my actual height. I felt like Peter Pan, that any minute it would detach and strike out on its own. And the silence! I was mesmerized by it, as if it were a color outside of the spectrum. I walked over to the edge. From a distance, the mesa looked like it reached all the way to the sky like a golden ocean, but when I got to the edge I could see it dropped down in a sweeping slope until far away, it reached the trees below. I was overwhelmed by a sense of wholeness. Nothing existed here but me. My fears, anxieties, regrets had left me.

As the sun rose higher, the silence was broken by what sounded like drunken partiers, laughing and yipping. *Some wranglers must still be out*, I thought, annoyed that they were ruining my morning quiet. When I went down to breakfast I asked Ivy about it.

She frowned. "Really?"

I explained the laughing and the yipping I'd heard.

"Are you sure it wasn't coyotes?" She pronounced it *kay-yotes*. I stared. "Seriously?"

She laughed. "Probably. They're everywhere."

"Ivy, I'm from New York. The only thing we have everywhere are rats."

The next morning, I listened more closely. But this time along with the yips I could now hear howls. It was coyotes! Eventually I began to think of them as my morning companions, singing up the sun and giving voice to these new wild mornings.

In the evenings, before bed I walked down to say good night to the horses that had not been turned out for the night. In New York, I was only ever aware of the moon as an accessory to the skyline, something that added to my enjoyment of the Brooklyn Bridge. Here I quickly became attuned to it as if it were a traffic light. The road out of the camp, the same one I walked in the morning, would first take me by the saloon, which most nights was booming with either music or guests and staff. The light spilled out the windows onto the roadway in golden squares. By the time I crossed over the stream that ran through camp and reached the gate, the noise of the saloon had almost entirely died off; all I could hear was the noise of the water running by. A little beyond the gate, the road dipped down, and I would pass through a pocket of cool air. On the nights when there was a moon, I was able to make out the roadway clearly in the dark— it glowed in the moonshine as if it were lit from underneath. Even when there was no moon, the light from the stars on clear nights provided enough glow for me to see where I was going. But if there was no moon and it was cloudy, I'd have to do the walk in the dark. Not dark, pitch-black.

The first time I did it I felt like I was in a closet with the door shut. I literally couldn't see my hand before my face. I had to force myself to keep walking, one foot in front of the other, and push thoughts of bears and coyotes out of my head. I was too loud, the camp was too near, the horses would alert me if there was something to be concerned about. I navigated my way by the sound of the gravel under my feet, by the cool pocket of air I blindly walked through, keeping my ears alert for the comforting sound of the horses, and then the warm smell of ammonia and hay. The dark was thrilling. It pushed everything else out of my head until my whole life was contained in this one stretch of gravel roadway.

After a while, I began to know the horses and was able to differentiate them by their appearance and personalities. Horses galloping through the wilderness were cosmic poetry. Horses grouped together in a paddock were a high school soap opera. There were cliques and bullies, weaklings, losers, and of course the popular crowd. Each night, I watched which ones grouped together and who pushed whom out of the way or nipped or sometimes even kicked (there were a few mustangs in the bunch), and who always came first when I held handfuls of hay out for them to eat.

"They are so bitchy!" I marveled to Ivy one evening over cold beers. "It's like a lunchtime cafeteria filled with preteen girls."

At the end of my first week J.D. showed up. J.D. was Dustin's friend whom he'd been talking about so much that week, and in such adoring terms, I was annoyed by the idea of him before he even arrived.

J.D. arrived one afternoon on a slim little motorbike he'd ridden all the way from Georgia. "Straight through," he drawled in an accent even thicker than Dustin's. "I stopped once for a four-hour shut-eye under a bridge." He told me he'd kept awake by taking swigs from a bottle of Jack Daniel's he kept wedged in the pocket of his leather jacket. He was twenty-eight, and so handsome that when I first bumped into him and Dustin coming around the corner of the kitchen, I'd nearly remarked on it out loud. Thick blond hair that appeared to have arrived directly from a seventies cop show, muscled body, and that accent.

I'd continued to go out on Tinder dates here and there since my sixty-year-old stunt guy fiasco. There was no end of messages in my account. But nothing held my attention for too long. "You have to make an effort," said my friend Marianne. "Dating is work." *But why?* I thought. *An effort for what?* I still wanted romance, sure. Of course I did. And sex. But "you have to work at it," suggested dating was the equivalent of paying my dues, a necessary evil on the way to a larger goal. I had no larger goal. And it made the whole thing much easier. *Maybe this could be something, he looks good on paper, I'll keep trying* became *This was not very interesting, see you later.* Men had become something to enjoy, not a means to an end.

I didn't see J.D. again until the next day I tagged along on another fishing trip, this time to a place called Crazy Woman Canyon, so named because according to legend the woman (depending on whom you spoke to, she was either white or Native American) who once lived here had been driven mad after her husband and children were killed by either (again, depending) Native Americans or white men. I was the only woman in a group of middle-aged, married male guests. As everyone fanned out, J.D. stuck close by asking me questions about what I was doing here, what sort of writer I was. What I wrote. I kept shifting the conversation just so I could hear his voice. After dinner, he came up to me at the saloon and bought me a shot of tequila. I knew it was the beverage of choice with the camp staff, but I'd stayed clear so far. The last time I'd drunk tequila I'd been twenty-four years old, and the hangover had been three days long.

It was square dancing night, and all the girl wranglers had put on their short dresses, were out on the floor doing swings and flips that made me dizzy. Out of their cowboy hats and jeans, they looked as though they could be competing in a Miss America contest.

By our second shot, J.D. was telling me about his childhood with a difficult single mother, describing how she would force him to exchange punches with her so he could learn to toughen up. He responded to my look of horror with a shrug: "The world is not a nice place. She wanted me to be able to deal." He told me about his time in the marines and the ex-girlfriend he had back home. "Does she know she's your ex?" I asked. He grinned and shrugged. Then he switched to politics and writers. He loved Vonnegut.

"Billy Pilgrim has come unstuck in time," I said.

He nodded, his eyes sparkling with recognition. And then he stopped and looked at me.

"How come you don't have a boyfriend?"

In the last few days a lot of the wranglers had been slowly working their way toward me, tossing out funny questions: "Is that dress you're wearing called a muumuu?" "In New York, it's called a caftan." "Who's that person on your t-shirt?" "Debbie Harry." But no one had yet been so direct.

I shrugged, a shred of the old feeling that I should somehow feel bad about myself flickered by and then promptly disappeared. "I just don't." I smiled. "Is there something wrong with that?"

"No," he said, shaking his head. "Not at all. It's just, you're so gorgeous, and the best conversationalist I've ever met."

If he'd simply said, "You're gorgeous," I would have chalked it up, like any other bar come-ons I'd received over the years, to alcohol and lack of imagination. But "the best conversationalist I've ever met"? It was a funny compliment coming from a gorgeous twenty-eight-year-old marine, currently drawing sideways eyes from nearly every woman in the room. I thought of all the dates I'd been on, phone calls made, and text messages I'd sent, where every word had been weighed as though I were making a court appearance. "Don't say the wrong thing!" is something women are taught from birth. I thought back—I had no idea what I'd been saying all day. I'd been too mesmerized by the scenery and keeping my eyes peeled for rattlesnakes. J.D. was still staring at me. This was a particular power I was not prepared for, I thought. No wonder intelligent older unmarried women were always cast as dangerous creatures. Furies and witches and sorceresses and harpies. Experienced, confident minds, bodies far from failing. I had all the power right now. To come and go, to unhook from one life and plunge into another, to drink with a sixty-year-old one day and a twenty-eight-year-old the next. Mine for the choosing. I had become unstuck in time, I thought. Absolutely untethered from any expectation, or lack of one, that I'd ever had regarding my life past forty.

An hour and two (or possibly three) more shots of tequila later, J.D. walked me to my cabin, sticking his arm out for me to loop mine through. For a while we stood on the driveway staring at the blanket of stars above, it appeared as though someone were shining a bright light through an empty pincushion, and listening to the coyotes cackling away in the hills. At my door, he did a little bow. "Good night, madam."

I opened the door and walked in, but he stayed on the porch.

"Aren't you coming in?"

"You have to invite me. Like a vampire."

"Honestly." I rolled my eyes. "Just come in."

We sat on the couch talking for so long I thought perhaps this was what it was going to be: a long night of talking. And then finally he leaned over and kissed me. Off came my dress, then the bra. For a brief moment, I considered what my body looked like compared to a twenty-eight-year-old's, and then just as quickly I forgot to think about it. I knew better. If there was one lesson I had learned by now, it was that how confident I felt was directly proportional to how much I was enjoying myself. And I was very much enjoying myself. We landed on my bed, the springs squeaking underneath us, the weight of his body pressed down on mine so heavily I could barely move. I pushed him back. "Slow down," I said, "here's what I want you to do."

I saw him only briefly at breakfast the next morning. An en-

tirely friendly lighthearted exchange free from any strangeness.
He was leaving later that day and wanted my email address so
we could keep in touch. An hour later, as I was sitting upstairs
in the saloon, I heard a rumble and looked up in time to see him
roar by on his motorcycle and disappear past the paddock and
over the hill. I stopped for a moment and stared at the dust settling on the empty road and then burst out laughing. *And then he
rode off into the sunset!* I thought. For the next week every time I
thought of it I'd start laughing again. At some point I realized I
had no idea what J.D. stood for or even what his last name was.

•

By my second week, I felt confident enough to go out for a hike by
myself. I'd done a few already with Laura, who knew all the trails.
She and Eve, a tall, willowy blond twenty-three-year-old who was
in charge of the children's program, and I had hiked up behind
the cabins to a pond filled with lily pads and small green frogs.
While I huffed behind, carefully avoiding the tree roots, which
seemed to be forever leaping out and grabbing my feet like hands,
they discussed their friends' wedding back home: the dress, the
invites, and what they planned on doing differently when their
turn came. For the first time that year I *felt* old. The years between us yawned out like an enormous gulch, and for a moment I
saw forty the way I'd seen it when I was twenty-three . . . a distant
point on the horizon so far away as to be meaningless.

When I'd been in my twenties, the mother of a close friend
would sometimes call me up and take me out. To the theater,
to dinner, to a book reading. She seemed to have an uncanny
sense for times when I most needed some caring for. She was a
successful professional and had a large family, and she always
seemed to burst with life. After one night out at the opening of
a new play, I turned to her and said, "You make me not afraid to

get older." I was fast approaching my thirtieth birthday at the time, and she must have been in her early fifties. But she didn't mock me, or take offense. Instead she laughed and took the compliment as I had meant it.

Another time over dinner she'd been recounting the troubled love life of one of her clients. "Some people are made to be in relationships, and some just aren't." She said it the way one might remark that some people were born with a good singing voice, and some were not. It was an offhand observation, but it was the first time it had been suggested to me that being alone might be a natural-born aptitude, and not a flaw. I'd never forgotten it.

I did not feel old. Me at twenty-three did not seem that long ago. Maybe that would have been different had I had children. Time is measured in experience as much as anything, and children, I thought, must both slow it down and speed it up. But I also didn't want to spend time trying to stay young. I wanted to live unafraid and fully in my life.

The talk turned to New York. The girls wanted to know how I had managed it. Could they move there? Do what I had done? I told them everything I could about my life, thinking that if they reached age forty and found themselves hiking through the hills of Wyoming, they'd be lucky.

Before I went out alone, I stopped by the office so Laura could explain my route to me. I'd done it the day before on horseback and thought I remembered it well enough, but she insisted on drawing me a map.

"Maybe you should take a radio."

I assured her I'd be fine. Phone service felt like an insult here. Plus, it was hard to think of anything being all that worrisome when the camp was so close by. I said so to Laura.

"Just don't ever leave camp without telling people where you're going," she said with a serious face. "Or where you *think* you're going." She handed me the hand-drawn map. "This should take you two to three hours. If you're not back by the time the talent show starts at eight, we'll send out a search party."

I laughed, but she wasn't joking. On the way out I ran into Ivy. "Are you taking a radio?" she immediately asked. I shook my head. "Okay," she said, walking away, "but just pay attention, things can go bad quickly out there."

I walked out into the hills. Up the long valley that the horses were let out into at night, and then into the trees. It was silent. I was alone. Not lonely, the way I'd been so many times in the last few years, but in solitude. I tried to follow Laura's map, but eventually I gave up, and instead kept my eyes peeled for hoofprints and piles of horseshit. When I came into open spaces I made sure the sun was to my left, in the west—I knew it set directly behind the camp. My whole body vibrated with alertness. I'd spent so much time since my birthday agonizing over how my life no longer hewed to a map, how I was unsure of where to go, and now here I was in the literal version of that fear. Off the trail, in the wilderness, without a map, feeling as focused as I'd ever been. I felt dazzled that I'd made this happen. That I'd gotten myself from where I was to here, where I wanted to be without even knowing I was doing it.

I struck a line of horse prints again and stuck to it this time. The trail took me through the wooded pines, and down through pastures surrounded by rock faces. I knew the coyotes (in my head now, I called them *kay-yotes*) lived up here, and I kept my eyes open for them, half terrified I'd see them and half hopeful. I walked on. Sometimes I'd catch groups of antelope frozen mid-graze, staring at me as though I were an alien emerging from a spaceship. The silence wasn't really silence. Not like the morning silence on the mesa. Here there were woodpeckers, and other birds I sadly couldn't name, and the constant hum of the leaves moving in the breeze. And the sound of my feet. The path led me back into the trees, and then across a stream,

and then up a steep, rocky hillside. No one knew where I was.
I thrilled to the thought as I walked, glancing behind me every
now and then out of habit, as though I were walking home along
New York City streets. I paid attention to my steps and crossed
the streams carefully, knowing if I fell and twisted or broke
something I'd be out here for hours on my own. Eventually, I
came through the woods to the top of a hill, below stretched a
valley; from the crest I could see the Bighorns, and to my right,
the aspens rolled away like a golden river. At the bottom, I connected back with the two track, which eventually led me back
into camp. I arrived just as the dinner bell was ringing.

"You're glowing!" said Ivy.

The hike became part of my daily routine. By the time I left
a month later, I knew the route the way I knew the streets of
New York. Eventually I was such a familiar sight on the slope
leading out of camp they named the trail after me. I didn't get
comfortable, though. *Things can go bad quickly out here*, I thought,
every time my foot slipped. They never did, though. For that
month, at least, I was merely a woman wandering alone in the
wilderness, who always found her way back to camp.

•

By the beginning of week three, I'd become friends with most of
the wranglers and was able to hang out with them at the saloon
at night and hear about their day. Fairly quickly the mystique
began to wear off. They worked with their bodies, lived their days
in the wild, and had very old-fashioned ideas about women. Down
from their horses, with their cowboy hats off, they were like su-
perheroes without their masks and capes. Cowboy Clark Kents.

Beau, the wrangler with the handlebar mustache who'd
mesmerized me on my very first day here with Jo, had finally
confided in me.

"I'm lonely," he said, staring sadly down into his drink.

"Well, surely there is no shortage of women who come here who are interested in you." I knew plenty of the female guests arrived here, as I had, and immediately asked about Beau.

He shrugged.

"Well, what sort of woman do you want?"

He finished off his rum and Coke. "I want a woman who makes me French toast." He looked up at me. "Not pancakes, French toast. And wears a slightly see-through dress while she's doing it, or maybe even a dressing gown. And we'd live in a cabin."

"You sound like you're describing the cover of a romance novel."

He looked at me like I'd hurt him.

"That's what I want."

I put my hand on his shoulder. "Well, I have to tell you, Beau, I think if you came to New York with me for a week or so you'd probably find a woman who'd be more than happy to do that for you."

He shook his head. "Too many people in New York."

I was starting to wonder myself if I was going to return to New York. I was shocked by my own indifference. "Who am I, if I don't want to be a New Yorker?" I asked Ivy one day as we drove into Sheridan to eat at the town's only sushi place, which we'd discovered was not terrible.

"Plenty of writers come out here from the east and set up shop," she said. "Hemingway wrote one of his books not far from here."

"Yeah. Probably with his wife to make him French toast every day." I'd told Ivy about Beau and it had become a running joke.

But I was going back, at least in the short term. I had to be in Philly in a week to officiate Jo's wedding.

I was scheduled to fly home on my birthday. The afternoon

before I left I went for my usual hike in the hills. It was amazing to think only one year earlier I'd been on a hot subway car on my way to the beach, feeling as though I'd been handed a death sentence. I thought of my mother, who had spent the year with an actual death sentence. My own fears once again felt like a luxury. I had known a year ago that I could do what I wanted, and had spent the last twelve months figuring out what that meant. What it required and what it afforded me. I had ridden off into my own sunset, and now I was about to turn around and ride straight back into my life. It was all my life.

The horses had been let out into the pasture already, and I wandered through them as I made my way up the slope, stopping here and there to rub their noses before continuing on. I wondered who I'd find when I arrived back in the city. What changes had been wrought in me while I was out here. I'd come here on a whim. Allowed myself to just be happy. This was good. All the terribleness of this year and all the greatness had culminated here, in this vast open space. I'd discovered that left on my own, away from phones and magazine racks, I was quite thrilled with who I'd turned myself into, and quite up for the task of navigating through what came next, whatever it was. Like walking in the dark to the horses or taking off into the hills on my own. Too exhilarating to ever consider turning back.

Behind me I heard a noise. I'd stopped habitually looking over my shoulder when I walked. There was no need. But now I turned around to see what was behind me and was greeted with such an extraordinary sight that I promptly burst into tears. All the horses in the valley had turned and followed me; they were trailed out behind me in a long line, as if I'd been nominated their de facto leader, following as I led them up the rise and through the trees to the other side. An entire herd of mythical creatures, as if out of a storybook. Except they, and I, were real.

There Are No Happy Endings,
Only Good Editing

My mother died a year and a half after I returned from Wyoming. Six weeks before she passed away, following some vague intuition that I should be there, I moved back to Toronto, renting an apartment downtown for the month of February so I could be closer to her while I finished the first draft of this book.

A few afternoons a week I trudged through the frigid, snowy, Toronto weather, the way I had as a child to catch the school bus, and took a commuter bus up to her nursing home, so I could sit and hold her hand. My sister went more regularly. For months she'd driven over three times a week and stayed for hours. It was Alexis who insisted my mother's painkillers be upped, arguing that the unrelenting stress on her body from being held rigid for hours at a time by the tremors of Parkinson's was an unfair exchange for keeping my mother conscious. My mother didn't recognize any of us anymore. She could no longer talk. She was being fed liquids only.

One afternoon I arrived and found her unexpectedly calm; even when heavily medicated she often thrashed in her sleep. Her eyes were closed and her breathing regular. I pulled my Kindle out of my bag and began reading her *The Lion, the Witch and the Wardrobe*, taking big, gulping breaths between sentences. I made it to the Mr. Tumnus's illustration at the end of the first chapter, before the nurse came around and said it was dinnertime. I leaned over her and kissed her forehead.

"I love you, Mom," I said out loud. "Thank you for being a good mother." She opened her eyes, looked into mine, and smiled. A real smile. Not the confused smile of politeness she'd greeted me with so many times when she was still able to speak and move, but a smile of unconditional love and recognition. The same one I'd been getting from her my entire life. She knew who I was. Later I would think back on it as my parting gift from her. It was the last time I saw her conscious.

After she died I was stunned by the response. She had been sick for so long, and I had been struggling with her illness for so long, I was taken off guard by the immediate outpouring of sympathy from so many people. This must be what it's like to be a bride, I thought wildly. To have a baby. To be at the center of a ritual everyone understands, and knows the language for.

A number of my friends offered to come to Toronto for the funeral. I told them not to worry about it. I was so accustomed to doing things on my own, it didn't occur to me that this would be any different. I thought I was prepared. I thought I'd be fine. No doubt they believed me. I'd always been fine on my own.

I didn't realize what a terrible error I had made until the morning of the funeral.

That morning I lay in bed absentmindedly scrolling through Twitter on my phone. I'd already discovered real reading was impossible, utterly beyond me. I couldn't make my brain follow the words. I'd picked up my phone hoping for messages from friends. Hoping, I realized, to find that someone had neglected my assurances and bought a plane ticket anyway, that someone was on their way. My oldest friend from high school, who'd lived next door to us, whom I still saw every holiday, and who knew my mother, was in Switzerland that weekend with her new boy-friend. She would cancel if I wanted her to, she'd said earlier that week. But those are not requests one can make of friends. Just of family members, spouses. The obligations of friendship are unwritten.

There were no messages. People think that death is some-thing to be avoided out of respect. No doubt I'd been guilty of it. But the truth was, all I wanted was to hear from everyone constantly, something to fill the void that had been left by my mother's body. Instead I scrolled through Twitter, spotting an interview with a *New Yorker* writer who'd just released a memoir about losing her son shortly after his premature birth. My eyes glanced over the words, but I couldn't make any of it stick, until I came across a line that detached itself from the context of the interview and jumped out and grabbed me by the throat. "I was childless and alone at thirty-eight," she told the interviewer, "I felt like a complete failure."

At the funeral home, I had no one to stand between me and all the people who wanted to extend their condolences. I'd never been more aware of the empty space people sometimes saw beside me; I felt like a ship being violently tossed on the ocean with no anchor, no port, exposed.

I gave the eulogy. I have no idea what I said, only that I didn't cry. After the service, the mother of an old friend stopped me and asked if she could put in a request to have me give the eulogy at her funeral. "You were so eloquent!"

When I sat down after the eulogy, my brother-in-law put his arm around my sister, and my uncle put his arm around my father. I was the solitary figure in the front row. The absolute loneliness of it was so intense it was painless—I felt like the blue center of a flame. This is why people get married, I thought once again, so they can have an arm around their shoulder; no matter how mediocre or disappointing the arm might turn out to be, it was still obligated to be there. I could feel the pitying eyes on my back and without warning the line from the interview I'd read that morning rose up and grabbed me again—but even now, facing this worst moment alone, I didn't feel like a failure. I felt like a warrior.

A strange thing had happened in the days after my mother had died. For so long her presence had been limited to a physical one. Her body, writhing and confused, was at least a real thing we could see. Her person, as it was leached away, was replaced by this body, until her physical presence was the only reality we knew, and the person, the woman whom I'd been raised and loved by and read to so carefully, was a distant memory that rarely entered into my mind.

Two days after her death I stopped at the bookstore on the way back to my sister's from the funeral home, largely for a distraction. It was a chain store, a favorite destination of my mother's and mine; we'd often come here together and spend an hour browsing. As I was walking aimlessly through the aisles, she was suddenly there beside me. Not in the *I'm thinking about my mother and how she would like this* sense, but literally. I could see her. I could see the outfit she was wearing. I could watch her as she walked away toward another aisle in that good-natured way she had of strolling absentmindedly with a half-smile on her face, holding a stack of books she'd picked up. I could hear her voice, "Oh, sweetie, look what I found," as she proffered a new Georgette Heyer edition or Ellis Peters mystery my way. I'd been here a hundred times on my own after she'd gone into the nursing home, but this was the first time I'd remembered us here together. It took my breath away. I stood gaping as I watched her walking around the store, tears streaming down my face.

After that I saw her everywhere. Heard her voice. Felt her nails on my back. Turned to see her coming up the stairs. It was as though the death of her body had finally released her person back to me. It was strange and wild—stranger and wilder than anything I had experienced—and so unexpected. *This must be what people mean when they say they are haunted*, I thought, except it wasn't bad or frightening. I didn't want it to stop. I was terrified of it stopping. I wanted to be haunted forever. Have her walk alongside me and never leave.

She was buried in the graveyard behind the house we'd lived in when I was younger and still dreamt about. In the same town where she'd attended high school. The plot had been bought by her parents. A space for each of them, and one for my mother. She'd been a teenager at the time, the middle child and only girl, beautiful even then, though apparently to her parents, for reasons I can now only guess at, an old maid in the making. I had played in this graveyard growing up, built Star Wars forts under trees that still stood. Raced around in my Princess Leia costume with the neighborhood boys. Gone on long bike rides through it with my mother and my sister. It was the scene of some of my happiest childhood memories, when the world felt very safe and filled with the same potential I found in the stories my mother read me.

It was raining as my father lowered my mother's urn into the ground. A dismal March rain, a funeral scene from a movie. But I didn't look down. Instead I looked around at the winding lanes and saw my eight-year-old self, dancing around the figure of my mother that had not yet left me, bursting with promise, thrilled with the possibilities of life and where it might take her.

ACKNOWLEDGMENTS

This book was made possible by the unwavering encouragement and support of a team of women. My brilliant editor Christine Pride, who saw the potential for this story immediately, and who believed in it even when my own resolve flagged. And my incredible agents: Lucy Carson (who once gave me a much-needed pep talk in the form of a seven-page letter with all her favorite lines), and Molly Friedrich, who has been giving me much-needed everything since I wandered into her kitchen fourteen years ago. It was an extraordinary experience to have beside me people in whose guidance I was able to trust unconditionally, and I'm forever grateful.

There are two people whose presence in my life is not properly reflected in this story:

My friend and business partner Rachel Sklar, who has her own story to tell about this year, and whose support as a friend and a colleague throughout my career has been unmatched.

The exceptional Kimberly Burns, who has been my cheerleader and confidante since we spotted each other across the room in 2007 and just *knew*.

Thank you to Mel Hamilton and Crispin Russell who, having not laid eyes on me in twenty years, offered up their home, sight unseen, so that I could have a place to write. It's wonderful when the instincts of your twenty-year-old self prove out two decades later.

Thank you to my early readers, Allyson Rapisarda, Lindsay Robertson, and Ivy Givens, for all their good reading and kind feedback. And my blood sister, Naama Bloom, who not only read many early versions of this but asked me to write a book with her.

Thank you to Clay and Leah Miller for their breathtaking generosity. And Laura-Ellen Brewer for hers.

I'm very lucky to have the friends that I do. Thanks to Lesley, Maddy, Mauri, Margeaux, Allyson, Kara, and Rachel, who all appear in these pages. *No one should come to New York to live unless she is willing to be lucky.* Thanks to Meghan Nameth, Greg Macek and Yaya, Amy Lemen, Jen Doll for her iMessage therapy, Carolyn Murnick, Rebecca Soffer, Aminatou Sow, Alison Gelles, Whitney Joiner, Jane Barratt, Elizabeth Plank, Jenn Romolini, Jess Bennett, Alyssa Mastromonaco, Anna Holmes, Julia Cheiffetz, Stacy London, Lori Leibovich, Chaédria LaBouvier, Melissa Lafsky, Kate McKean, Mary Traina, Mary Kate Flannery, Ashley Ford, Erin Edmison, Julia Carson, Vass Bednar, Carita Rizzo, Heidi Moore, Eve Panning, Cathrin Wirtz, Kathleen Fox, Bernie Shanahan, Benjamin Peikes, Benjamin Heemskerk, Nick Aster, Matt Lambert, the Perekoppis, and TheLi.st. Thanks also to the amazing Sarah Reidy and Elizabeth Breeden at S&S.

Special shout-out to my manly reading club: David Bloom, David Gelles, and Justin Soffer.

Thanks to the kids: Quinn, Hannah, Oona, Connor, Scarlett, Ruby, Desi, and my niece Zoe, who felt strongly this book should be called *About an Aunt*.

Thanks to Jo Piazza for her constant advice and counsel and for making it possible for me to leave when I needed. And thanks to Maddy for feeding me, and always, always making sure I have a place to come home to.

And finally, thanks to my family for their love and support. Also, Carrie Fisher and Laura Ingalls Wilder for existing, and then telling us about it.

ABOUT THE AUTHOR

Glynnis MacNicol is a writer and co-founder of TheLi.st. Her work has appeared in print and online for publications including ELLE.com, where she was a contributing writer, *The New York Times*, *The Guardian*, *The Cut*, *New York Daily News*, *W*, *Town & Country*, *The Daily Beast*, and Shondaland. She lives in New York City.